# FRIEDRICH THE BLACKSMITH

From The Promised Land of Catherine the
Great to The Gulags of Comrade Stalin

A Non-fiction Novel
By
Norman Fischbuch

Note for Librarians: A cataloguing record for this book is available from Library and Archives Canada at www.collectionscanada.ca/amicus/index-e.html

Printed in Victoria, BC, Canada.

ISBN: 978-1-4269-1294-8 (sc)

ISBN: 978-1-4269-1295-5 (dj)

ISBN: 978-1-4269-1296-2 (e-book)

*We at Trafford believe that it is the responsibility of us all, as both individuals and corporations, to make choices that are environmentally and socially sound. You, in turn, are supporting this responsible conduct each time you purchase a Trafford book, or make use of our publishing services. To find out how you are helping, please visit www.trafford.com/responsiblepublishing.html*

*Our mission is to efficiently provide the world's finest, most comprehensive book publishing service, enabling every author to experience success. To find out how to publish your book, your way, and have it available worldwide, visit us online at www.trafford.com*

*Trafford rev. 5/3/2010*

 www.trafford.com

North America & international
toll-free: 1 888 232 4444 (USA & Canada)
phone: 250 383 6864 ♦ fax: 250 383 6804    email: info@trafford.com

The United Kingdom & Europe
phone: +44 (0)1865 487 395 ♦ local rate: 0845 230 9601
facsimile: +44 (0)1865 481 507 ♦ email: info.uk@trafford.com

10  9  8  7  6  5  4  3  2  1

i

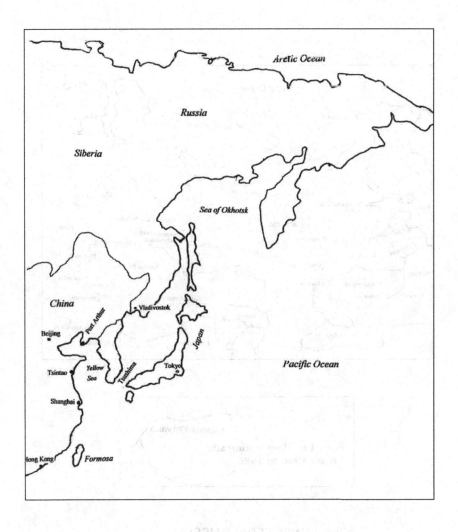

# EASTERN RUSSIA and JAPAN
## 1900 - 1906

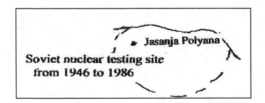

Jasanja Polyana

Soviet nuclear testing site
from 1946 to 1986

## WESTERN RUSSIA
## 1900 – 1928

# Table of Contents

# ACKNOWLEDGEMENTS

My first obligation is to thank my cousins and their descendants for the vast amount of information that they have shared with to me during the last twenty-five years about their lives in Russia. They patiently did this despite my limited capabilities in the German and especially the Russian languages. In 1982, my cousin Elfrieda (Fischbuch) Bergstreser, the daughter of Johann, began by telling me about the first 22 years of her life that she spent in Russia. She was born there in 1906 and along with the rest of her family lived through the 1915 deportation and the subsequent terror tactics of Lenin and Stalin before they came to Canada in 1928. During our discussions, she allowed me to copy the pictures she had brought with her from Russia including the picture that was taken for Friedrich shortly after he left to serve in the Tsar's navy.

We both agonized over the fact that from 1928 onward there was only silence from behind the Iron Curtain. Nothing was heard of or known about our Russian family ties. In 1997, a nephew in Hanna Alberta got a letter from a Gerhard Fischbuch in Lohmar Germany in which he gave the name of his grandfather Emil Fischbuch and his great-grandfather Michel Fischbuch who were from the village of Nataliendorf. This of course matched all of the family connections that Elfrieda Bergstreser had recorded for me in 1982. I then went to Germany in 1997 where over the next 10 years I found descendants of all of the six brothers who remained in Russia after 1928. One of my first encounters was with a cousin who got out to Germany in 1990. This was Margarita (Fischbuch) Krieger the daughter of Emil. She was born in 1930 and told me about her childhood years in Nataliendorf including when her father was taken away by the secret police. Then there were her accounts of her mother and the remaining children's deportation to the Woroschilograd kolkhoz their forced removal to a collective in northern Kazakhstan, her marriage and her ordeal of having to seek out her husband Otto Krieger. During the times that I visited them in Germany from 1997 to 2008 Margarita and her seven children patiently told me about how they unknowingly lived in the nuclear wasteland of Karaganda, Semipalatinsk, and Pavlodar until their final escape in 1990.

Margarita's brother Reinhold came to Germany in 1992 but died there in 1993. I spoke at great length with his son Gennadij, his wife Lydia and his sister, Lydia (Fischbuch) Gohr who accompanied me to St. Petersburg and was instrumental in our efforts to get Friedrich's naval history from the Russian Naval Archives.

Another cousin, Gerhard Fischbuch Sr. Margarita's brother, had died in Russia in 1961 and his son Gerhard Jr. came to Germany in 1988 (this was the first person to greet me at Frankfurt in 1997). He told me much about his life in Kirgistan including how he had risen to become head of the food and goods distribution centre. Every year he was sent to Moscow to study the science of management. Distribution of food and any other commodity was a major problem in Russia since there was no incentive for anyone to do anything more than to fulfill their daily allotment of work and collect their subsistence allowance; no one cared about marketing food or anything else. The fact that he had risen to manage a distribution centre of this sort was unusual since descendants of German colonists rarely rose above menial labour; they were rated very low on the Communist ethnic scale. When it came to graduation time he was told to russify his name and to join the Communist Party. He refused and told them that his father and mother had died in Communist slave labour camps under their ancestral name and said to them that in view of their sacrifice, he would not join the Communist Party and he too would die with his ancestral name. They immediately sent him back to Kirgistan to work as an ordinary labourer. Upon meeting him in 1997 and discussing our family ties, he took it upon himself to search the Fischbuch name in all of Germany and found descendants of the remaining brothers who now also were in Germany. He eventually found descendants of Friedrich, Robert, Gustav and Zamel.

Waldemar Fischbuch a grandson of Friedrich came to Bad

Zalzuflen, Germany in 1989. After Gerhard Fischbuch discovered his whereabouts, I went to Bad Zalzuflen in 2000 and spoke at length with him, his wife Erica and their sons Willi and Hari about their lives in Jasnaja Poljana. Waldemar spoke of the times when Friedrich had told him and his two brothers about his time in the Tsar's navy. Regrettably, Waldemar died in 2007, however, I again met with his wife Erica in 2008 and heard more about their lives in Jasnaja Poljana and as well spoke with Waldemar's next youngest brother Gerhard who had just recently come to Bremen, Germany.

Gregor Fischbuch the son of Robert Fischbuch another of my cousins came to Germany in 1992 with his wife Alma (Leicht) Fischbuch and their two children Waldemar and Irina. Gregor told me much about his life in the Trudarmee, the Gulag, the coalmines and slave labour on the railroad at Lake Balkhash in east-central Kazakhstan.

Albin Fischbuch, the grandson of Gustav Fischbuch, Friedrich's brother, was discovered by Gerhard near Munich in 2002. They came to Germany in 1989 from the general area of Kerchevo in Siberia where Gustav had been sent by Stalin's secret police in 1930. Again, they told me many of their experiences of their Siberian exile.

Zelfia (Fischbuch) Stahl the daughter of Zamel came to Essen, Germany in 1990 from Syktyvkar, Komi. This is where Zamel his wife Beate (Lauch) Fischbuch, Zelfia and her two brothers Ernst and Artur were sent as slave labourers to work in the forests of Russia's far north. Another sister Maria was born there in 1939. Zelfia's accounts of their treatment while they worked long hours in the bitter cold of the forest were very disturbing.

Further thanks must go to the people who had the fortitude to write about the fall of the Romanov dynasty and those that had the courage to publish their experiences during and after Bolshevism, Leninism, Stalinism and the continuation of the Communist atrocities that have ravaged Russia for nearly a century. Firstly, there are the courageous treatises of Aleksandr Solzhenitsyn. As well as the telling works of several published accounts of forced labour in Stalin's Trudarmee that populated the Gulags and kolkhozes, these are publications that reveal much of Stalin's atrocities and are listed in the following references.

The sources of Friedrich's service in the Russian Navy were obtained from the Naval Archives in St. Petersburg and from other publications listed in the references. Many of the details of Admiral Rozhdestvensky's guidance of the "The Tsar's Last Armada" to the Battle of Tsushima was derived from a book written by Constantine Pleshakov, and from a book "The Fleet that had to Die" written by Richard Hough. Without these well-researched and detailed accounts of the Second Pacific Squadron, the story of Friedrich's role in the disastrous Russo-Japanese War would not be complete.

# FOREWORD

Born and raised in Russia Friedrich Fischbuch a young man of German descent served in the Russian Navy from 1899 to 1906, shortly after Tsar Nicholas II was crowned supreme autocrat of the Russian Empire.  During the turbulent years after the October Revolution in 1917, the Romanov dynasty crumbled and Bolshevism and Communism arose.  During this time, Friedrich and his family suffered through the confiscation of their homes, deportation, hunger, humiliation and degradation.  Firstly, they were deported from their treasured farming village of Nataliendorf in 1915.  This was followed by the Bolshevik Revolution which labelled German colonists as spies and traitors to the Empire; then came Stalin's Communist reign of terror which lasted for the next seventy years.  From the time Friedrich was discharged from the navy he and his family struggled to survive the slave labour and starvation tactics of the growing Communist regime.

With the advent of Gorbachev and Perestroika, the descendants of some of the German colonists who had been invited to Russia by Tsarina Catherine the Great nearly two centuries earlier finally were allowed to flee the Soviet Union in the 1990's.  Two of the three grandsons that were with Friedrich during the last days of his life fled to Germany and have recounted some of the stories he told them about his younger days and his naval career shortly before he died as a blind and broken captive of the Soviet system.

Born in 1879 Friedrich grew up in Nataliendorf a little farming community located in southwestern Russia near the Polish border. Nataliendorf was one of many German colonies in Russia established by disenchanted Germans originally invited to Russia by Tsarina Catherine the Great to develop the resources of the vast tracts of fertile land on the broad prairie-like steppe areas of Odessa, Ukraine, the Volga River basin and Kazakhstan.  Her manifesto of 1763 offered the artisans and workers in the tiny principalities of Germany free land, freedom of religion and exemption from military duty. She knew from her German heritage that the workers in the little principalities of her native country were obligated to provide for an ever-expanding royal family from limited tracts of land. They eked out a hand-to-mouth existence under the feudal burdens imposed on them by the petty princes who ruled each tiny principality. Each prince at all costs was obliged to maintain a royal front. It followed that many of the farm labourers on these little feudal kingdoms were more than willing to answer the call of Tsarina Catherine II.

In the early 1800's, Friedrich's ancestors trekked across Poland to western Russia. They eventually settled not far from the Polish border near the city of Novograd Volinskiy in the Russian province of Volhynia. From the time that the German colonists first arrived in Russia they were at last grateful that they could have land of their own and through hard work and diligence their farmsteads became some of the most productive and picturesque in all of Russia. It was in this environment that Friedrich's parents Michel and Justina Fischbuch raised their fourteen children thankful that they could provide for such a large family in a nation that they were now proud to be part.

Friedrich was the fourth child of Michel and Justina's eleven sons and three daughters and his boyhood ambition was to become a blacksmith. Very early in his life he was intrigued by how his neighbour August Wendtland could deftly mould red hot iron into plough shares, horse shoes, wagon wheels and a multitude of working tools. Friedrich spent much time in the Wendtland blacksmith shop cranking the forge for August and was delighted when he was offered to apprentice under this master blacksmith. As he became adept at his trade, he took pride in the fact that he was on call to many German villages in the area.

On December 19th, 1900, when Friedrich was twenty-one-years-old he was conscripted into the Russian navy, undoubtedly because of his background of working with iron. Steam power had just been established to propel ships and this revolutionary mode of transportation made travel by sea no longer dependent on sails and the vagaries of the wind.   It followed that ocean-going vessels propelled by steam needed skilled ironworkers to build and man the boilers and propulsion systems of these new ships.

The family and especially Friedrich's younger brothers spread the word through the community that their son and brother had been chosen to serve their country's navy and the Tsar.  Michel and Justina were pleased that their ancestors had found a nation that allowed them to prosper on lands that were now their own and were proud that their son was called to serve their country.

Friedrich was posted to Kronstadt the naval base on the Baltic Sea at St. Petersburg.  Since the Tsar had alerted his navy that war was imminent against the Japanese, ordinary seaman Friedrich immediately began his training as a stoker's helper on ships operating in the Baltic Sea.  With his background of working with iron Friedrich was soon put in charge of tending the ship's boilers, which quickly led to his being promoted to Engineer First Class.  By early 1903, war against the Japanese was becoming imminent.  The Tsar alerted the navy to bolster the fleet at Russia's far-eastern ports of Vladivostok and Port Arthur.  In April of 1903, Friedrich was sent to Toulon, France where the French were building a Borodino-class, armour-clad, pre-dreadnought battleship for the Russian navy. Friedrich, who was now well versed in the steam power of various ships, was delegated to supervise the assembly of the twenty boilers to serve the propulsion system of the new ship.  This battleship was the seventh ironclad pre-dreadnought in the Russian navy and was launched on August 18th, 1903.  It was christened the Tsesarevich (son of the Tsar).  Undoubtedly, the name was prompted by the Tsar himself since Tsar Nicholas was hoping that after having four daughters that the next pregnancy of Empress Alexandra would finally provide a son and heir to the vast Russian Empire.  His prayers were answered exactly one year later, on August 18, 1904, a son, Alexei, was born.

After the launching, the Tsesarevich was under the command of Friedrich's naval mentor Captain Ivan Grigorovich.  Friedrich had served under Grigorovich on one of the training ships in the Baltic Sea.  Grigorovich had requested that Friedrich supervise the assembly of the boiler system of the new battleship being built in Toulon. Upon its launching the Tsesarevich left immediately to supplement Russia's First Pacific Squadron at Port Arthur the ice-free port that Russia had acquired from China in 1895. Little did the crew of this new armour-clad vessel know that this would be the only battleship of the entire Russian navy that would survive the Russo-Japanese naval battles.

On the journey to the Yellow Sea, the Tsesarevich steamed from Toulon across the Mediterranean Sea, through the Suez Canal to Djibouti and then continued on the long eastward journey along the equator to the South China Sea. Friedrich and his stokers were exposed not only to the heat of the boilers but also to the stifling temperatures along the equator as they passed from Djibouti through the Straits of Malacca to Singapore and then on to Port Arthur. When they reached Port Arthur on October 8th, 1903, they were greeted by the playboy Commander of the First Pacific Squadron, Admiral O.V. Stark. Stark was soon to be replaced by Admiral Makarov. They did not know that only five months after their arrival at Port Arthur, on March 31, 1904, that the new commander of the First Pacific Squadron, Admiral Stepan Makarov, would be killed along with most of his crew during the sinking of his flagship the Petropavlovsk. Admiral V.K. Witgeft was sent to take command of the squadron and selected the Tsesarevich as his flagship.

Following orders directly from the Tsar to take the fleet to Vladivostok, Admiral Witgeft was confronted by the Japanese fleet under Admiral Togo Heihachiro on July 28, 1904. This battle resulted in the epic defeat of the Russia's First Pacific Squadron in the Battle of the Yellow Sea. As the Japanese fleet confronted the Russians Friedrich was on the bridge with Admiral Witgeft when the first salvo of Japanese shells struck the Tsesarevich. By chance, one shell hit the bridge and a shell fragment decapitated Admiral Witgeft. Now with no directive signals from the flagship Captain Grigorovich signalled the second-in-command an admiral on the battleship Peresviet, a royally appointed admiral with little naval experience, that Admiral Witgeft had been killed and that the Peresviet must now take over as flagship. Surprisingly, there was no response from the

Peresviet since the new commander had panicked and with no signal to the rest of the fleet reversed direction and fled back to Port Arthur. In the confusion that ensued, four of the other Russian battleships followed the Peresviet leaving the wounded Tsesarevich and the rest of the fleet in disarray. As daylight was fading Admiral Togo's battleships took full advantage of the confusion among the remnants of the Russian fleet and bombarded whatever craft they could see.

When the first salvo had hit the Tsesarevich, not only was the admiral killed but also the wheel of the ship was struck killing the helmsman. With the steering of the ship being jammed the ship heeled over and nearly capsized. Other shells had struck at the water line and Friedrich quickly had the stokers man the pumps to fight the fires, which had been ignited in the coalbunkers. Friedrich requested volunteers to take the hoses and follow him into the hold below deck to brave the raging inferno. Inevitably, several of his men passed out and two of them could not be rescued and died because of the coal-fed fires. Despite the loss of his men Friedrich's crew were able to put the fires out before they reached the magazine housing the ships ammunition. Friedrich then found that nearly half of the boilers were damaged and out of commission.

Fortunately, he and his stokers were able to repair several of them. Now, with enough boilers in operation and as night was falling Captain Grigorovich was able to slip away with all lights out and in the moonless cover of darkness slowly limped to the neutral Chinese port of Tsintao, which at that time was a German protectorate. Here under international law the ship and its crew were interned until after the end of the war. Russia surrendered Port Arthur to the Japanese in January of 1905. Humiliated by this defeat Tsar Nicholas informed his Admiralty to assemble as many ships as possible. He launched a Second Pacific Squadron and had it sail all the way from the Baltic through the English Channel, around the African Horn, across the Indian Ocean and into the Sea of Japan to avenge the sinking of the Petropavlovsk, the Yellow Sea disaster and finally the surrender of Port Arthur. However, after the long and arduous voyage of the Second Pacific Squadron insult was added to injury when Russia's Second Pacific fleet under the command of Admiral Z. P. Rozhdestvensky was handed a humiliating defeat by Admiral Togo in the Battle of Tsushima on May 27th, 1905. Finally, in August of 1905 a peace settlement between Russia and Japan was negotiated by United States President Theodore Roosevelt.

During this time, the damaged Tsesarevich was still interned at Tsintao. Since Friedrich and his chief stoker were the only ones on the ship that could speak German, they were able to converse with the German port authorities to help with the repair of all of the damage sustained during their encounter with the Japanese flagship. In October of 1905, the Tsesarevich was allowed to leave Tsintao and made the long voyage back to the Baltic and home to St. Petersburg. The Tsesarevich was the only Russian pre-dreadnought battleship that was not sunk or captured by the Japanese in the disastrous naval encounters between the Russian navy and the Japanese from early 1904, and to the final defeat of the Rozhdestvensky armada in May of 1905.

Upon the arrival of the Tsesarevich in St. Petersburg in early January 1906, the Tsar was thankful that at least one of his battleships had returned from Russia's humiliating defeat in the Far East. He immediately promoted Captain Ivan Grigorovich to admiral; later during World War I Grigrovich became Minister of the Navy. Upon his promotion to admiral, Grigorovich asked the Tsar to recognize the efforts of the one member of his crew who was instrumental in saving and repairing the Tsesarevich. In a ceremony at the Winter Palace on January 22nd, 1906, the Tsar presented Friedrich with the Cross of St. George, the only Russian sailor that was decorated for his service in Russia's devastating naval battles during the Russo-Japanese War. The next day, January 23rd, 1906, Friedrich was discharged from the navy and immediately set out to get back to his family, and home, at Nataliendorf. After travelling by train to Kharkov and then by horse and buggy to Nataliendorf he happened to arrive home on the day that his sister Justina-Gustel was being married. Great rejoicing followed as the family greeted Friedrich. They had all heard of Russia's naval defeats in the North China Sea and during this time feared for the life of their son and brother.

Along with his parents, Michel and Justina and his thirteen brothers and sisters, Friedrich quickly settled back into the comfortable life he had always known. The younger brothers were intrigued by his adventures of sailing halfway around the world. They listened intently to his accounts of the Battle of the Yellow Sea, the sudden death of his admiral and the subsequent measures that were taken by him and the boiler crews to save the ship. It was not long before Friedrich resumed his association with his neighbour and blacksmithing mentor August Wendtland, and in a short time he was again called upon to travel to other German colonies to ply his trade. However, he now noticed a distinct animosity toward the German villagers by their Russian neighbours. He soon learned that it stemmed from Tsar Nicholas's policy of ethnic cleansing that had been established by his father Tsar Alexander III two decades earlier. In addition, it was becoming obvious that with the devastating loss of the war against Japan Tsar Nicholas now found his autocratic power was being eroded; not just by his fawning bureaucrats, but also by the social upheaval of the masses.

Dissension of the general population had already begun much earlier, in 1897 and 1898. Massive crop failures resulted in famine, which triggered a steady exodus of peasants to the cities where they found conditions even more deplorable. Most of these peasants were ex-serfs and the descendants of serfs who had been freed in 1861. Since attaining their freedom, they had learned little about farming or the trades. They roamed the broad forest and steppe of Russia and survived by pilfering, odd jobs and living off the land. With this background, they were ill adapted to supply the agricultural needs of the country. To make matters worse Tsar Nicholas continued to implement his father's policy of russification, which meant ridding the Empire of the very people that produced the most grain, vegetables, cattle and farm machinery for the country.

Continued ethnic cleansing escalated and resulted in not only the purging of ethnic Germans but also Jews, Poles and any identifiable group that was alien to the true "Russian culture" as had been defined by Tsar Alexander III. What resulted was that Tsar Nicholas's pursuit of russification led to annihilation of whole communities through pogroms, incarceration, deportation and death camps. Therefore, it was inevitable that much bitterness ensued. Nevertheless, the Tsar rationalized it all by stating that through his supreme autocratic power his wishes emanated directly from the will of God and that this divine intervention would eventually ensure the salvation of the Russian Empire. Through all of this turmoil, the Tsar and his family submerged themselves in their cloistered palatial environment in St. Petersburg and surrounded by their fawning bureaucrats were unaware of the magnitude of the unrest. They spent their time worrying about the health of Alexei their haemophiliac son and heir to the throne. Empress Alexandra became obsessed with the powers of the wily peasant Rasputin who portrayed himself as a reincarnation of Jesus Christ and promised to perform a miracle cure for the heir apparent.

Inevitably, by 1905 the demonstrations, strikes and violence grew stronger as the social upheaval grew. Finally, a minor strike in St. Petersburg quickly escalated into a massive protest drawing hundreds of unemployed, destitute and hungry people who were led by individuals that eventually would be the leaders of the revolution that was about to erupt. Many of the demonstrators who basically still felt the Tsar was compassionate to his people set out to march to the Winter Palace with a genuine request for sympathy from the Tsar. Some even sang the imperial anthem "God save the Tsar." However, when the Tsar was informed of the magnitude of the demonstration rather than appearing and calming the demonstrators he ordered his troops to intervene. The marchers were told to desist and that the Tsar was not at the Winter Palace and as the crowd pressed forward the soldiers opened fire. As some of the lead marchers were shot, those behind moved forward and the soldiers were obliged to continue firing. The result was that hundreds of people were killed including women and children. From then on, this event was known as Bloody Sunday, January 22nd, 1905. Subsequently, "Bloody Sunday" became the battle cry of the revolutionaries as they gained momentum while the Romanov dynasty of Tsar Nicholas II continued to crumble.

While still interned at the Chinese port of Tsintao the crew of the

Tsesarevich were unaware of the discontent that was brewing at home. They were busy repairing their ship and waiting patiently to be released so they could return to St. Petersburg. Consequently, when Friedrich settled back into what he thought would be his old comfortable life at Nataliendorf he was soon to realize the impact that "Bloody Sunday" was having on his community. From 1906 on life at Nataliendorf became untenable. Friedrich's next oldest brother August left for Canada under trying family circumstances. The younger brothers who were still entranced by seeing the Tsar's soldiers parading through the nearby city of Novograd Volinskiy and hearing Friedrich's stories of navy life were reprimanded by their father and older brothers since the animosity toward anyone of German ancestry was growing stronger.

This was difficult for the German colonists to comprehend. Even though the German settlers had been productive citizens of Russia for nearly a century and were well versed in the Russian language their obvious affluence set them apart from the Russian peasants, especially from the transient ex-serfs who had previously roamed through the countryside and pilfered from their established colonies. The Russian peasantry were now fired with revolutionary zeal and the petty pilfering from the German colonies escalated into full-scale looting, vandalism and arson. By 1914, rumblings of war against Germany became more evident. This resulted in suspicion that the colonists were collaborators with the enemy and triggered even more violence against the German colonists.

In 1914 Eduard, Friedrich's oldest brother was conscripted into the Russian army and sent to the Crimea. With the advent of war against Germany and the dissension among the populace by 1915 the entire Russian nation was in a state of disarray.

**Emil & Albert Fischbuch 1915**

In early 1915, Emil and Albert two of Friedrich's younger brothers also were conscripted and they too were sent to the Crimean front. Since Tsar Nicholas's hold on the Empire continued to disintegrate there was little support for the armed forces. Guns and ammunition were at a premium and to survive the soldiers were not only practically defenceless but had to feed themselves by stealing vegetables, chickens, dogs and even trapping rats to fend off starvation.

Shortly after Emil had been conscripted, he was promoted as a non-commissioned officer, which was surprising since anyone with German ancestry was considered with suspicion by the Russians. Surprisingly, after serving a short time in the Crimea he was sent to the western front to fight against his ethnic brethren as the German army was advancing into Poland. While stationed in the Crimea Emil served for a short time in the same unit as his brother Albert. Before Emil left and when he was saying goodbye to his brother Albert told him that he knew how to take care of himself against the Turks but that Emil should be careful since the German army was better trained than the Turks were. He also told his older brother not to worry and that it would not be long before they would see each other back home again in Nataliendorf. Unfortunately, Emil later found that

Albert would never return to Nataliendorf; undoubtedly, he was either shot or starved to death in the service of Russia and the Tsar. By chance his body was discovered by their oldest brother Eduard who, just before he died of his own war injuries, told his mother about finding the body of his brother, and her young son, Albert.

Only a short time after his arrival in Poland to fight against the advancing German army Emil was severely wounded and since the Russian army had little or no medical facilities at the front he crawled to a nearby farmstead. The kind Polish farmer bound his wounds and fed him or he probably would not have survived. By this time, the Tsarist regime was near collapse and the army was in chaos with many of the Russian soldiers deserting and drifting off into the Polish countryside. Emil also quietly left and somehow found his way back home to Nataliendorf.

In the meantime, a directive was issued by the Russian Commander-in-Chief Nicholas Nikolayevich on July 10th, 1915, that all those of German ancestry in the district of Novograd Volinskiy were to be deported within forty-eight hours to an undisclosed vicinity in eastern Russia. The reason for this was that the German colonists were regarded as spies and collaborators with the German enemy. Michel and Justina assembled the family to discuss how they could pack up some belongings and somehow make their way to this distant and unknown destination. They covered their wagons harnessed their best horses and let their livestock into the pastures to fend for themselves. They quickly butchered some pigs, chickens and cattle for meat and baked bread for their journey. Since Friedrich's brother Eduard had been conscripted into the Russian army, he was away fighting the Turks somewhere in the Crimea. Friedrich helped Eduard's wife Henrietta and her three children, a boy twelve and two girls eight and ten-years-old to get ready for their deportation into the unknown. Gathering their belongings and food Friedrich, Henrietta and the children loaded what they could into Friedrich's wagon and they were on their way. The revolutionary police, or "strazhniks," who oversaw their exodus, were part of the Bolshevik cause only by the fact that they had never owned property, and prior to the rise of Bolshevism were nothing more than vagrants.

The strazhniks forced the colonists to travel day and night and as the wagon train moved slowly onward, the strazhniks whipped the horses pulling the wagons until the horses collapsed from exhaustion. The strazhniks then shot the horses and made the families of each wagon travel on foot carrying what few belongings they could. As they walked along Friedrich tried to stay behind the three children to keep them ahead of him. However, the strazhniks rode their horses close to the stragglers and lashed their whips on anyone that fell behind. The children were able to avoid the beatings as Friedrich urged them forward; however, as the strazhniks were right behind him he was exposed to the brunt of their attacks. Friedrich's coat was ripped apart by the fine leather thongs of the whips and he soon felt the warmth of his blood trickling down his back.

Friedrich had no way of knowing that this was just the beginning of his long journey into hunger, misery, terror and sadism that would last for the rest of his life. As history unfolded it not only lasted through his lifetime, but plagued the remnants of his family for the next 70 years under the oppression that was yet to come with the advent of the Bolsheviks, Lenin, Stalin and the emerging Communist regime that were soon to rule his cherished Russian homeland. A homeland that he had served the Tsar's navy for and his ancestors who had toiled for nearly a century in this forested swampland to establish their picturesque and productive farmsteads.

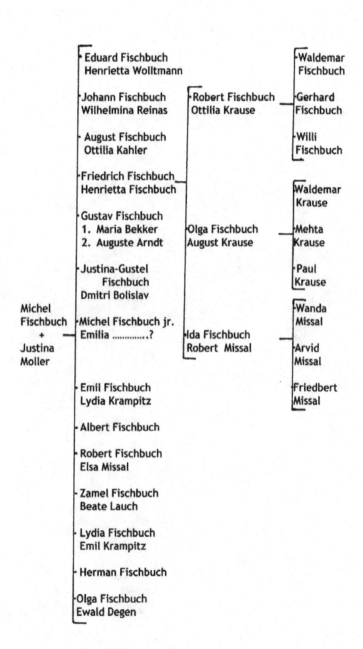

Michel
Fischbuch
    +
Justina
Moller

- Eduard Fischbuch
  Henrietta Wolltmann

- Johann Fischbuch
  Wilhelmina Reinas

- August Fischbuch
  Ottilia Kahler

- Friedrich Fischbuch
  Henrietta Fischbuch

- Gustav Fischbuch
  1. Maria Bekker
  2. Auguste Arndt

- Justina-Gustel
      Fischbuch
  Dmitri Bolislav

- Michel Fischbuch jr.
  Emilia ..............?

- Emil Fischbuch
  Lydia Krampitz

- Albert Fischbuch

- Robert Fischbuch
  Elsa Missal

- Zamel Fischbuch
  Beate Lauch

- Lydia Fischbuch
  Emil Krampitz

- Herman Fischbuch

- Olga Fischbuch
  Ewald Degen

- Robert Fischbuch
  Ottilia Krause

- Olga Fischbuch
  August Krause

- Ida Fischbuch
  Robert Missal

- Waldemar
  Fischbuch

- Gerhard
  Fischbuch

- Willi
  Fischbuch

- Waldemar
  Krause

- Mehta
  Krause

- Paul
  Krause

- Wanda
  Missal

- Arvid
  Missal

- Friedbert
  Missal

# Part 1

# Chapter 1

## Michel's History Lessons

During the years from 1879 to 1900, when Friedrich was growing up in the cloistered and comfortable affluence of the little colony of Nataliendorf, he often wondered why there were so many Germans living in Russia.  However, as Friedrich grew into manhood he methodically learned of his family's history by listening to the stories of his father.  During the long winter evenings, after the days work was done his father would sit with the family and tell them about how both Russian and German history had evolved.  He explained why and how this had influenced the Fischbuch ancestors to come to Russia and build their farmsteads in this pleasant and productive land.  Including, how through the invitation of Tsarina Catherine II they had arrived in Russia.

Friedrich could recall that starting when he was about five-years-old in the long winter evenings as the family sat around the warmth of the open fire in the wood burning stove, his father first started telling the story of what prompted their ancestors to come to Russia. Michel's first accounts were about their adopted homeland and the rise of the Russian Romanov dynasty. The first Tsar was a nephew-by-marriage of Ivan the Terrible, and Michael Romanov became Tsar Michael I. He was crowned in 1613 and ruled until 1645 and upon his death he was succeeded by his daughter Elizabeth.

The most notable Emperor of the Romanov regime, however, was Tsar Peter I, better known as Peter the Great and ruled from 1689 to 1725. He was well aware that Europe was far advanced both economically and culturally compared to Russia's vast Empire that languished under the feudal system  He sought to remedy this by encouraging Russia's nobility to invite skilled German artisans to modernize Russia's economy. Peter the Great often visited major centres in Germany, Holland, England, Italy and France and brought back many skilled workers to modernize the backward Russian commercial and cultural system. It was not long before German artisans settled in German-speaking enclaves in various parts of the nation. In fact, so many migrated to Russia that a large community of Germans was established in what was known as Moscow's "German suburb" which began to emerge during the reign of the predecessors of Peter the Great, Tsar Michael I and Tsar Alexis I, which marked the first incursion of German influence into the Russian Empire. To institute even further Russian connections to the west Peter the Great also instituted a policy whereby Russian royalty could intermarry with the royalty of the principalities of Germany. He knew that to bring about ties with German royalty it would not take long before Romanov connections would eventually extend to the royal houses of other countries as well. During the next few generations, Romanov descendants appeared in Denmark, England, the Netherlands, France and Greece. As foreign influence continued to flourish, the "German suburb" continued to grow and became part of Muscovite culture.

During Russia's war against Sweden in 1702, Peter the Great was personally in command of two Russian frigates in Russia's arctic-bound White Sea. Here he waited patiently for the winds to change to carry them around the Scandinavian Peninsula and into the northern part of the Baltic Sea where he intended to attack the Swedish fortress at Noteburg, which blocked the entrance to the mouth of Russia's Neva River. He soon grew tired of waiting for the winds to change so Tsar Peter assembled hundreds of Russian serfs who, along with his sailors and teams of up to 100 horses, pulled the ships 110 miles across land to Lake Onega. The frigates were launched into Lake Onega and sailed on to Lake Ladoga and then into the Baltic Sea. Here they surprised the Swedes at Noteburg and captured this barrier to the delta of Russia's river Neva. Gaining control of the entrance to the broad delta allowed Kronstadt to evolve at the old Swedish fortress of Noteburg. Kronstadt eventually became Russia's maritime link to the outside world. Little did

Friedrich realize, as he listened to his father's accounts of Noteburg, which became Kronstadt that he would start a naval career at this old Swedish fortress.

Another connection to Friedrich and his family that would occur some 35 years later is that in 1932 Stalin in an attempt to eclipse the glory of Peter the Great declared that a canal would be built permanently linking the White Sea with the Baltic Sea. He had it christened "The Stalin Belomor Canal," which was to perpetuate his name in history forever. To accomplish this he ordered 170,000 slave labourers from his Gulags and slave labour camps to begin excavations using primitive tools and their bare hands. Later, he had 36 Soviet writers write a book about "his" canal. This propaganda about the virtues of Russia's new socialist industrial power was published with great fanfare in 1934. As Michel and Justina's evening history lessons progressed and as Friedrich's life was to unfold, he would later find that among the 170,000 prisoners that Stalin drew from the Gulags as slave labourers that both his future son-in-law, his granddaughter and several other relatives would perish among the 170,000 Belomor slave labourers that vanished without a trace. These were men, who along with their wives and their children, had been arrested merely for being property owners. These landowners worked side by side with a variety of convicts, murderers and wayward serfs who found various ways to prey on their fellow inmates. Today, no statistics are known of the 170,000 people most of whom perished building this monument to Comrade Stalin.

In 1704, Tsar Peter declared that the capital city of Russia would be built along the marshy shoreline tributaries, which wound their way through the delta of the Neva River that was now Russia's major waterway that spilled into the northern margin of the Baltic Sea. His vision was that the location of the capital city would expose it to the culture and industry of all of the countries bordering the coast of the Baltic Sea. In time St. Petersburg exceeding all of the Tsars' expectations and was eventually influenced not only by the Baltic States but also by all of the European countries. It was through this influence that today it boasts some of the most diverse and fascinating architecture in the world. Unfortunately, upon the death of Peter the Great in 1725 his efforts to Europeanize Russia waned considerably. Under the rule of his daughter, Empress Elizabeth, the new Tsarina, who ruled from 1725 until her death in 1761, her country remained as stagnant as ever. During this thirty-six year interlude, the Russian Empire continued to wallow in feudal isolation and retained only a veneer of western influence, which was restricted to and practiced exclusively by the Russian royalty and nobility. Over ninety per cent of the population remained in the grip of serfdom untouched by the attempts of Peter the Great to modernize the country.

The next sovereign to institute major advancements in Russian culture, trade, industry, commerce and territorial expansion was Tsarina Catherine II who in 1763 through her manifesto brought about a massive migration of Germans to Russia.

Michel and Justina Fischbuch continued their educational entertainment for the family during the long winter evenings and Friedrich eagerly looked forward to each session of his father's version of their history. He constantly pressured his brothers to finish their chores early so that they could all hear further episodes of the family history as it emerged and how it was intertwined with the history of the two countries that moulded the lives of his family. Michel suggested that the family also should know some history of their native country and proceeded to continue with accounts of the early history of Germany and how a minor German princess from Pomerania was instrumental in the migration of the Fischbuch settlers to Russia. The tribulations of Friedrich's ancestors who were workers and artisans on a little German principality arose from the way Germany as a country had evolved. The earliest inhabitants of Germany varied with the warring factions that migrated northward from the inhabited areas along the northern coast of the Mediterranean Sea. In the early 1700's Germany was a crazy quilt of nearly three hundred states or principalities that ranged from estates consisting of a few hectares to the large nation states of Prussia and Austria. All of these principalities were part of the Holy Roman Empire, however, the Emperor in Rome himself had little influence.

Consequently, the minor prince of each principality even if he owned only a few hectares had his own laws and jealously guarded his territory. This set the stage for much petty squabbling, fighting and warring between the principalities that the peasants, serfs, or farmers of each property had to endure. A large number of princely houses also led to financial problems since each royal family had to be maintained in a dignified and luxurious lifestyle including castles, courtiers and all of the associated trappings. The task of maintaining this royal front and providing all of the required luxuries to their royal masters fell to the few lowly workers in each minor kingdom. They were expected to provide for their royal masters, but were allowed little for their own sustenance. Consequently, much was wrought from the prince's farmers who had to pay up to ninety-five percent of their produce in taxes which was standard in Germany's feudal system of the day.

Each royal family of course was intent on perpetuating itself and since there were so many of them considerable effort was made to marry the offspring to foreign royalty, as an estate of only a few hectares could ill afford to be split. Examples of ones who married into famous foreign royal families are the Hannoverian Georges who became kings of England and of course the German princess from a minor principality in Pomerania who became Tsarina Catherine II of Russia.

During the middle ages, while Germany was closely allied to the Roman Empire there was a relative but uneasy religious stability. With the advent however of Martin Luther the country soon was split into warring factions and there followed a century of religious wars with the Catholic Empire on the one side and the Protestant north German princes on the other. After indescribable devastation and decimation of the population, these wars ended in 1684, mainly due to complete exhaustion and frustration on both sides. The Treaty of 1684, gave each prince the right to choose the religion for the people of his principality. However, this did not succeed too well since most states had minority religious groups sometimes Catholic, sometimes Lutheran and sometimes dissident Protestants. Even the ruler himself in some cases was of a minority faith in his own principality.

Consequently, religious confusion and persecution continued. It is apparent that the German working class of 1763 had much reason to be unhappy. They groaned under the feudal burdens imposed by the petty princes who at all costs had to maintain a royal front. Their sons were dragged off to fight in never-ending local or foreign wars. The passing armies confiscated their grain, ravaged their women and quartered in their houses. Taxes were exorbitant and they were always on the verge of poverty and starvation.

In the midst of this depressing existence in 1763, came the Golden Manifesto of Tsarina Catherine II of Russia. This was a masterpiece of immigration propaganda, which laid the groundwork for a century long influx of thousands of Germans to the "promised land" of southern Russia. The manifesto indeed gave an alluring vision of Russia: large tracts of fertile land, virtually uninhabited, in well-watered regions that would provide a wealth of agricultural products. Furthermore, she offered free transportation to Russia with freedom to settle anywhere in the country, freedom to practice any trade or profession, generous allotments of free land, interest-free loans, local self government, freedom from military service and above all freedom of religion. Since Catherine had grown up in the tiny German principality of Anhalt-Zerbst, she was well aware of the plight of the German working class. The sales job done by Catherine's manifesto was magnificent and the agents she sent to the German cities attracted entire villages that migrated en masse—after all who could refuse this ascension to paradise?

Fascinated that she had such an influence in expanding the German population of Russia, Friedrich and his older brothers insisted that their father tell them as much as he could about the life of this unknown princess who became Catherine the Great and had emerged from a tiny German principality, much like the one the Fischbuch ancestors came from. Consequently, Michel devoted nearly a month of evenings expounding on the life of this German princess.

Catherine was born as Sophia Augusta Frederica in 1729 at Stettin in Pomerania. Her father was the prince of a small principality called Anhalt-Zerbst but like many small German principalities Anhalt-Zerbst had fallen on hard times and her father was employed as an officer in the Prussian Army to make royal ends meet. Sophia's ambitious mother Johanna was twenty-seven years younger than her Prussian soldier husband. Princess Johanna had rated all of the various German principalities and found that Anhalt-Zerbst was quite low on the royal ladder. Setting her sights higher for her daughter, Sophia was tutored in French, history, theology and philosophy.

In the latter part of 1743, while Princess Johanna was casting about for a royal suitor for Sophia, Empress Elizabeth the Tsarina of Russia who had ascended the Tsarist throne upon the death of her father Tsar Peter the Great in 1725, designated her young German nephew Peter as the heir apparent to the Tsarist throne. In fact, due to the decree of Tsar Peter the Great that promoted royal intermarriage young Peter and Sophia were second cousins. Princess Johanna seeing an opportunity, lost no time in using this as an excuse to pay a visit to Moscow even though it was in the dead of winter and travel in those days was harsh. Upon her arrival in Moscow Johanna found that Empress Elizabeth was sceptical of Sophia, but Johanna undaunted pressed on until Elizabeth was convinced of Sophia's many attributes. Once convinced, Elizabeth promptly set a wedding date, since she was anxious for Grand Duke Peter to produce an heir to continue the Russian Romanov lineage of German origin. Sophia was received in the Orthodox Church and was given the name Catherine. They were married with great fanfare in August of 1743; he was seventeen, she sixteen.

Moreover, what of Grand Duke Peter? Unfortunately, he was a bad match for Catherine, he was not studious he was not clever, in fact he was somewhat retarded both physically and emotionally. He liked military training but this was limited to playing with toy soldiers. Catherine soon became tired of his childish antics and spent her time reading Plato and Voltaire. With reading and studying, she unwittingly prepared herself for the role that fate would soon bestow upon her.

Empress Elizabeth became more and more exasperated in her quest for an heir since the wedded couple seemed to have no physical attraction for each other. In a mood of desperation, she had them imprisoned together in a portion of the palace, but to no avail. After seven years, she gave up and let them roam the palace at will. Catherine had continued her self-education while confined with the Grand Duke. Nevertheless, now that she was free, twenty-three and quite attractive she soon caught the eye of Serge Saltikov, a Russian nobleman. An affair followed and in 1754, this union produced a son, Paul. The Empress was elated that an heir finally had been born although deep in her heart she must have known that the child was not Peters. Paul eventually ascended the Russian Throne as Tsar Paul I. Empress Elizabeth, in her joy sent an emissary on a special mission to Sweden's monarchs and court to announce the birth of the heir. Ironically, it was none other that Serge Saltikov.

Catherine lost Saltikov as a lover, but she quickly set her sights for another. They fell on the handsome Stanislaus Poniatowski the Polish nobleman who would soon become the King of Poland. In 1756, they had a daughter, Princess Anne who died a year later. Soon afterward in 1758, Poniatowski was recalled to Poland but Catherine did not grieve for either her dead daughter or her delinquent lover for she had become enamoured with a commoner, Gregory Orlov. Orlov was a guardsman of a family of professional soldiers and had distinguished himself for bravery in the Seven Years War against Prussia and was somewhat of a hero in St. Petersburg. Gregory Orlov had four brothers who also were soldiers. In concert, they were known for their fighting, debauchery and drinking. Her liaison with Gregory Orlov lasted for fourteen turbulent years (1759-1773) and changed the course of Russian history forever.

Gregory Orlov's affair with Catherine must have set him thinking about the line of power and what would happen when old Empress Elizabeth died, and if Grand Duke Peter somehow was forced to abdicate. He must have discussed this with his brothers because it was not long before they were spreading the gospel of Catherine among the military. The seeds of a grand plan were being sown.

Empress Elizabeth, the daughter of Tsar Peter the Great died in 1761, and Grand Duke Peter ascended the throne as Tsar Peter III. At this time, the Seven Years War with Russia, Austria and France against Prussia and England was progressing satisfactorily. Empress Elizabeth's armies had driven the Prussians westward and had occupied Berlin; the Prussians were about to surrender. In a moment of unbelievable ignorance newly crowned Tsar Peter III called back all of the armies and Prussia, instead of being conquered emerged as the victor and again became a major power.

The animosity between Peter and Catherine was increasing and she was becoming more and more uneasy for she feared that he might make some fickle move against her as having her divorced, banished, or even worse, put to death. He was extremely fond of his current mistress, which made Catherine even more apprehensive. In June 1762, while Peter visited in Germany and was well engrossed in his favourite pastime of playing war games, the Orlov brothers took this opportunity to inform Catherine of their devised plan. She was agreeable so they set off to St. Petersburg where the Russian military was stationed. When they arrived at the barracks, the Orlov brothers informed the commanding officer to assemble the troops for the Tsar's wife wished to make an announcement. Here she was a pathetic woman among a sea of soldiers. In a quiet voice, she said she came to them to seek protection since she feared the Emperor intended to kill her. The soldiers rushed forward to kiss her hand and swore allegiance to her as Empress Catherine II. The military now was at her command and as a result so was all of Russia.

Tsar Peter was informed of the revolt the same evening and he spent the night agonizing as to what to do. By morning, completely confused, he abdicated—a decision that cost him his country and his life. He was confined to a small estate under the watchful eye of Alexis Orlov. A few days later Alexis informed Catherine that Peter had quarrelled with someone during a drinking bout and was killed. Catherine probably was relieved since a dead dethroned Emperor could never be reinstated. She immediately announced to the world that Tsar Peter III had died suddenly of a severe attack of hemorrhoidal colic and that all of Russia was in mourning. Catherine did not hesitate to show her gratitude to the Orlov brothers. Her lover Gregory of course got special status as a Prince and on the other four, she bestowed the titles of Count. Count Alexis soon became Admiral of the Russian Fleet and was instrumental in decimating the Turkish Navy.

Gregory fell from Catherine's favour in 1772, when she became fed up with his philandering, even though he had provided her with three sons. From this time on, she became infatuated with at least eleven more lovers ranging from her private secretary to various guardsmen and cavalry officers. In 1792, she had her last fling and installed a handsome twenty-two year old Horse Guards Officer into her quarters. That Russian royalty was a hotbed of international gossip and intrigue did not faze Catherine in the least. Her attributes of persistence, stamina and ambition are reflected in her accomplishments. No other Romanov ruler matched her territorial expansion of the Russian Empire. She drove the Turks from the Black Sea area and progressively took slice after slice of territory from Poland, much to the dismay of her former lover Polish King Poniatowski.

Catherine died in 1796 at the age of sixty-seven. She left behind a country that would never forget her. On the one hand, her unabashed love affairs were the gossip of every royal household around the world. On the other hand, she engineered her rise to power and her territorial and domestic expansion like a master chess player. Among her many accomplishments was her Manifesto inviting the German farmers and artisans, among whom were Friedrich's ancestors who toiled for nearly a century to clear and till the forest and swampland of southern Russia and made their fertile land bloom.

# Chapter 2

# Hannover to Danzig to Pilipovitschi

The massive influx of German colonists that came to Russia in the late 1700's and early 1800's occurred mainly through the invitation of Tsarina Catherine II. Upon her accession to Tsardom in 1762, Catherine immediately saw this opportunity to develop the vast relatively untouched fertile regions of her country that ranged from Ukraine, to the Volga and into Kazakhstan. Shrewdly looking back on her own German heritage, she was well aware of the plight of the harassed and over-worked farm labourers that were treated like slaves in Germany. There is little wonder that when in 1763 the Golden Manifesto of Russia's Catherine II was presented by her agents in Frankfurt, Munich, Cologne and Hannover that the German peasants responded en masse. Michel pointed out that this is undoubtedly why his fore-fathers could not resist this wonderful invitation—up to eighteen hectares of free land, no taxes, freedom from military service, freedom to practice any religion, plus other incentives.

It was in this atmosphere that young Friedrich's ancestors left a tiny principality somewhere near Hannover in central Germany in about 1800. On their way through Poland, they were stopped in the Danzig (now Gdansk) area of northern Poland to wait for further instructions from Catherine's agents. These instructions never came so they again were forced to work more or less as slave labourers for Polish nobility clearing and draining land while they waited and waited.

Some time in 1815, twenty-five German families in the Danzig area were approached by a Polish nobleman by the name of Pilipovitshi. Several of these families were Michel Fischbuch's ancestors. Pilipovitshi owned several large undeveloped estates adjacent to the Ukrainian city of Novograd Volinskiy. Realizing the plight of these displaced German farmers he shrewdly capitalized on their dilemma and invited the twenty-five families to come to Ukraine to sell them parcels of forested land on his estates that needed much draining and clearing. He told them that to develop this land would require much work and it was for this reason that Pilipovitshi said he would sell the land to them for only three roubles per hectare, and that the colonists could buy whatever land they were able to put into agricultural production. However, he made the stipulation that title could be obtained only when the land was properly cleared and drained and that the first two settlements be named after his two daughters, Annette and Josephine. As fate would have it, Michel was born in Josephine and his future wife was born in Annette.

Since the twenty-five families were well experienced in the adversities of clearing and draining land in the Danzig area, and had fled the rigours of near serfdom in a tiny German principality, they were easily convinced. By this time they were very frustrated by Catherine's unfulfilled promises, consequently, they were overwhelmed by the fact that they could at last have their own property by perseverance and hard work.

After a long and arduous trip by wagon train, they finally arrived at the Pilipovitshi estate. They soon found that to clear, log, drain and cultivate these forested areas was a monumental task. To cut down massive oak trees up to six feet in diameter, tamarack, birch and evergreen trees with only axes and handsaws took much time, patience and hard work. The only other help they had was the strength of their horses and oxen. The twenty-five colonist families then had to ditch and drain the swampy land, which was their next formidable challenge.

It was fortunate that the Danzig colonist brought with them the seed grains necessary for their livelihood. This included wheat, oats, barley, corn and hops. They also brought steel shares for their mould-board ploughs, a multitude of steel farm tools, and their wagon wheels were steel rimmed as well. The Russian peasants, on the other hand worked only with wooden implements modelled after what they had worked with in the days when they were serfs. Until

1861, serfs made up ninety per cent of Russia's population, they were bought and sold like cattle, beaten for the most minor offences, and indeed were considered as livestock. They were owned by the Tsar's royal family, the elite of the church and the nobility. However, in 1861, the serfs were freed by one of the more benevolent Tsars, Tsar Alexander II. Before they were freed they had little interest in the day-to-day welfare of their masters, their only goal was to survive to live another day. Nevertheless, even though the serfs were now free they remained a culture unto their own. Some of them attempted to make a living by using the primitive farming tools they used as serfs, but many of them just roamed the vast forested and steppe areas of Russia and survived by what they could find in the wild and by stealing from established farmsteads and villages. Inevitably, it was not long before the German colonies were producing far greater per capita yields of grain, fruit and vegetables than the backward Russian farmers were.

When the Fischbuch ancestors arrived at the Pilipovitshi estate, they settled on a parcel of land in the new colony of Josephine. As their children were born and grew up new colonies adjacent to Annette and Josephine were carved out of the Pilipovitshi estate. Friedrich's father Michel was born in 1849 at Josephine. In 1871, Michel married Justina Moller whose family was one of the other pioneering families that had settled in the second mother colony of Annette. After Michel and Justina were married they cleared, and then bought, an eighteen-hectare parcel of land in the new and nearby colony of Nataliendorf. From 1874 to 1901, Michel and Justina had fourteen children, three daughters and eleven sons. As the other settlers in Makowetz had children more land again was needed, and Nataliendorf continued to grow. It was in Nataliendorf and Makowetz where all fourteen of Michel and Justina's children were born. Friedrich, their fourth son was born in 1879. From the time that they were married Michel, Justina and their growing family worked diligently to clear the huge oak trees and drain the swampy land. As Friedrich grew up he, his ten brothers and three sisters were assigned more and more tasks to maintain their prized property.

As Nataliendorf grew, the cleared land was carefully put into production. Michel and his immediate neighbour August Wendtland, who was another new arrival in Nataliendorf, saw to it that no one was allowed to build their houses immediately adjacent to the street or roadway that ran through the village. Instead, three or four rows of fruit trees were planted between the houses and the road and in springtime, the aroma of flowering plum and cherry blossoms filled the air. As the families grew and other colonists moved into the village fruit trees continued to be planted along the roadway. When outsiders approached and entered Nataliendorf, it was as if they were entering an orchard.

The children continued to grow and the five oldest boys were delegated more and heavier tasks. The farm animals were a treasured part of every colonist's life and they were treated with great care and affection. This was especially true for Michel and his sons; at the top of the list of course were their horses since they were used to do most of the heavy work on the farm and especially were necessary for travel therefore proper care was justified. By the late 1880's, during planting time or harvest Friedrich would wait for his older brother August to return from the fields after a long days work with the tired and sweating horses. August spent most of his time working with horses, which seemed to be his sole ambition, and it is ironic that some twenty-five years later, in his new home country of Canada he would be killed by his favourite horse. Friedrich, who at the time was about eleven-years-old would help August un-harness the horses and let them run free in the barnyard, where they would roll on the ground and shake themselves before being let into the barn for a feed of oats and hay. It was then that Friedrich was allowed to take the horses down to the nearby Sluch river to let them drink and swim. It always amazed Friedrich that the young colts could swim the first time they entered the water, yet it took him nearly a year of practice before he himself could swim across the river.

Friedrich's best friend was Gustav Wendtland who lived directly across the roadway that ran eastward toward the Sluch River. Gustav had four brothers and together with the five oldest Fischbuch brothers, they made quite a contingent when it came to working on a community project or being caught up in neighbourhood shenanigans. Friedrich became intrigued with the Wendtland blacksmith shop where August Wendtland spent all of his spare time making horseshoes, ploughshares, wagon wheel rims, hay rakes and a multitude of tools. August Wendtland had learned his trade by trial and error and his expertise of working with iron had become known throughout the area surrounding Novograd Voliniskiy. He soon was referred to as that "Master Blacksmith from Nataliendorf." August Wendtland was intent for at least one of his sons to take up the blacksmith trade. However, after suffering through hours of cranking the forge the intense heat from the hot coals and the constant clanking of August's hammer on the anvil, they were soon overcome by boredom. As often as they could they would slip away to their nearby fishing haunts along the Sluch River where they would join their friend, an old bearded Mouzhik (ex-serf) who would occasionally lend them his boat when he was not fishing himself. Friedrich would often join his friend Gustav Wendtland when he was at the river watering and bathing his brother's horses. Since fishing was not Friedrich's main interest he would help Gustav cut small willow shoots. From these Gustav's father would make baskets, which he would sell at the market in Novograd Volinskiy. Friedrich, however, was always drawn to the music of the hammer on the Wendtland anvil and every spare moment he would have he would crank the forge; fascinated how slabs of iron could so easily be moulded into sharp ploughshares and the more delicate tools such as sickles and scythes.

Since his own sons had little interest in his blacksmith shop August Wendtland was delighted that Friedrich would so willingly crank the forge. One day August Wendtland showed Friedrich how to take a red-hot length of iron from the fire, how to place it on the anvil, and how to hammer it into the shape of a horseshoe. From that time on Friedrich spent every free moment in the Wendtland blacksmith shop and loved to hear the ring of hammer on anvil. During the next few years, Friedrich became more and more adept at the blacksmith trade and when he would accompany August Wendtland to other villages he eventually became known in the whole area as that "other blacksmith from Nataliendorf."

On longer journeys with heavy loads, Michel Fischbuch or the older boys would take along an extra horse and would stop at regular intervals to rest the horses. Their Russian neighbours, on the other hand, would not take care of their horses and would drive them unshod on the hard gravel roadways until they were lame or even until they dropped from exhaustion. In contrast, Michel's horses always were superior in strength and stamina that was coupled with the fact that Michel and the boys had always kept their wagons with their steel-rimmed wheels in good condition. When they met an oncoming Russian wagon that would not give them passing room, they would force the Russian wagon off the road, and the Russian wagons with only wooden wheels often were broken. This then would lead to much name-calling and in some cases even fisticuffs where again Michel and the boys would excel since they were always well fed and strong from hard work.

As time went on, the whole family was so busy with looking after their fields, orchard, horses, oxen, cattle, pigs, chickens, geese plus many other chores so they did not have time to visit far from home. Consequently, the only contact with other communities was to visit relatives in the nearby Lutheran villages of Annette, Josephine or Makowetz. Consequently, little contact was had with other German colonies that were of the Baptist or Catholic faith, and there was even less contact with Russian villages. The exception to this was individuals who were specialists in certain trades and travelled to nearby German and even some Russian colonies to ply their special trades. For example, August Wendtland became the travelling blacksmith. Michel Fischbuch became the travelling sexton (Kuster). Another neighbour from the adjacent colony of Josephine, Johann Kahler, was the travelling lay doctor (Felscher). He had acquired his medical skills when he had served as a medic in the Crimea during the Russo-Turkish war in 1877.

In the rather cloistered environment of the Nataliendorf colony, the younger boys always were curious about outside events and were particularly entranced when they heard of soldiers passing through the area, since at that time there was escalating tension along the Polish-Ukrainian border. In the early 1890's, whenever they would hear of the military activity along the Polish frontier Friedrich, his brothers and the Wendtland boys would often secretly slip into the nearby major centre of Novograd Volinskiy. They would watch the spirited horses prancing to music while the soldiers in full uniform strutted arrogantly by them in their polished boots leaving the boys to look down at their own calloused bare feet. However, for Michel this show of military bravado only heightened his apprehension about the promise of Catherine the Great in her manifesto to exempt the colonists from military service. This promise however had been conveniently ignored by Tsar Alexander II and was revoked by him in 1874. Thenceforth, all young men when they reached the age of twenty-one were required to serve in the Russian army. Michel was concerned about the military conscripting one or even all of his eleven sons since he could vividly recall the stories of his father about the way the young men in the principalities of Germany were forced to fight in never-ending wars. On the other hand, Michel felt that since his grandfather, his father and now he had prospered, were diligent in paying their taxes and were model citizens that he would be proud if his sons were called to serve their country and their Tsar.

Milking cows and looking after the farm animals, other than the horses and oxen was the task assigned to Justina and later to the three girls. Working in the fields with horses and oxen, cutting wood, building fences and other heavier tasks were performed by Michel. However, m.ore work was accomplished as the boys became older. Michel had become the Sexton (Kuster) of the village prayer hall (Bethaus). He would perform regular Sunday services, religious instruction, baptisms and funerals. However, confirmations and marriages could only be performed by an ordained clergyman from Novograd Volinskiy, who travelled from village to village as the latter events arose. The Nataliendorf Bethaus, or prayer hall, also served as a school and all of the children of the village were required to attend. In the first few years they were only able to take five years of schooling that was taught by those in the community that were versed in various subjects. Later, as the residents prospered, a full-time teacher was brought in and all subjects were taught in both German and Russian, and the students were required to take at least eight years of study.

The rare times when outsiders came to Nataliendorf Michel and Justina saw to it that the whole family greeted them cordially especially the aged who were treated with special respect. This also extended to Russian, Ukrainian, Tartar and Gypsy elders when they arrived. However, whenever the transient Gypsies appeared they were always found entertaining but often were caught pilfering fruit, vegetables or anything that was not out of sight. One time Friedrich saw a young Gypsy boy taking pears from their orchard and tucking them into his shirt. Friedrich ran to tell his father and as he ran to where the Gypsies had gathered and were entertaining the villagers he heard an anguished scream from the young Gypsy boy. Bees had been burrowing their way into some of the pears and since they were entrapped in his shirt they exposed the young boy's thievery by stinging him under his shirt.

Eduard, Friedrich's oldest brother was the first of the family to be married. He had met Henrietta (Yeta) Wolltmann at the colony of Adolin, which was a colony settled by Germans directly under the auspices of Catherine II. It was located about fifteen kilometres south of Annette. The residents of Nataliendorf had been called to fight a fire that was ravaging the community. As fate would have it, Eduard was on the bucket brigade that saved the home of Henrietta's parents. Wedding customs of the colonists did not include a betrothal or engagement period and a Matchmaker commonly singled out eligible couples. In Henrietta's case, however the matchmaker was "instructed" by her parents to accommodate the arrangement. Eduard and Henrietta were married in Novograd Volinskiy in late October of 1894, and the three-day wedding reception was held at Michel and Justina's home at Nataliendorf.

On November 1, 1894, during the last day of the festivities they heard of the sudden death of their current Tsar, Alexander III. Tsar Alexander had been ailing with kidney problems ever since 1888, when on a return journey from Livadia, the summer palace in the Crimea the royal train derailed somewhere near Kharkov and the Tsar's coach had overturned trapping all of those inside.

Tsar Alexander using his enormous strength lifted the steel roof of the carriage and held it while the royal travellers escaped. From this over-exertion, his kidneys were damaged. He survived with sheer will power for the next six years before he finally succumbed in 1894. Tsar Alexander III was a huge imposing hot-tempered ruler who revelled in his role as the supreme autocrat of the Russian Empire. Indeed, he portrayed himself as an example of the legendary Russian Bear and often demonstrated his brute strength by lifting massive weights to embarrass his battery of bodyguards.

His son Nicholas, the heir to the Russian throne was born in 1868. However, he was not endowed with his father's domineering will, strength or roughshod lifestyle. Nicholas was a quiet, thoughtful and retiring youngster who was made even more insecure by his father's constant urging him to be more aggressive. His father who constantly scoffed and ridiculed Nicholas at his reticence to take on responsibility, made Nicholas even more introverted. In fact, when Nicholas was twenty-five-years-old Tsar Alexander's advisors suggested that Nicholas be put in charge of overseeing the final stages of the construction of the Trans-Siberian railway. Tsar Alexander scoffed at the suggestion and said that his son did not yet have the mettle to take on such a task, since he was still only capable of childish responsibilities. Consequently, as the future unfolded, and upon his father's death, Nicholas was faced with the fact that as Emperor and supreme autocrat of the Russian Empire he would be totally unprepared to fill his father's iron-fisted role in dealing with the huge Romanov domain.

Nicholas's future wife in family terms was his second cousin. Princess Alexandra's royal lineage included that she was the granddaughter of Queen Victoria of England. Alexandra hailed from the principality of Hesse in central Germany. The capital city of Hesse, Darmstadt, had one of numerous palaces inhabited by Ludwig IV, the Grand Duke of Hesse and his family. Furthermore, Alexandra, the Grand Duke's third daughter had an impeccable pedigree and could trace her lineage back to Charlemagne. She was well educated by a complement of astute governesses that were hand picked by her grandmother. Alexandra spent much time being coached to read and study the classics, which kept her from indulging in idle gossip, as was the norm for most royal princesses. The early death of Alexandra's younger brother, due to his inherited haemophilia was an omen for things to come for Alexandra. This was followed by the death of her mother when Alexandra was only six-years-old and shortly after that, her younger sister died of diphtheria. This had a lasting effect on Alexandra who became devoutly religious and turned to God whom she felt would bring about the ultimate reunion between her, her mother and her siblings. This obsession of reaching out to God stayed with her and her religious devotion was a major factor in Nicholas and Alexandra's future during their reign as Emperor and Empress of the Russian Empire.

By the late 1880's and early 1890's, Tsar Alexander III had no qualms about his dislike of Alexandra. He had even less respect for her grandmother England's Queen Victoria, who he felt was a doughty old biddy who was constantly meddling in the affairs of international royalty. Even more irritating to Tsar Alexander was the Queen's interference in the politics of other countries. Inevitably, this made the relationship between Russia and England tenuous at best. Queen Victoria, in the same vein also was strongly against the union between Nicholas and Alexandra, and felt that any German princess that went to Russia would be overcome by the cold winters in this desolate and godforsaken land. In fact, since she had so much contact with the Hessian Empire she felt it was her royal duty to select the spouses of all four of the Hessian princesses.

Tsar Alexander, to counter Nicholas's interest in Alexandra, selected a seventeen-year-old ballerina to divert Nicholas's ardour away from Alexandra. Nicholas, as usual wishing always to please his domineering father meekly bent to his father's wishes. At first, he was a bit hesitant, however, he soon became comfortable in the company of his tiny, attractive and ardent mistress and for the time being pushed Alexandra out of his mind. Alexandra nevertheless kept thinking of the prestige of becoming the Empress of the vast Russian Empire. Her devout religious connection to the Lutheran faith was a definite roadblock since, to become Empress she would have to convert to Russian Orthodoxy. Nevertheless, in 1890,

Alexandra travelled to Russia to visit her sister with more on her mind than just to keep in touch -- Alexandra wanted to keep her options open. Her arrival made Nicholas quite uneasy and he began to have second thoughts about his ballerina mistress after all, she had no connection to royalty and here was Alexandra with her sterling pedigree.

The health of Alexander III continued to fail and by 1894, his unbending will and superhuman resolve to live diminished to the point where he even relented in his opposition to Nicholas's marriage to Alexandra. His doctors told him that he would soon die from nephritis and if he should die, he felt that a firm hand would be necessary to continue the Romanov lineage. The Emperor saw in Alexandra the domineering spirit that he had not been able to instil in Nicholas and for this reason felt that Alexandra would bolster his son's timidity in his future role as supreme autocrat. Just before he died on November 1st, 1894, Alexander III gave Princess Alexandra his blessing to wed Nicholas. Twenty-six-year-old Nicholas was overwhelmed with grief at his father's death but he was also smitten with terror at now becoming the new Tsar. Nicholas and Alexandra were married in St. Petersburg on November 26th, 1894, in the chapel of the Winter Palace. The celebration that followed had all of the ritual trappings of Russian royal weddings of the past even though it was announced that it would be a quiet wedding in deference to the death of Alexander III. The so-called subdued celebration included a ride along the Nevsky Prospect in a golden coach to the accompaniment of a twenty-one gun salute fired from the Fortress of Peter and Paul as the entourage wended their way to a grand reception at the Winter Palace.

Since Nicholas had led a sheltered life by his aggressive father, he grew up very insecure and was very shocked by the fact that he was now supreme autocrat of this vast Russian Empire. Maturing into a kind and gentle man he therefore was very uneasy in his new role. He depended much on his new wife Alexandra as well as the vast array of Romanovs and courtiers surrounding him. Nicholas was oblivious to the magnitude of his power and shrouded in his role as this timid but supreme autocrat unknowingly made his advisors constantly afraid of disagreeing with him. Nicholas was unaware that if their advice offended or irritated him he could demote them, ban them to Siberia, or even put them to death. Inevitably, since he was terrified of the power he had witnessed in his father, he blanked this out of his mind and governing the country became a minor interest to Nicholas. He was more concerned with the pursuit of being accepted by everyone including God, making it difficult for his hangers-on who naturally would always say what they thought the Tsar wanted to hear. If they were unsure of voicing their opinions, they would conveniently fall into silent idolatry whenever they were asked for controversial advice. Consequently, most of them shrewdly kept a low profile so as not to alienate his Royal Highness, since they never knew just when they could be in line for an admiralship, a governorship or some other bureaucratic plum.

Now as Tsar, Nicholas not only had absolute autocratic power over the entire country, it naturally extended to presiding over the royal Romanov family. The family was composed of many egotistical individuals who were spoiled by a lifetime of grandeur from living under the Romanov umbrella. The dynasty itself extended to other European families as well which included Kaiser Wilhelm of Germany who was the grandson of Queen Victoria, cousin to Nicholas as well as a cousin to Alexandra, Nicholas's new wife. Both Wilhelm and Nicholas thus were nephews of King Edward VII of England. Nicholas's grandfather was Denmark's King Christian IX and his grandmother was Denmark's Dowager Empress Maria Federovna.

Again, Nicholas with his timid and introverted personality was overwhelmed by the power as the supreme being of the dynasty. It is small wonder, therefore, that Tsar Nicholas II was greatly influenced by his older and domineering cousin, Germany's Kaiser Wilhelm II. Indeed, many of the other aggressive Romanovs influenced Nicholas as well. Yet, on the other hand, Nicholas knowing that he had this ultimate power became quite harsh with the less assertive members of his diverse royal entourage. State affairs were run by a bureaucracy with the Tsar at the top and all of the senior ministers and administrators held some connection to the Romanov dynasty.

Since many of them had been appointed by some casual whim of the Tsar, most of them had little or no background in their selected fields.  Consequently, wide ranges of senseless bureaucratic decisions were made that resulted in major disasters.  Members of the royal hierarchy were constantly in competition with each other to climb this royally devised ladder.  They all knew that once they were appointed their authority was never questioned; allowing them to languish unchallenged in perpetuity at some ministerial, foreign or military post -- paying little attention to their duties as heads of state.

# Chapter 3

# Nataliendorf

Shortly after their wedding, Eduard Fischbuch and his new wife Henrietta set about establishing their own farmstead in Eduard's home colony of Nataliendorf. However, the news of the death of Alexander III made everyone in the whole district of Novograd Volinskiy concerned about what the future held for them. They had grown to know Tsar Alexander as a harsh and dictatorial ruler and had for some time been distressed about the Tsar's emerging policy of russification and the beginnings of his brutal ethnic cleansing. They now anxiously looked forward to the reign of the new Tsar, Nicholas II and what his view would be of their own German background. They had heard that he was a much kinder and gentler person than his tyrannical father. The Tsarist regimes had been relatively tolerant of the influx of German workers since the time of the first Tsar, Michael I who in 1613 was the first to bring in German workers. This policy was followed in 1645, by the next Tsar, Alexis I and in 1690, further efforts were made by Tsar Peter I (Peter the Great) who tried to Europeanize his backward Russian Empire by inviting specialists not only from Germany but also from many other countries.

However, the major influx of Germans occurred from 1763 to the mid 1800's due to the Golden Manifesto of Tsarina Catherine II in which she invited not only artisans but also colonists to the far reaches of the Russian Empire. During all of this time and until the latter part of the 1800's it led the German immigrants and Michel and Justina's own migrant ancestors to feel comfortable in their adopted country. However, in 1881, when Tsar Alexander III became Emperor and instituted his policy of russification all ethnic minorities became aliens.   Since the German colonists became the most prosperous minorities, they were now visible targets.

In the summer of 1898, as Eduard and Henrietta were settling in their new home Johann, the next oldest son, was the next to be married.  The wedding took place in Novograd Volinskiy, however, the grand reception was held at the home of the bride, Wilhelmina Reinas.  The Reinas family lived in the village of Marianin some six miles to the northwest of Nataliendorf.  Marianin was established during the 1830's by German colonists who came directly from Germany, without any forced sojourn in Poland.  Johann and Wilhelmina did not take up residence in either Marianin or Nataliendorf, but bought an established farmstead in the mother colony of Josephine.  During the next fifteen years, they had six children.  If they only knew that during the upcoming fall of the Romanov dynasty and the rise of Bolshevism that their two youngest sons would die of starvation and the oldest daughter would perish in a slave labour camp.

With the maturing of Michel and Justina's family the next eligible candidate for marriage was Friedrich's next oldest brother, August.  August's bride had been selected by the local Matchmaker who had chosen the daughter of the widow of the local community Felscher, or lay doctor who had died in January of 1900.  His name was Johann Andreas Gottlieb Kahler and the number of given names signified that his ancestral connections went well back into early German history.  Although his duties took him to many of the surrounding communities his home was in the mother colony of Josephine.  Johann Kahler's medical training started when he was a medical corpsman in the second Russo-Turkish war that was fought in the Black Sea region from 1876 to 1880.  His widow, Ottilia Kahler was left with three daughters: Ottilia Jr., Martha and Emma.  Not long after the death of her father in the early summer of 1900, Ottilia Jr. was surprised when the Matchmaker came to call.  She had only seen her prospective husband a few times at church.  Being only sixteen-years-old young Ottilia was somewhat frightened by the prospect of leaving a home of four women to enter into a union with a man who had ten boisterous brothers and just three sisters.  Nevertheless, as tradition would have it the wedding date was set for the 15th of June 1900. The wedding ceremony took place in nearby Novograd Volinskiy where an ordained Lutheran minister performed the service. Ottilia's two younger sisters were at her side during the ceremony. Friedrich thought that if Martha, who was only fourteen-years-old was a bit older he would have a serious talk with the Matchmaker.

After the church services there was the usual race to the site of the festivities that were held at Michel and Justina's home. Each brother of course had harnessed his fastest team of horses and the competition turned out to be quite intense. Friedrich, driving his buggy with several of the younger brothers on board became entangled with the buggy of the bride and groom. August, with an adept sharp turn had forced Friedrich's team off the road and into the adjoining forest. This created much damage to Friedrich's buggy, which resulted in them being dead last in the race, much to the dismay of all seven of the younger brothers. Furthermore, this journey frightened the young bride Ottilia, which made her even more apprehensive about joining this boisterous family. She soon found that during the three days of festivities that work around the farmstead had to continue in spite of the celebration. One chore that had to be performed on a daily basis was milking the cows that was a task performed solely by the women of the household. Consequently, each morning during the first three days of her marriage celebration Ottilia was awakened early by her new mother-in-law to join her and August's sister Justina-Gustel to help milk the cows.

Through the summer of 1900, Michel and Justina were becoming more and more concerned about the tenure of their new Tsar, Nicholas II. Following his coronation Tsar Nicholas now in his new role as supreme autocrat of all of Russia was afraid to rock the dynastic boat. Consequently, he retained nearly all of the controversial decrees of his predecessor such as the process of ethnic cleansing of the Empire, and what disturbed Michel and Justina even more was the fact that their eleven sons were reaching the age for induction into the military. Kaiser Wilhelm of Germany, Nicholas's older and very aggressive cousin, was quite persuasive in counselling timid Tsar Nicholas to militarily expand the Russian Empire in the Far East. Nicholas, of course, then felt that expanding the Empire would undoubtedly bolster his image as a leader; it was not long before he announced an expansion of his armed forces. When Michel and Justina heard of the Tsar's edict, they nevertheless felt that it would be their duty to see that their sons serve in the Russian military. After all, this was their adopted country where their family had been allowed the liberty to work hard and to establish a comfortable lifestyle. As anticipated word came on the 13th of November 1900, word was received that Friedrich was to report to a naval recruiting board in Novograd Volinskiy. Here he was informed that he was to serve in the Russian Navy from January 1, 1901 to January 1, 1908, and to report to the Naval Academy at St. Petersburg on December 19, 1900, where he would be assigned to serve at Naval Depot number five at Russia's Baltic Naval base at Kronstadt.

When he came home and announced that he must leave immediately the family elders, Michel, Justina, Eduard, Johann and the recently married August were uneasy that their son and brother was going so far away. In contrast, the younger brothers were enthralled and wasted no time to inform their friends in the neighbourhood, especially the boys next door in the Wendtland family about Friedrich's naval calling. Together the boys had often seen soldiers as they passed through Novograd Volinskiy and now were impressed that their brother and neighbour was not only in the military but in the navy. The family celebrated Christmas early since Friedrich had to leave as soon as he could get away. His last request was that he would like to have a photograph of the family. However, assembling a photographer and all of the associated paraphernalia would take too much time before he had to leave. Nevertheless, they all promised that it would be done later and the photo would be sent to him after this major undertaking could be done. The closest rail link to St. Petersburg was at Kiev, which was over 50 miles from Nataliendorf. Newly married brother August who was the horseman of the family was assigned to deliver Friedrich to the rail station as quickly as possible with his best team of horses, and in the family's most reliable buggy. It took the best part of two days to get to Kiev, but August delivered Friedrich to the train in time for him to make his long rail passage to St. Petersburg. By the time August arrived home, Michel and Justina had all of the arrangements made to have the family photograph taken. Everyone was aligned according to age with Michel and Justina at the centre and a space was left between August and Gustav the next youngest brother for the place where Friedrich would have been standing. The three youngest of the fourteen children, Lydia who was 7 years-old, Herman 4, and Olga 2 were carefully instructed by the photographer to sit very still during the long period when the bright lights were on. When the photographer finally developed the picture, it was immediately dispatched to the Naval Academy at St. Petersburg. In their hearts, they knew that it would be Friedrich's treasured reminder of his family in any of his long and trying sea voyages.

When Friedrich arrived at the Naval Academy at St. Petersburg, he and the other recruits were housed in large barracks near the wharf where tugs, barges and ferries were docked to transport men and materials to the Naval base at Kronstadt. On their second day at the Naval Academy, the new recruits were quickly assembled and told that the Supreme Commander of the Baltic fleet, Vice-Admiral Stepan Makarov was coming in from Kronstadt and he might pause at the Academy on his way to a meeting with the Naval Ministry and Tsar Nicholas at the Winter Palace. Friedrich and his group of recruits were aligned in a very unmilitary formation outside the barracks as the admiral and his staff approached. However, the admiral looked neither to right nor left and proceeded unconcerned directly toward the Winter Palace.

As Friedrich would later find, Vice-Admiral Stepan Osipovich Makarov was one of the most brilliant and versatile naval officers in the history of the Russian Navy. Stepan Makarov's father had been at sea most of his life as a naval petty officer. Since his father was just an ordinary citizen with limited resources, he worked desperately hard to get his son a foothold in the Russian naval hierarchy. He finally got his son into the Naval Academy at Nikolaevsk. Stepan graduated in 1865 at the top of his class, far ahead of any of his classmates. His inventiveness and astute leadership qualities immediately put him far ahead of the multitude of naval appointments made by the Tsar and his royal hangers-on. Over the next thirty years Makarov accomplished a vast array of academic, exploratory and naval inventions that advanced not only Russian, but worldwide naval technology. Some of his many accomplishments were as follows: In 1870, he invented a ship's collision mat that was eventually used by every navy in the world and resulted in his promotion to lieutenant with a 200-rouble award. While serving in the Black Sea he had the ships use Welsh coal to reduce the amount of smoke that would always herald the approach of enemy ships. In addition, while serving in the Black Sea in 1878, he designed a much-improved torpedo boat. In 1882, he was transferred to the Baltic fleet and from 1886 to 1889, he circumnavigated the globe and during the voyage wrote a book about the performance of his ship, the Vitiaz. In 1890, when he was forty-one-years-old he became Russia's youngest admiral and shortly thereafter invented an armour piercing shell that became known among other navies as the "Makarov tip." In 1895-96, he again travelled around the world—through the Suez Canal to the Far East, across the Pacific, traversing America and the Atlantic and back to St. Petersburg. In 1897, he published his most famous work "Discussion of Questions in Naval Tactics" that was translated into seven languages. Ironically, the Japanese studied the textbook for their war against the Russian fleet in the Battle of the Yellow Sea and the disastrous defeat of Admiral Rozhdestvensky's armada in the straits of Tsushima. From June to August of 1899, Makarov took his ship north of Spitzbergen to the Barents Sea seeking a northern passage to the Pacific and during this time published yet another book "Without Sails," a guide to naval education in this new era of steam-powered ships.

In December of 1899, the same month that Friedrich left for St. Petersburg, Makarov was appointed Supreme Commander of the Baltic fleet at Kronstadt. He was well aware that the Russian fleet at Port Arthur, the ice-free port that Russia had recently acquired from China would have to be expanded and that war with Japan was imminent. Consequently, several warships were soon to leave the Baltic for Port Arthur to supplement Russia's First Pacific Squadron.

Friedrich's first assignment was as a naval deckhand. Along with several of the other recruits, he was put to work on a barge loading ropes, pulleys and fishing nets. The largest body of water that Friedrich had ever seen had been while he was fishing with the Wendtland boys on the Sluch River and now was amazed at the vastness of the Baltic Sea that lay before him as the barge was slowly pulled to the naval base at Kronstadt. When the barge arrived at dock number five they were guided to an old rusted trawler whose shabbiness was emphasized by the fact that it was anchored among an array of sleek warships. He soon found that the role of this trawler named the Evgeny, was to stock the warships, such as the torpedo boats, cruisers and also the stately battleships with fish during their exercises before the much anticipated long voyage to the Far East. As they boarded the Evgeny, the first person to greet them on this decrepit old craft was the grizzled captain by the name of Kozlowski. They soon found that he was a veteran who had served many years in the navy, which made Friedrich wonder why he had been relegated to this rusty old trawler. However, as their service on the Evgeny unfolded Friedrich would find out much from him about the political intricacies of the Russian Navy.

Friedrich's assignment was to help stow the equipment that had arrived with them on the barge and in the process of carrying the supplies down to the hold, he was able to see the wonders of the coal fired boilers that powered the propulsion system of the ship. However, he was not allowed much time to ponder for he was immediately put to work by the stoker in charge to bring coal from the bunkers to the mouths of the furnaces firing the boilers. Here, the coal was carefully shovelled into the furnaces by the stoker who constantly watched gauges to maintain a constant steam pressure. It was not long before the Evgeny set out on its role to supply food for the warships preparing to go to the Far East. Friedrich however, was not involved in the laying of the fishnets or any of the duties on deck; his task was to take wheelbarrows of coal from the bunker to the stoker who tended the boiler. He soon found that his work in the warmth of the hold was much better than the work on deck where the cold north winds that swept across the Baltic Sea whipped the icy January sea spray across the deck. This, in no time soaked the fishing crew to the skin, numbing their limbs as they worked the nets.

As the winter days passed, Friedrich after he had put in his twelve-hour shift in the coalbunkers would spend as much time as he could in the galley sipping tea with the deck hands. He used his tiny bunk only for sleeping; since it was wedged in among twenty others, there was hardly room even to turn over. While he was in the galley, he found that the only officers on board were the captain and his first mate. Most of the crew was composed of Mouzhiken, the descendants of serfs who had been conscripted at random wherever they roamed the forest and steppe of southern Russia. About a month after he arrived on the Evgeny Friedrich received the family picture from Nataliendorf. He kept it hidden under his straw mattress since many of his personal belongings had already been stolen by his Mouzhiken shipmates.

Working among this motley group Friedrich found there was one conscript whom he could trust and that they could communicate with each other in both the German and Polish languages. This allowed them to converse without the others understanding them. The Polish man's name was Lubomir Radomski and he was from Lutsk, a city just across the Polish border from Nataliendorf and Novograd Volinskiy. They often talked about home and found that their upbringing had much in common. Quite often, they would listen to the conversations between the captain and his first mate and from this evolved the story of how Captain Kozlowski had been relegated to the Evgeny. He was the son of an impoverished family that eked out a living on the estate of a Russian nobleman near Moscow. His father worked as a tailor at night to gather enough money to send his only son to Kronstadt to study at the Naval Academy. Early in his career, Kozlowski had risen to captain a cruiser on the Black Sea during Russia's war with Turkey in the late 1870's. However, even though he had distinguished himself by fending off a Turkish battleship, Kozlowski was unceremoniously replaced by a nephew of Dowager Empress Queen Olga of Greece.

This Royal Prince had little naval experience other than entertaining Tsar Nicholas on the royal yacht Standart whenever the Prince visited the Royal Family at St. Petersburg. Friedrich soon saw how the traditional Russian maladies of bureaucracy and corruption that afflicted the Tsarist regime were especially rampant in the naval hierarchy. While Friedrich listened to the stories of his captain's accounts of his naval career, he learned that the Tsar casually made many royal appointments of naval officers. Many of these new officers had little or no sea-going experience or training. On the other hand, there were some qualified and dedicated officers that had honestly risen through the ranks from rather common roots. They had earned promotions by diligent apprenticeship and by quietly working hard and methodically learning their naval strategies. They further realized that to maintain their rank they had to play shrewdly to the Tsarist tune so as not to offend the Tsar, his naval confidantes or members of the Romanov nobility. However, when it came to seagoing experience it was not difficult for them to outshine the royal appointees. As a result of the Tsar's helter-skelter appointment of captains and admirals by 1903-04 the Russian navy had far more officers than any other navy, boasting more than one-hundred admirals. England, with the largest fleet in the world had sixty-nine admirals; France had fifty-three and Germany only nine.

During the next five years from the time he started his career in the Baltic on the Evgeny, Friedrich was later to find that the three admirals that he would serve under in the ill-conceived war against Japan were seamen who had risen through the ranks from modest beginnings. One of these admirals was to be the very admiral that now commanded the Baltic Fleet, Admiral Stepan Makarov. Even though these admirals had to struggle through the Tsarist bureaucratic maze to build a viable naval force to confront the Japanese Navy halfway around the world, they were competent leaders who not only were respected by their subordinates but were also admired by their international naval peers. As fate would have it however, the first admiral Friedrich served under who was sent to the Far East was none other than Stepan Makarov. His flagship the Petropavlovsk struck a Japanese mine and sank within minutes with the loss of over ninety per cent of the crew including the admiral. Secondly, the next admiral that Friedrich served under, V.K Witgeft was decapitated by the first salvo from a Japanese battleship in the Battle of the Yellow Sea. With the flagship incapacitated it left the whole fleet in disarray—and without a leader this led to the subsequent defeat of Russia's First Pacific Squadron. Finally, after an 18,000-mile voyage to confront the Japanese the third admiral, Z. P. Rozhdestvensky also was physically incapacitated early in the Battle of Tsushima and was taken unconscious from his sinking flagship leaving Russia's Second Pacific Squadron in disarray and finally, defeat.

# Chapter 4

## Baltic Training

As spring came to the Baltic, the weather became more moderate and Friedrich was able to spend more and more time with the stokers as they tended the boilers, which provided the power to the screws that propelled the craft so easily through the sea. As time went on the stokers would often let Friedrich tend the boilers and oil the bearings of the propeller shafts while they took a break. They were pleased that at least one of the recent recruits was so willing to help and learn since most of the Mouzhiken conscripts had no interest other than eating, sleeping and doing as little work as possible. Captain Kozlowski also noted Friedrich's diligence and interest and on April 1st, 1901, he was the first of the new conscripts to be promoted. As Seaman 2nd Class he was now allowed him to spend more time with the stokers and gave him the freedom to help maintain and repair the boilers and the propulsion system of the old Evgeny, which frequently broke down forcing the ship to drift out of control, much to the exasperation of the captain and the first mate. Consequently, Friedrich spent much of his time on the forge and anvil in the repair shop deep in the ship's hold, as he straightened bent and twisted propeller shafts and steering linkage rods and levers.

Some time toward the end of June, 1901, when they were in port and while the Evgeny was docked and unloading its catch on the battleship Mikhailovich, Captain Kozlowski was visiting with the captain of the battleship and found that he was one of his classmates at the Naval Academy. Captain Grigorovich had guarded his captaincy very carefully by not offending anyone in the Tsar's naval hierarchy and even though his background was entrenched in lower Russian nobility, he followed naval tradition religiously. After all, his grandfather, Rear Admiral Konstantine Ivanovich Grigorovich rose to nobility solely through his service in the Russian navy. Ivan Kostantinovich Grigorovich entered the Naval Academy in 1871 and upon his graduation began his naval career as an officer cadet. He remained at sea for the next eight years. During this time, he was advanced in rank to midshipman. However, while many of his fellow officers, and of course those appointed through Romanov connections, sought less demanding postings onshore, Grigorovich remained at sea. Grigorovich told Kozlowski that it was rumoured that he might be chosen to command one of the new armour-clad Borodino-class battleships that was being built in France for the Russian Navy. However, unknown to Grigorovich at the time his organizational abilities had become evident to the naval administration and a move was afoot for him to be sent to Britain as naval agent.

As they recounted their experiences, they had on their respective ships Grigorovich mentioned to Kozlowski that when they were on exercises along the Finnish coast near Helsinki, they were forced to veer sharply toward shore to avoid one of their own ships that was piloted by a newly Romanov-appointed captain. In the process Grigorovich had ran aground damaging one of the ship's propellers and driveshaft. However, they were able to limp to port and he felt that he probably would have to take his ship into dry dock at Kronstadt to remove the damaged screw. Kozlowski said that his blacksmith on the Evgeny had repaired much of his old ship's decaying machinery and could probably help with the repair. Friedrich and his Polish friend, Lubomir Radomski, were dispatched to examine the damage. After they had surveyed the problem and found that, without going to dry dock, if someone could dive and remain underwater long enough to detach the propeller, and if the drive shaft could be pulled onto the ship, the propeller could be lifted to the deck with cables. Radomski was quite willing to do the underwater work since he had done this once on the Evgeny. However, the Evgeny had a much shallower draft and a smaller screw making the same task on the Mikhailovich much more challenging.

It took Radomski three tries but he finally got the screw detached allowing it to be hauled aboard. When Friedrich saw the size of the propeller, he wondered how he would be able to heat such a large piece of iron. However, with much help from Grigorovich's stokers he was able to put two forges together in the blacksmith shop allowing them to heat the whole screw at once. One of the blades of the screw had been shorn completely off, so Friedrich had to cut and mould a piece of iron to the exact size and thickness of the others blades so that the screw would be fully balanced. This took nearly a week of continuous work, but with perseverance, Friedrich completed the task. Grigorovich was pleased that he did not have to go to dry dock since the accident would undoubtedly be a reflection on his seamanship rather than any blame being put upon the royally appointed captain of the ship that had forced him into shallow waters. Grigorovich was so impressed by Friedrich and Radomski, that he asked Kozlowski if he would agree to let the two join the crew of his battleship. Kozlowski was in no position to decline the request of this senior captain since he could hardly afford another demotion. Kozlowski's replacement by a Tsarist appointed captain on his cruiser in the Black Sea adventure continued to haunt him.

Even though the Mikhailovich was nearly ten years old, it was in much better condition than the old and decrepit Evgeny. Friedrich and Radomsky were relieved that there was much less repair work to do on their new assignment. As it turned out Friedrich and Radomski spent the rest of their naval duties on the Baltic Sea while on the Mikhailovich, even though that later there would be a change of captains. Friedrich found that working for Grigorovich was far different from serving under Kozlowski on the Evgeny. Grigorovich was a much more rigid disciplinarian and his crew had to follow the captain's orders smartly. Many times shore leaves were denied and much time was spent by the offenders swabbing decks and painting the superstructure. Nevertheless, once they satisfied their captain that they were willing to perform their assigned duties he soon reinstated their status. Grigorovich had a well-established reputation in dealing with the seamen under his command. Early in his career, the Admiralty assigned him to serve as an officer on the cruiser, Admiral Kornilov, and he was specifically ordered to clean up this dirty ship and its undisciplined crew. Within six months the vessel was in ship shape, the crew was orderly and no disciplinary measures were needed. This obviously was the result of his positive attitude about his ship and the ensuing respect the men showed for him. In mid-summer of 1901, Grigorovich informed his crew that the commander of the Baltic Fleet was coming aboard the Mikhailovich to make an announcement.

When Admiral Makarov arrived, he said that Grigorovich was to be reassigned to serve as naval agent in Britain. In addition, sometime early in 1903 he was to go to Toulon, France to captain and supervise the final fitting of the new prototype ironclad Borodino-class battleship being built there for the Russian Navy. He also stated that a new captain had been chosen for the Mikhailovich, and that twenty of the crew of the Mikhailovich had been selected to join Grigorovich in Toulon to be the nucleus of the first crew of the new battleship. Friedrich and Radomski found that they were the first two of the twenty seamen selected, and that Friedrich was to start training under the new captain of the Mikhailovich. He also was assigned to head the stoker contingent of the new battleship being built at Toulon. The Tsar on the advice of Captain Grigorovich and Admiral Makarov had selected the new captain of the Mikhailovich. To the surprise of both Friedrich and Radomski, it was none other than Captain Kozlowski who was to be transferred from the old fishing vessel, Evgeny.

All of the ships stationed at Kronstadt went through various military exercises for the rest of the summer of 1901. As the cold winds of winter approached, rumblings of Japanese discontent with Russia's intent to bolster their ground forces. Their naval strength in the Far East had now become the main topic of conversation among the ship's crews. As the waiting game progressed, it became evident that an intense rivalry was brewing between the two senior admirals at Kronstadt. One was Admiral Makarov the Supreme Commander of the Baltic Fleet with his sterling reputation of twice circumventing the globe and fresh from his quest to find a northern passage through the Barents Sea in June to August of 1899. Through his books on seamanship and his leadership qualities, he was held in high esteem, not only by his fellow officers, but also by naval scholars around the world.

The other was Admiral Zinoviev Rozhdestvensky, the son of an ordinary military doctor whose social status was just high enough for him to afford to put his son into the Naval Academy. The Academy was small and accepted only fifty cadets a year. Standards were quite rigid and those who graduated were well versed in seamanship, as opposed to the captains and admirals who were randomly appointed at the whim of the Tsar, regardless whether they had sea-going experience or not. To put Zinoviev into the elite regiments of the Army was out of the question for his father since the cost of purchasing the required thoroughbred horse alone would have been out of the question for the senior Rozhdestvensky. Furthermore, to wine and dine the army's upper echelon at St. Petersburg's exclusive clubs would have been mandatory and, consequently, even more financially prohibitive for a lowly military doctor. Zinoviev graduated at the top of his class in 1868 and during his time at the Academy, he pursued his studies with a fervent zest. He spent a record 227 days at sea and would while away his evenings and Sunday's reading of the latest developments in naval cannonry. As well, during this time he mastered both the English and French languages. He graduated three years after his future rival and compatriot, Stepan Makarov, who in 1865 also graduated at the head of his class. Upon graduation, Rozhdestvensky was immediately assigned to the Baltic Fleet aboard the first big Russian ironclad battleship, the Pervenetz. Here he spent the next twenty months where he impressed his superiors and fellow sailors by diligently observing the finer points of the technical aspects of the new ironclad battleships. After his tenure on the Pervenetz, his request was granted to enter the Mikhailovskaya Artillery Academy to hone his skills on the firepower of the guns arming the ironclad ships. Here again he graduated with honours in 1873 and was promoted to the rank of lieutenant. Rozhdestvensky fixed his career goal mainly on seagoing warfare. Makarov, on the other hand, concentrated on the finer points of oceanography, naval technology and in opening new frontiers. Rozhdestvensky was a workaholic who not only was deeply engrossed in his naval career but also had other far-reaching interests. On his brief periods of shore leave he discovered the titillating nightlife of St. Petersburg, which included generous portions of wine, women and song. During this time, he also found time to wed—a union that soon produced a daughter.

In 1877, shortly after the war with Turkey began, Rozhdestvensky went to the Black Sea Fleet as an artillery supervisor. He was assigned to the schooner, Vesta, which was quite an old and small steamship. Nevertheless, Rozhdestvensky was pleased that it had relatively new cannonry with which he could practice his newfound artillery skills. At this time Makarov also was serving the Black Sea Fleet as Naval Tactician and the two rising stars of the Russian navy warily watched each others performance. The Vesta's orders were to seek out and attack any Turkish ships that were of equal or smaller size. However, when they left the seaport at Odessa the first Turkish ship they encountered was one of Turkey's finest battleships. As soon as the Turkish battleship spotted the Russian flag on the Vesta, it immediately began shelling the little schooner. Rozhdestvensky was ordered to return the fire but after the first salvo with his smaller guns, he advised the captain that they would have to move closer. The captain felt that this would be suicidal and summoned the crew to flee. The Turkish battleship, hungry for an easy target, followed and continued to fire at the Vesta. The helmsman of the Vesta guided the ship in a zigzag pattern so that its stern presented as small a target as possible when all the while Rozhdestvensky carefully and continuously fired his guns at the bridge of the battleship. Finally, a shell struck and momentarily disabled the helm. The Turkish battleship had to stop for repairs and the Vesta soon was out of range. Rozhdestvensky was credited with saving his ship and, in turn, was promoted to lieutenant captain. In addition, he was given two honours—the Order of St. Vladimir and the Cross of St. George. At first, he basked in the publicity that was lavished upon him; however, he felt uncomfortable receiving this continuous barrage of accolades. He soon found to his dismay that all of this publicity stemmed from the efforts of the Romanov Commander of the Navy, Grand Duke Constantine. The Grand Duke's reason for this was that the Russo-Turkish war had been won mainly by the efforts of the Tsar's land armies and, as far as the navy was concerned, outside of the Vesta's damage to one Turkish battleship, the Russian navy played rather a minor role in winning the war. However, what irritated Grand Duke Constantine most was that none other than Constantine's two brothers, Grand Dukes Nikolai and Mikhail, commanded the land armies. Sibling rivalry was always rampant in the royal dynasty, and now that very little credit was being given to the navy, Grand Duke Constantine's ego was bruised since his brothers were basking in the St. Petersburg limelight. Constantine, therefore, in his anxiety to elicit kudos for himself sang the praises of his navy's accomplishments and with nothing much else to offer he trumpeted the Vesta's victory over the Turkish battleship. This made Rozhdestvensky understandably uneasy with his promotion and honours, especially being bestowed with the Cross of St. George, which was a cherished prize for anyone in the military. He did not want to be regarded as a hero since essentially the Vesta really had been in full retreat. It soon became evident that this overplay of Rozhdestvensky heroics also irritated many of the senior officers in the navy, especially Stepan Makarov. This criticism, however, did not deter Rozhdestvensky; it only increased his zeal to prove himself in his naval career.

After his service in the Black Sea on the Vesta Rozhdestvensky was sent to Germany to monitor Russian military orders which, if nothing else, allowed him to polish his German language skills. His stay in Germany was short-lived, however, for in 1883 to his surprise he was assigned an entirely new role—as commander of the Bulgarian navy. The task sounded impressive but after the war with Turkey Russia had annexed Bulgaria which was now a Russian satellite state. Bulgaria, therefore, had little interest in its military, let alone its naval defences. Already, Russian bureaucrats had replaced the Bulgarian government and the Bulgarian minister of war was a minor Russian aristocrat. Unfortunately, the navy consisted of only a handful of Russian cast-off wooden steamers and cutters;

consequently, Rozhdestvensky's stay in Bulgaria was fraught with frustration. The armies of most countries commonly spent at least one third of their military budget on the navy. In Bulgaria, however, Rozhdestvensky was allotted only one-twenty-fifth of the military budget. Then to add insult to injury they used his decrepit naval craft mainly to transport cargo. After two long years of service in Bulgaria, it is not surprising that he was relieved when, in 1886, Tsar Alexander III recalled him to the Baltic to serve as an administrator. This really was a demotion and added further to his frustration for he yearned to be in command of a ship on the open seas. His wish finally came true in 1890 when he received an assignment to go to Vladivostok as the captain of a sleek and sturdy clipper ship to patrol the North Pacific. Although he faced no impending battles, he relished the task of taking his ship out of the Baltic Sea, into the Atlantic Ocean, through the Mediterranean Sea and the Suez Canal, across the Indian Ocean past Singapore and Hong Kong and through the South China Sea and on to Vladivostok.

On one of his patrols in the stormy North Pacific, his ship ran aground on uncharted rocks. He quickly had the crew jettison coal and any heavy cargo that they had on board and succeeded in freeing his ship and was able to bring his ship back to Vladivostok. In 1892, he was ordered back to the Baltic and his home port of Kronstadt. By this time, his value as a mariner was well established. The ordinary seamen under him respected and admired him for his devotion to his shipmates. He was a rigid disciplinarian and if a sailor did not tend his task of keeping the ship in perfect order the iron fist of the captain often loosened teeth or bloodied noses. Even though he was stern with his men, he also could be thoughtful and compassionate. After one harrowing time at sea, when they had sailed through a violent north Pacific storm, they had to stop to load coal. Seeing that his crew was exhausted Rozhdestvensky at his own personal expense hired men on the dock to load the coal, something that very few captains would have done. By now, his superiors could hardly ignore his talents, especially his naval commander Grand Duke Constantine. The Grand Duke, still smarting from being overshadowed by his brothers in the Russo-Turkish war, was intent to demonstrate to the Tsar that his navy was of international calibre. Unfortunately, he too had to constantly keep in mind the traditional Russian priority of accommodating the Romanov aristocracy with plum ministerial, foreign or military appointments. The navy was not immune and the Tsar had anointed many Romanov relatives and hangers-on as captains and admirals, many of whom had never even been to sea. Consequently, sailors who trained at the Naval Academy were the only ones really qualified so any senior admiral or captain with Naval Academy credentials usually were quietly selected for any major naval task. Nevertheless, on rare occasions a Romanov appointment turned out to be competent. With all of these bureaucratic complications in mind the Grand Duke, looking back on the performance of Rozhdestvensky on the schooner Vesta in the Black Sea encounter, selected him for yet another task.

Since the English had been masters of the high seas from time immemorial the Grand Duke felt that it would be in his navy's best interests to send a knowledgeable seaman to get a first hand look at what lay behind the power of the British Navy. In the autumn of 1892, Naval Commander Grand Duke Constantine sent Rozhdestvensky to Britain as a naval attaché to seek out details of the efficiency and firepower of Britain's vast armada. In fact, the British naval fleet was being enlarged to become twice the size of any other navy in the world and when Rozhdestvensky arrived in London, the normal hustle and bustle was accentuated by ship building activity and gossip. He settled comfortably into his new role among the naval and political elite and especially enjoyed the nightlife where, with poise and dignity, he charmed the British aristocrats especially the women who found themselves enthralled by this handsome and charismatic foreigner. He would conveniently switch from one language to another as the occasion demanded since by now he could be eloquent in four languages and used them to full advantage among the well-travelled British as well as the military visitors from abroad. Socially he now had become a direct contrast to his Russian naval competitor, Stepan Makarov, who was concentrating solely on naval research, had a rather unkempt appearance, and studiously avoided public appearances.

With his exposure to so much of Britain's naval, military, political and social elite Rozhdestvensky gleaned much interesting information about England's naval operations and expansion, which he religiously relayed to the Russian naval command. In early 1894, Rozhdestvensky was relieved of his duties in Britain and reassigned to command a relatively old but competent battleship, the Vladimir Monomakh. The ship was to join the Mediterranean squadron under the command of none other than Admiral Stepan Makarov. Rozhdestvensky was uneasy having to serve under his main naval competitor; nevertheless, he was not deterred and concentrated on keeping his crew attentive and his ship in top condition. He remained stern with his men, held regular artillery practice and was the first to accept any task demanded by the admiral. Makarov, still disdainful of the honours that Rozhdestvensky received during the retreat of the Vesta during the Russo-Turkish war, grudgingly had to admit that Rozhdestvensky was the best captain in his squadron. The fleet harboured at many of the major ports bordering on the Mediterranean Sea from Spain to France to Italy and to Greece. In Athens Makarov and his captains were personally received by the Greek Queen, Olga. Who, incidentally, was none other than the daughter of Russia's naval commander, Grand Duke Constantine.

Queen Olga made a point of keeping in touch with royalty in other countries and especially if they were members of her Romanov family. Consequently, she was quite distressed when she heard of the rapidly failing health of Tsar Alexander III and rushed to be at her grandfather's bedside. The Tsar, who throughout his lifetime had both a physique and a will of iron, died on October 26, 1894, at the age of only forty-eight, which resulted from his over exertion during the derailment of the royal train at Kharkov while they were on their way back from the Tsar's summer palace in the Crimea. His demise was followed shortly by the coronation of his only son, timid and introverted Nicholas, as Tsar Nicholas II.

Queen Olga, always aware of her Romanov ancestral duties, made a point of greeting any ship of the Russian Navy whenever one entered her realm. Rozhdestvensky, ever the gallant gladiator and connoisseur of fine wine and women, would make a point of attending the soiree's that the Queen would lavish on her naval countrymen. Makarov, on the other hand, remained steadfast in his studious avoidance of public functions. However, his wife, Capitolina Makarova, who accompanied the admiral on this Mediterranean venture, was a product of St. Petersburg's social elite and missed the elaborate nightlife of the Russian capital. Consequently, she looked forward to Queen Olga's gala events with as much enthusiasm as Rozhdestvensky. In fact, they both revelled at these celebrations and came to enjoy each other's company to such an extent that an affair began, which persisted throughout the remainder of the squadron's stay in the Mediterranean, and well beyond. Understandably, this then made the relationship between the admiral and his wayward captain somewhat tenuous. Nevertheless, no major confrontations were ever documented probably because attention was being drawn elsewhere since tensions with the Japanese were escalating.

Shortly afterward, in January of 1895, Makarov was ordered to dispatch his most readily available battleships to the Far East to demonstrate to the Japanese the power of the Russian Navy. The Vladimir Monomakh, as could be expected, was the first to be ready to sail and Rozhdestvensky was immediately on his way. His departure, however, was marred by the fact that Makarov, apparently looking for a way to get revenge for his wife's indiscretions, insisted that Rozhdestvensky be accompanied by an admiral who had recently arrived with great fanfare from Kronstadt. Admiral Evgeny Alexeev was a spoiled and egotistical Romanov appointment and Makarov had already noted that no love was lost between Rozhdestvensky and Alexeev. This probably was due to the fact that not only was this admiral a royal appointee but he also was a graduate of the Naval Academy. Then to add insult to injury Alexeev immediately insisted that his royal flag be flown on the Vladimir Monomakh. Another irritant to Rozhdestvensky would have been the fact that Alexeev was not even a full-blooded Romanov. He was the bastard son of the new Tsar's grandfather, Tsar Alexander II. Rozhdestvensky wasted no time on his voyage through the Suez Canal, across the Indian Ocean, through the Straits of Malacca, across the Sea of Japan and arrived at the Japanese port of Nagasaki in less than two months. During this time he treated his royal passenger as one of the crew and at every opportunity had him perform the most menial tasks, much to Alexeev's irritation. From Nagasaki Admiral Alexeev was taken by Tsarist decree directly to Port Arthur where he would soon receive further royal appointments. Upon their arrival at Nagasaki Rozhdestvensky immediately sought out the leaders of the Japanese Admiralty and, in his charming and persuasive manner, he opened the door for the further negotiations that took place upon the arrival of Makarov. Through the diplomatic efforts of both Makarov and Rozhdestvensky Japan grudgingly agreed to curb their aggression in China and stated that they had no interest in threatening Russian holdings in Manchuria. Once negotiations were over Makarov's squadron, including the Vladimir Monomakh, returned to the Baltic and their home base, Kronstadt.

Now that he was back at Kronstadt and in the thick of Russian naval and bureaucratic activity Rozhdestvensky was faced with the old conflicts that again came back to haunt him. Even though he had performed duties as a naval attaché, a gunnery expert, a disciplined captain, an outspoken and unrelenting diplomat he, nevertheless, still faced criticism for having been decorated and overly heralded for his performance on the Vesta in the Black Sea encounter, as well as his defiance of the Romanov appointments, i.e. Admiral Alexeev. However, the most significant of his exploits that spread most quickly through the naval establishment was his on-going relationship with Capitolina Makarova. Consequently, Admiral Makarov was in no mood to lavish compliments on Rozhdestvensky nor were many of his Kronstadt compatriots. As a result, Rozhdestvensky's first assignment was to captain the old battleship Pervenetz, a demotion that would have infuriated any other captain, let alone a seasoned mariner like Zinoviev. Nevertheless, he made the old ship and its crew into a battle ready craft.

However, to add to his duties he had to supervise several other ships in artillery practice and adding further to his workload he was in charge of a shore-based rifle unit. Despite this amount of work he bent his iron will to the tasks and, being the workaholic that he was, he excelled in all three of them, much to the dismay of his fellow officers, and especially Admiral Makarov. Finally, in December of 1898, the Admiralty had to admit that despite his brash and unpredictable character Rozhdestvensky had proven his abilities as a naval leader and when this was passed on to the Tsar he was promoted to rear admiral. Now he had finally won respect and even envy from the other officers and especially from the rank and file ordinary seamen. With his background in cannons and artillery, he was put in total command of the Baltic Artillery Practice Unit, which salved the new admiral's ambition for the moment. However, his satisfaction in becoming equal in stature to Makarov was short lived for in December of 1899 Makarov was appointed Supreme Commander of the Baltic Fleet. This was the same month that a young and inexperienced naval conscript arrived at Kronstadt from the tiny village of Nataliendorf.

# Chapter 5

# From The Baltic to Toulon to Port Arthur

In December of 1899, young Friedrich Fischbuch was conscripted into Russia's navy and had to forego his duties as Nataliendorf's village blacksmith.  After his arrival at Kronstadt, it was not long before he was introduced to the intricacies of the Russian naval establishment and he soon witnessed the competition between the two senior admirals.  From 1899 to 1901, Friedrich served on the old fishing vessel, the Evgeny, under Captain Kozlowski and later under Captains Grigorovich and Kozlowski on the battleship Mikhailovich.  During this time, Friedrich diligently honed his skills on the steam propulsion systems of Russian battleships, and it was not long before he became intrigued by Russia's cumbersome naval hierarchy.  In the early summer of 1902, Tsar Nicholas paid a visit to the Kronstadt naval base and was impressed by how Rozhdestvensky's regimented and well-kept ships moved smoothly in well-rehearsed manoeuvres and he was equally taken by the fine artillery performance.  Later in the summer, Tsar Nicholas invited his overbearing cousin, Kaiser Wilhelm II of Germany, to come and have a first-hand look at his Baltic fleet.  The Kaiser for some time had been pressuring the Tsar to expand his Empire beyond Manchuria and into the entire Pacific theatre.  However, knowing how sensitive Nicholas was, Wilhelm would make a point to irritate his Tsarist cousin and at every opportunity would scoff at Russia's naval capabilities.  The Tsar, having recently witnessed Rozhdestvensky's artillery expertise and his well-kept ships, chose him to demonstrate the firepower of the Russian navy.  The Russian battleships were ordered to assemble with all hands on deck to watch the proceedings.  The Mikhailovich was first in line adjacent to Rozhdestvensky's flagship so Friedrich and

Radomski had a first-hand view of the cannonry performance.

Tsar Nicholas and his esteemed guest, Kaiser Wilhelm, with a full contingent of German and Russian military elite arrived from St. Petersburg aboard the Tsar's royal yacht, the Standart. The dignitaries were squired directly onto the bridge of the Artillery Practice Unit's flagship where Rozhdestvensky graciously greeted them to the spit and polish of his flagship, and in flawless German introduced them to his entire crew. With crisp orders, he had his gunners aim carefully at a distant target being towed by a tug. The first gunner's salvo struck the target perfectly. Nevertheless, to Rozhdestvensky's irritation, the second gunner missed the target completely in three consecutive attempts. The admiral exploded and shouted a tirade of expletives at the errant gunner and in a fit of frustration threw his field glasses overboard and immediately ordered the gunner to be replaced by the second in command. The Kaiser was impressed and told the Tsar and the other dignified observers that this is something he would have done himself. Nicholas beamed and was pleased that his ruthless cousin was so impressed with this efficient but vulgar artillery commander.

Friedrich was on the bridge of the Mikhailovich with Captain Kozlowski who was appalled at Rozhdestvensky's outburst and from his own experience observed that Rozhdestvensky would undoubtedly be reprimanded, or even demoted, by the Tsar. However, in fact the opposite occurred; the way that Rozhdestvensky ruled his sailors with an iron hand brought back memories to the shy and mild Nicholas of his domineering father. Upon the departure of the German Kaiser Nicholas, much to the chagrin of the other admirals, promoted Rozhdestvensky to general adjutant. Later, as Tsar Nicholas learned more about his adjutant admiral his admiration grew even stronger so that later, in March of 1903, he again promoted Rozhdestvensky to Head of the Naval General Staff. This now would set him somewhat above his brilliant adversary, Admiral Stepan Makarov.

After witnessing Rozhdestvensky's artillery exercise for the Tsar and Kaiser Wilhelm and seeing the damage done to the target vessels, Friedrich wondered what it would be like to be in a sea battle, what the consequences would be if a shell struck them amidships and what would happen if the fires in the boilers spread to the coalbunkers. As a stoker, he now wondered what the future held for him. During the remainder of 1902 and into the winter of 1903, the Mikhailovich continued to patrol the Baltic Sea and during this time Friedrich learned more and more about the intricacies of the steam propulsion system of their ship. Each time they docked at Kronstadt they heard more and more about the approaching conflict with Japan. Everyone then wondered which of the two senior admirals would be sent to monitor the defence of Port Arthur. Many of the senior officers in the Kronstadt naval community wondered if and when the Romanov state figureheads in the Far East, such as Alexeev, and his Commander of the First Pacific Squadron, Admiral O.V. Stark, would be replaced by competent military commanders.

In March of 1903, Captain Kozlowski announced to the members of his crew that he had received word from Admiral Makarov. Apparently, Grigorovich had left his post in England and was now at the shipbuilding yards at Toulon, France. There he would observe and supervise the final stages of construction of the prototype of five new pre-dreadnought ironclad, Borodino-class battleships for the Russian Navy. On April 1, 1903, Admiral Makarov arrived on board the Mikhailovich and announced that the twenty-crew members that Grigorovich had selected to go to Toulon would be leaving shortly. Furturemore, Friedrich was to be promoted to Senior Stoker First Class and to act as the Chief Stoker of the new Borodino-class battleship about to be launched at Toulon. There also was a promotion for Lubomir Radomski to Stoker Second Class. On April 27, 1903, Friedrich, Radomski and the other chosen seamen were taken by ferry to St. Petersburg where they boarded a train for their long trip to France. When they arrived at the Toulon dockyard Captain Grigorovich who had arrived from London a month earlier formally greeted them. Friedrich was amazed at the magnitude of the shipbuilding industry in France and found that not only were they building battleships for Russia but were building ships for several other European countries as well. Accommodation for the Russian seamen was provided in barracks near the dry-dock site where their new battleship lay.    The French company that was in charge of building the ship was Forges et Chantiers Mediterranee de la Seyne who had laid the keel of the ship in May of 1899.

Up until the time of the arrival of the Russian crew, nearly four years of construction had taken place.    To Friedrich the ship appeared to be massive compared to the old battleship, Mikhailovich, on which they had steamed through the Baltic waters.    Their Baltic ship had been built back in 1880; it was 90 metres long with a maximum speed of 15 knots; it had six boilers and at its age, it had been rigged for sails.    By comparison, the new ship was 118 metres long and had 20 boilers, which would propel this new battleship at a maximum speed of 18 knots despite the fact that it was heavily clad with an iron belt 125 to 200 millimetres thick and with this enormous displacement it laid low in the water.    Friedrich and Radomski anxiously inspected the ship and especially its propulsion system. They saw that the newly designed Bellville water tube boilers had been installed but were not yet linked to the propeller shafts.    The coalbunkers were in place by the boilers and each bunker had the capacity to hold 40 tons of coal.    Thus, the total volume of coal that the ship could carry was 800 tons.    This was very different from their old battleship at Kronstadt that had only six boilers and maximum coal storage for only 200 tons.    Since each boiler required a senior stoker in charge on each shift, Friedrich knew that only four stokers including Radomski were among the twenty seamen that Grigorovich had requested to come to Toulon.    Consequently, he immediately told the captain that at least thirty-six more stokers would have to be brought from Kronstadt.    In examining the ship and assessing the crew, Captain Grigorovich soon found that the ship would need a total crew of at least 780 seamen, which would include a minimum of 25 officers.    For the next few days, the telegraph system was busy with messages to the Russian Admiralty at St. Petersburg with requests for sailors.    Fortunately, fifteen of the seamen that Grigorovich had brought from Kronstadt among the original twenty men were senior officers who had served on several of the Baltic battleships. Nevertheless, he still had to have ten more officers to fill the duties on the new ship.    During the next three and one half months much activity took place to ready the ship for its departure date which was estimated to be sometime in the middle of August of 1903. Grigorovich finally got a return telegraph from the Admiralty in St. Petersburg that ten officers and thirty stokers would arrive by train in Toulon by July 15 and another 700 men, to make up most of the crew, would be arriving by ship by the end of July. Grigorovich had been told that they would be coming to Toulon on the armour-clad cruiser Bayan, and that the Bayan would accompany their new battleship to Port Arthur. This would add another battle-ready vessel to Russia's First Pacific Squadron.

The captain of the Bayan, Robert Nickolayevich Wiren, was well known to Grigorovich and he had served with Wiren on shore duty at Kronstadt prior to their assignment as captains. When the trainload of officers and stokers had previously arrived Grigorovich and Friedrich found that all had been taken from different ships, so assessing their sea-going experience took considerable time. Consequently, much training and familiarisation had to take place during the next month. They then anxiously awaited the arrival of the Bayan but when it arrived they were somewhat disappointed and found that many of the new recruits had little sea-going experience. In fact, some of them were criminals who had been liberated from prison, apparently for the sole purpose of filling the quota. Others were Mouzhiken (ex-serfs) who probably were conscripted at random from the Russian backwoods. Fortunately, the officers and stokers who arrived previously by train had spent various amounts of time at sea, were quite interested in this new ship and were willing to learn the intricacies of its operation. To Friedrich's relief only six of the Mouzhiken who had arrived by ship were assigned to train as stoker's helpers. To train and discipline forty stokers and forty stoker's helpers became a challenging task for Friedrich during their long voyage to Port Arthur. In early August, Captain Grigorovich announced that the ship would be leaving Toulon on August 18, 1903. Shortly after this announcement, word was received from the Admiralty in St. Petersburg that the Tsar's request was that Russia's first Borodino-class battleship be named the Tsesarevich (son of the Tsar). His wish was that after having four daughters his wife,

Empress Alexandra, would have a son and heir to the Russian throne. The battleship Tsesarevich must have been a good omen for exactly a year later, August 18, 1904, Alexandra finally had a son and heir to the throne—Tsarevich Alexei.

The Tsesarevich and the Bayan left Toulon with very little fanfare; Captain Grigorovich on the Tsesarevich had made only three practice runs prior to their departure so it took all of his attention to maintain order among his inexperienced crew. Nevertheless, once they were on their way, much in the manner of Rozhdestvensky, the captain maintained a stern and orderly hold on the crew. He was pleased to find that the new ship glided easily through the Mediterranean waters and had no difficulty maintaining a speed of 18 knots despite the fact that it had an enormous displacement due to its heavy steel belt of armour. As Grigorovich had planned, they sailed directly to the friendly port of Soudha on the Greek island of Crete. Prior arrangements had been made and friendly emissaries and Queen Olga herself gave them a Romanov welcome. Surprisingly, coaling went relatively smoothly with only minor grumblings about the heat and exposure to coal dust from the ex-convicts and Mouzhiken. As he supervised the untested crew, Friedrich knew that trouble would be encountered later since much of the heavy loading at this stop had been done with help from men who were working on nearby Greek colliers. When the two warships left Crete, Grigorovich was worried about the next stop, which was Port Said at the entrance to the Suez Canal. Port Said was controlled by the British who were instrumental in the construction of the Suez Canal, which stretched some 100 miles and joined the Mediterranean Sea to the Indian Ocean via the Red Sea and the Gulf of Aden. It was built 35 years previously and was now a convenient shipping shortcut for many nations—a route that the British jealously guarded. With this in mind, Grigorovich was apprehensive about the fact that the British had signed an alliance with Japan in 1902, which was an agreement that both countries would oppose any Russian territorial expansion into the Pacific theatre beyond Manchuria. However, British interests were not necessarily devoted only to the protection of Japanese sovereignty for they had their own underlying ambitions to expand the British Empire into the Far East. Consequently, the movement of Russian warships through British shipping lanes, on their way to Vladivostok and Port Arthur, aroused enough concern with the British that considerable efforts were made to stall or even block Russian naval traffic to the Far East whatever route they travelled. Consequently, Grigorovich wondered what greeting they would receive when their new Russian battleship and cruiser arrived at the entrance to the Suez Canal. When the Tsesarevich and the Bayan steamed into Port Said, the British port authorities refused to let them through. Then, for two days cables were sent back and forth to St. Petersburg and several communications were exchanged with Denmark. Further negotiations took place directly with the Danish Consulate at Port Said and finally the Danish Consul himself was brought in to negotiate. Grudgingly, at last their ships were allowed to continue on their way through the canal. For the crews the weather was considerably warmer in the Mediterranean than the cold and blustery gales they were so familiar with on the Baltic Sea. Now, as they steamed closer and closer to the equator, the heat became more and more oppressive, especially for the stokers and their ill-prepared helpers. Friedrich thought about the cold blustery days on the Baltic when he would welcome the heat of the boilers; however, he now found that it was much more comfortable to be on deck to sample even the slightest breeze. When they reached Djibouti, which was the French controlled gateway port leading to the Indian Ocean, Grigorovich again was concerned for he feared that another diplomatic ambush might be awaiting them.

The Admiralty at St. Petersburg had advised Grigorovich that in 1900 Japan had formally notified France that they were opposed to their allowing passage of Russian ships through French controlled ports and that this would be a violation of France's neutrality. However, the fact remained that the Tsesarevich and Bayan would again need a full supply of coal, food and water at Djibouti to last them for the long voyage along the equatorial route to Singapore. It would be necessary for the Tsesarevich to take on at least 1000 tons of coal. This meant that they would have to overload by 200 tons to allow them to cover the nearly 3500 miles across the Indian Ocean to the Straits of Malacca where they likely would face yet another questionable supply rendezvous at Singapore.    Singapore was a British port and, even though it was far removed from the mother country of the British Empire, Grigorovich felt that they would undoubtedly face the same problem that they had at Port Said.

As they neared Djibouti and before they entered the port, a French launch signalled them to stop and they were hailed by the Commander of the Djibouti port authority.  Since France was still a staunch ally of Russia the Commander was now caught in a delicate diplomatic situation, he carefully welcomed them and offered full assistance but with the caveat that coaling in port was out of the question.  However, they would be allowed to coal, stock water and take on any other supplies as long as they remained outside of the port of Djibouti.  He said that Japan and now England had protested that French ports were neutral territory, therefore, by international law could not service belligerent warships in their ports.  Fortunately, Kaiser Wilhelm, in his efforts to persuade the Tsar to expand the Russian Empire to the Far East, had assured Nicholas that if Russian ships had any difficulty coaling at foreign ports he would see to it that German colliers would be available from German friendly anchorages along the route.  It now appeared that Grigorovich's only alternative was to summon German colliers to their aid.  However, as Friedrich feared from the time of their departure from Toulon that coaling in the open ocean would be a tricky operation especially now that the weather was stormy and the ocean swells were running high.  To add to his fears there was the inexperience of the crew with several of the new recruits still steeped in their Russian criminal and Mouzhik maladies of being adept at avoiding physical labour of any kind.

Grigorovich, on the other hand, was just as happy to stay out of Djibouti's harbour even though it was large and well protected from wind; it had a very narrow entrance fringed by coral reefs.  While they were waiting for the German colliers the Commander of the port authority, who was still uneasy about being caught in the middle of a diplomatic stalemate, invited Grigorovich to come into Djibouti on his launch to seek out what provisions and fresh water he required and to arrange for its transport to the Tsesarevich.  The Captain agreed and Friedrich with several of the officers accompanied him into Djibouti on the Commander's launch. It was nearing mid-day and Friedrich found that his shirt was already wet with sweat and for him the heat already was stifling. As they entered the port, he could see that there was very little activity and he asked the Commander why everything was so quiet. The Commander said that it was part of life near the equator that only work that was absolutely necessary was performed between 10 a.m. and 3 p.m. Generally, offices and shops were closed. The military did not leave their barracks and any European workers soon learned to avoid any physical exertion during this time of the day.

When they arrived on shore, the Commander took them to a shaded area where they were served cool drinks and everyone rested quietly until late in the afternoon. The Port Commander, anxious not to jeopardize his port's neutrality, graciously offered to arrange the gathering and transportation of fresh water and provisions to the Tsesarevich, which was a pleasant surprise to Captain Grigorovich. He further announced that he had arranged for them to dine that evening with the port officials and the French naval contingent stationed at Djibouti. That night Friedrich and especially Radomski were amazed with the variety of food that was lavished upon them. They found it hard to curb their appetite since there was so much fresh fruit and a variety of delicacies that were continuously set before them. Friedrich made a point of asking the Commander if an ample supply of fresh fruits and vegetables could be sent to the Tsesarevich. He knew that this would endear him to his crew of stokers and helpers. He felt that it would ease their grim task of loading coal over the next few days. Very early the next morning when they arrived back on the Tsesarevich, two German colliers were anchored beside the battleship and one beside the Bayan. Unfortunately, they found that the Djiboutian authorities had been obliged to contact Paris via telegraph. Grigorovich was amazed that with the new technology of telegraph that information could be so rapidly transmitted to announce to the world of the arrival of Russian battle-ready vessels. It followed that it was not long before London also was aware of the Russian incursion into French territorial waters.

The Port Commander was now obligated to inform them that even though they were not directly in port, they were in French territorial waters and, consequently, they were breaching French neutrality. Caught in a diplomatic dilemma the Port Commander, grasping for a solution, said that it would take him at least 24 hours to muster his military forces in Djibouti to escort the Russian battleship out of the area and that perhaps Grigorovich could load enough coal to proceed to a friendly port. As the morning progressed and the temperature rose, frantic orders were issued to begin coaling. The sea swells were high and the German colliers rose and fell so had to keep their distance from the Tsesarevich. By 10 o'clock, coaling began as Friedrich hastily organized the stokers. Grigorovich announced that not only the stokers and their helpers would be loading coal, but also the rest of the crew including the officers would be pressed into service. Every able bodied man aboard was put to work to load and make room for the 1200 tons of coal that they needed for the long journey to Singapore. As the heat of mid-day approached the temperature rose to well over 100 degrees Fahrenheit. The coal dust rose from the holds of the colliers and the Tsesarevich was soon smothered in a cloud of coal dust so thick that the workers on board all of the five ships could only see the sun as a barely discernible red spot in the darkness above them. Soon hardly anyone was recognizable as the thick black dust clung to the sweat streaming from their bodies.

As the day wore on many of these dark, strange-looking caricatures collapsed from thirst and exhaustion and had to be revived by being doused with fire hoses. Even the drinking water was warm and barely alleviated their thirst. In addition to the heat and choking coal dust, some of the men became seasick from the heaving waves in the open sea. As severe as conditions were on deck it is hard to imagine what conditions were like for the stokers in the bunkers below deck where the temperatures were a stifling 120 to 125 degrees Fahrenheit. As Friedrich felt the choking coal dust burn in his lungs, he found that by holding a piece of cotton waste in his teeth it blocked at least some of dust. He searched the pharmacy and all of the ship for cotton remnants and gave the men working in the bunkers wads of cotton to hold in their teeth somehow to keep the coal dust out of their lungs. Even then, every few minutes someone below deck would collapse from the heat and had to be carried onto the deck to be revived by being sprayed with sea water from the fire hoses. Friedrich finally had to rotate the men in short shifts and have each shift go up and lie on the deck to recuperate where the air was somewhat fresher. When night came, they had over 700 tons loaded however, the heat dropped only a few degrees and they yet had to accommodate storage for coal on the deck. By 4 o'clock the next morning, they had completed loading the coal but now came the task of cleaning the ship. To keep all of the men in line during the stifling heat of this dust-laden marathon, the loading process was a monumental task not just for Friedrich but also for the Captain and the other officers. The stokers and their helpers now realized that once they were underway the fires in the boilers would accentuate the unbearable heat below deck. They were soon to find that this would plague them for the rest of their long voyage along the equator.

The day after they steamed away from Djibouti they were struck by heavy rains that came in bursts of showers that would last for only a short time, but with great intensity. The sharp rain squalls cleared the decks of remaining coal dust but soaked the sailors working on deck or on the bridge. As the morning sun came out and the temperature rose the heat brought an itching rash to the sodden sailors. Fresh water was the only known cure but had to be conserved for drinking only. Being doused with seawater only made the itching worse yet most of the men could not resist the temptation to get temporary relief from the cool seawater. The tortured sailors thirst became unbearable which was relieved somewhat by drinking anything they could get their hands on: any available fresh water, or even their slim rations of beer, wine and vodka. Everyone looked forward to nightfall when the temperature would fall, if only by a few degrees. Sighs of relief could be heard as nightfall arrived suddenly at 6 o'clock. There is no twilight in the tropics there is only a blaze of red and then darkness. At night, the ocean was calm and relatively motionless resulting in a silence that was interrupted only by the sound of the churning screws as they pushed the Tsesarevich and the

Bayan toward their next coaling stop, which hopefully would be at the British controlled port of Singapore. The next seven days were relatively uneventful as they steamed their way through the Indian Ocean at a steady pace of 15 to 18 knots. The seas were relatively calm, however, the heat persisted much to the discomfort of the stokers who grumbled incessantly to Friedrich. As was his nature he tried to accommodate them in every way he could but there were incessant complaints of heatstroke, headaches, seasickness and many other maladies real or imagined that were accompanied by requests to see the ships doctor to somehow get away from the heat of the boiler rooms.

Finally, Grigorovich reprimanded Friedrich for being too lax with his boiler crews and intervened by sending one of the Mouzhiken conscripts to the brig for insubordination. This for a short while calmed the stokers and their helpers but the heat drove them to others ways of seeking relief. Indeed, one conscript after finishing his twelve-hour shift shouted that he could stand the heat no longer and leaped from the deck into the cool ocean waters below. In a short time sharks that had been continually following the Tsesarevich and Bayan made short work of devouring him. Those who witnessed their co-worker being torn limb from limb by the sharks realized the reality of their situation and dreaded going back to work the next day again to face the heat of the boilers and both the heat and coal dust in the bunkers. They now were over half way to Singapore and they could clearly see the coastline of Ceylon far to the north. There had been the possibility of coaling at Ceylon's main port city Colombo but this plan was abandoned since word was received from Kronstadt just as they left Toulon that Russian intelligence agents in Ceylon had observed Japanese torpedo boats anchored in the Colombo harbour.

It took another five days for them to cross the remainder of the Indian Ocean and agonize through the gruelling heat along the equator. On the fifth day, they finally reached the Straits of Malacca, the narrow oceanic channel that extends for 500 miles separating Malaysia in the north from Sumatra to the south. By now, their supply of coal was running low and it was imperative that they get permission to load coal at Singapore. Fortunately, Rudanovsky the seasoned Russian consul at Singapore had been fully briefed by his superiors in St. Petersburg about the need for coal for the Tsesarevich and Bayan. Rudanovsky had spent much time in Britain as a diplomat where he became well acquainted with the man who had recently been appointed as the British consul in Singapore. Through this amiable relationship, he was able to convince the British consul that even though the Russian ships were warships they were being sent only to protect Russia's recent acquisition of Port Arthur. As a show of welcome Rudanovsky even made a point of greeting the Russian warships in his launch as they approached the Singapore harbour and guided them to the coaling stations. Through his close connections with the British Rudanovsky had been able to smooth the way for Grigorovich and Wiren to load coal for the remainder of their passage to Port Arthur.

To Friedrich's surprise, the British port authorities even had dock workers help them load the coal. much to the relief of the stokers and their helpers who continued to suffer from the heat of the boilers and the sticky equatorial temperatures. Rudanovsky also spent a considerable amount of time ensuring the Russian ships were not only generously supplied with food and water but also had an ample supply of vodka for the remainder of their voyage. Captain Grigorovich was pleased, but also relieved when two days later the Tsesarevich and Bayan steamed comfortably out of the Singapore harbour through the narrow Singapore Strait and out into the South China Sea; the third sea on their voyage to Port Arthur. In a few days, the temperatures gradually began to moderate as they steamed northward much to the relief of Friedrich and his stokers. Now the crew of the Tsesarevich, both the seasoned sailors and the recruits, were becoming accustomed to their duties on this new ship. This left Grigorovich able to spend more time planning the remainder of the voyage and less time on advising, refereeing and disciplining his sailors. Now that the ship's atmosphere was more relaxed, the seamen began to think and talk of home and what it would be like to have a home-cooked meal of freshly fried potatoes, onions, tomatoes, cucumbers, perogies and of course, staples such as smoked garlic sausage. Real and imagined stories of their prowess in the Toulon brothels were passed from helper to stoker to midshipman to helmsman to officer and finally to the captain. Each story was embellished as it passed from sailor to sailor. With the boilers and propulsion system now running smoothly Friedrich also found time to think and wonder what was going on back at Nataliendorf. He would often look at the picture of his family that was delivered to him at Kronstadt and think about his family, the rowdy brothers, and the little sisters, blacksmithing with his mentor, August Wendtland and swimming in the cool fresh water of the Sluch River.

Grigorovich estimated that if they could maintain a pace of sixteen knots it would take about as long to go from Singapore to Port Arthur as it took going from Djibouti to Singapore. Early one morning as they passed Formosa and entered the East China Sea Grigirovich called Friedrich to the bridge and told him that they were right on schedule and should arrive at Port Arthur on about the 7th or 8th of October. He also said that as chief of the Tsesarevich's stokers Friedrich deserved a further promotion to Engineer First Class, however, Admiral Stark Commander of the First Pacific Squadron at Port Arthur could only make this official. Friedrich was pleased that Grigorovich recognized the tribulations that the senior stoker contingent had gone through in training the stokers and the motley crew of stoker's helpers that were sent to Toulon from St. Petersburg. Friedrich immediately passed the news on to his friend Stoker Second Class Lubomir Radomski who also had played a major role in keeping the crews that toiled in the coalbunkers in line and helped Friedrich service the boilers that had been in near continual operation during their 12,000-mile journey. The captain fully agreed to Friedrich's request that Radomski be promoted to Stoker First Class and promised that it would be taken into consideration when they arrived at Port Arthur. It was not long before they passed Shanghai, the major port on the northern Chinese coast. As they passed into the Yellow Sea that lays between Korea and China the whole ships crew were relieved that they were at last approaching their destination for it was now a matter of only a few days before they would finally be in a friendly Russian port.

At the time that Port Arthur was acquired from China in 1895, little thought had been given to the qualifications of the Russian political elite who would be put in charge of the new port. It followed that some time after Rozhdestvensky's trip to Nagasaki, when he was accompanied by the Romanov admiral Evgeny Alexeev, that Nicholas appointed Alexeev as the Viceroy and Commander-in-Chief of all of Russia's holdings in the Far East. From the time that Nicholas had become Tsar Alexeev had fawned on the new Monarch at every opportunity and despite the fact that he had a somewhat troubled Romanov lineage he had become a favourite of the Tsar. Upon his appointment Alexeev, who was now the Tsar's mouthpiece in the Far East, convinced Nicholas to name a non-Romanov fellow playboy, O.V. Stark, as an admiral. Alexeev immediately appointed Admiral Stark as Commander of Russia's First Pacific Squadron at Port Arthur. However, by late 1903 it soon became painfully clear to the Tsar as the Japanese situation became more and more menacing that he now needed a competent naval Commander at Port Arthur to replace the royal figureheads that had been so casually appointed. It was therefore inevitable that a replacement would have to be found, especially for Admiral Stark, and speculation was that Rozhdestvensky would be the Tsar's first choice. Nicholas was still enthralled with the artillery commander's brash and domineering personality and Rozhdestvensky's superb handling of his ship and crew in the Tsar's earlier show of naval prowess in the Baltic to his cousin, Kaiser Wilhelm. Timid and introverted Nicholas undoubtedly was still looking back at the stern character and bold exploits of his father the late Tsar Alexander III.

# Chapter 6

## Port Arthur

On the morning of the 8th of October 1903, as the Tsesarevich and the Bayan approached Port Arthur, all hands were on deck to witness their approach to Russia's naval stronghold in the Far East. They were all surprised to see that several ships of the First Pacific Squadron were not in the port but were anchored at the roadstead outside of the narrow and winding entrance to the harbour.  To Friedrich's surprise, they had to be delicately guided through the entry to the harbour by a tug, which took nearly 24 hours.  As Captain Grigorovich assessed the scattered ships of the squadron at the roadstead and the hazardous approach to the harbour, he became more and more apprehensive about the vulnerability of Port Arthur. He could see that if so much of the fleet was anchored at the roadstead, they would be sitting ducks for a surprise attack by the Japanese who could easily approach the roadstead from the open sea under cover of darkness or overcast weather.  Furthermore, any ship that would be emerging from the harbour behind a slow-moving tug would become a naked target.  The only protection they could have would be from shore-based batteries and he could see none.  This was only his first of many doubts about the defences of Port Arthur, which were under the guidance of Evgeny Alexeev and Admiral O.V. Stark.  When Alexeev arrived in Nagasaki in 1895, with Captain Rozhdestvensky on the Vladimir Monomakh, he had somehow impressed the Tsar to such an extent that only four years later in 1899, he was put in full command of the First Pacific Squadron. Alexeev's continuing close ties with the Tsar soon led to his promotion to full admiral in June of 1903, and was followed only one month later by another plum appointment—Viceroy of all of Russia's holdings in the Far East.

As the tugs wedged the big battleships carefully into the inner harbour, the Tsesarevich and the Bayan were towed to the main wharf where they anchored. Here they were greeted by an honour guard with a band playing the Russian national anthem. The Viceroy himself flanked by the Commander of the First Pacific Squadron Admiral O.V. Stark, both of whom stood at attention as Captain Grigorovich and Captain Wiren came down the gangplanks of their respective ships. Captain Grigorovich was impressed by this welcome of the two new Russian warships to Port Arthur; however, he also was amused by the fact that the Viceroy was already making a public display of his importance as the man now in supreme command of Russia's Far Eastern Empire. Viceroy Alexeev announced to the two newly arrived captains that they would have a meeting at his residence. Grigorovich commented that two of his crew were to be promoted and asked if they could also attend so that Admiral Stark could formally present them with their new status. They were escorted to a waiting carriage and were taken to a high promontory overlooking the city, called Quail Hill.

When they arrived at the mansion, they had a breathtaking view of the harbour. It had been the home of the former Chinese governor, and Alexeev had made sure that as Viceroy he must have the finest accommodation in Port Arthur. Friedrich, Radomski and the two captains were quite taken with the luxurious surroundings: vast impeccably manicured lawns, bubbling fountains, and small streams flowing down through terraced flower gardens. They were equally impressed with the interior of the Viceroy's elegant dwelling, which was furnished with tables and chairs of green jade surrounded by beautiful silk screens and wall decorations. However, as their stay at Port Arthur progressed Grigorovich and his seamen soon found that this blatant show of power was made even more obvious by the fact that the Chinese population were required to live in relatively squalid conditions outside the walls of the port city. They were kept completely separate from the heterogeneous mix of Russians as well as the foreigners of many nationalities that had gravitated to Port Arthur in the hope of cashing in on the generous Russian construction and ship maintenance contracts. Control of the influx of money from St. Petersburg of course was solely in the hands of the Viceroy; which obviously would enhance his image as Russia's Supreme Commander in the Far East. Even though he was in control of the money, he paid very little attention to such mundane affairs as building contracts and harbour maintenance. It followed that Alexeev's casual approach led to much graft and corruption with many of the newcomers exploiting obvious opportunities to take advantage of the Viceroy's negligence.

Upon their arrival at the mansion on Quail Hill Alexeev announced that the first point of business would be Admiral Stark formally presenting Friedrich with his credentials as Engineer First Class and Radomski with his credentials as Stoker First Class. Stark rose to the occasion, and gave an eloquent speech about the arrival of such fine battleships. Later, in their meeting with Admiral Stark and Alexeev at the Quail Hill estate Grigorovich and Wiren asked several questions about why so many ships were moored out in the roadstead, and why the ones in the harbour had to be squired by tugs through the narrow entry channel. Surely the helmsmen of each battleship or cruiser would be able with practice to get through much faster. Stark's response was that one cruiser had run aground on its way through the channel, and had blocked the entry for a full week, therefore, he had decided that the cruisers and battleships were better to anchor out in the roadstead. Grigorovich asked as to what would happen to the anchored ships if the Japanese came in under cover of darkness or fog, would the whole fleet not be exposed to broadsides even before they could lift anchor? Stark's response was that the Japanese had not yet declared war and when they did he would have ample time to put the First Pacific Squadron to sea or take the squadron into the harbour.

In any case, they all knew that declaration of war by the Japanese was imminent. For the next three months, both the Tsesarevich and the Bayan were outfitted in preparation for action. Friedrich had his stokers clean and ready each of the twenty boilers so that they would easily be able to propel the battleship at its top speed of eighteen knots. On one practice run to the open sea, Grigorovich insisted that he steam through the channel without the help of the slow moving tugs and found that he could make much better time alone in the more open stretches. Each time thereafter, the Tsesarevich went through without an escort, and Grigorovich found that each time he was able to avoid the shallowest shoals and increase his speed accordingly. Nevertheless, Admiral Stark insisted that the battleships should be anchored out in the roadstead. His reason was to have the firepower of the battleships ready for any attack that the Japanese may initiate on the Korean mainland adjacent to Port Arthur. He neglected to take into consideration that the Japanese navy might attack the battleships from the open sea—war being declared or not. On the 20th of January 1904, Alexeev had Admiral Stark send several ships on a sortie out into the Yellow Sea to see if the Japanese were assembling any naval offensive. Nothing of consequence was observed, so on their return on the 22nd of January Alexeev ordered Admiral Stark to anchor all of the battleships and cruisers at the roadstead to watch for any landing of Japanese ground forces on the mainland adjacent to Port Arthur.

On January 26th, 1904, under cover of early morning darkness, the Japanese Navy suddenly attacked the outer row of the resting Russian fleet at the Port Arthur roadstead. The lookout on the bridge of the Tsesarevich spotted the first Japanese battleship as it emerged from the darkness and he immediately rang the alarm. The harsh clatter of the alarm awoke Friedrich from a deep sleep for he had been up late checking the boilers the previous evening to make sure that they were in top working order. As he and Radomski ran to the upper deck to see what the crisis was a violent explosion shook the ship to such an extent that they both were brought to their knees. They raced along the upper deck to the bridge where they saw Grigorovich signalling to them. The captain told them that a torpedo had struck them broadside on the port side just below the water line and for them to go down to the hold to check the damage. When they got to the place where the torpedo had struck, they found that the armour plating was bent and was still in place but some of the rivets holding the plates had broken. Water was streaming in along the ruptured seams and was already ankle deep. Friedrich sent Radomski to get the other stokers and the pumps, as well as lengths of boards and beams from the carpenter shop to staunch the flow of water. With the planks that were brought, Friedrich wedged the boards against the broken seams with the beams anchored against the opposite wall. Then he and Radomski went to their blacksmith quarters and heated several containers of tar, which they then put around the boards to further stop the inflow of water.

Meanwhile, Grigorovich waited patiently on deck while the repairs were being made. When they were finished he anxiously came down to see the extent of the damage. He and the First Mate decided that it would be too risky to lift anchor and challenge the approaching Japanese warships. Instead, he ordered his gunners to fire at any Japanese ship that was in range. When he returned to the bridge he noticed that Admiral Stark's flagship the Petropavlovsk along with three other Russian battleships and five cruisers were already well on their way to challenge the Japanese attackers. However, the two ships adjacent to the Tsesarevich, the ironclad battleship Retvisan and the first-rated cruiser Pallada also had been struck and were still at anchor. Admiral Togo Heihachiro, Commander of the Japanese fleet was surprised by the speed at which the Russian flagship and the other eight warships retaliated. He feared that all of the other Russian craft would soon join the fray and not realizing that three of Russia's warships actually now were disabled he immediately ordered his ships to retreat even though he had fifteen battleships and cruisers in his squadron. Admiral Stark pursued the Japanese fleet for only a short distance and when he saw that they did not turn to resume battle he turned and took his ships back to the roadstead to see what had happened to his two best battleships. The new Russian shore batteries, that had been installed after Grigorovich had pointed out the necessity of firepower from the mainland to Admiral Stark, were unable to fire a single shell at the Japanese warships. Even though they had plenty of ammunition they had no oil to lubricate their cannonry—another oversight by Alexeev and his Naval Commander Admiral Stark. Later, in his communications to St. Petersburg Alexeev laid the blame of the failure of the shore batteries solely on Stark. Nevertheless, even though Stark had repulsed the Japanese torpedo attack his days were now numbered as Commander of Russia's First Pacific Squadron.

Disabling three of Russia's best warships marked the beginning of the naval battles to come that would see few Russian naval victories—but many acts of heroism. As soon as the Admiralty in St. Petersburg received the news of this unprovoked attack on Russia's anchored fleet at Port Arthur Tsar Nicholas telegraphed a formal declaration of war to Japan. The telegraph lines were now humming between St. Petersburg and Port Arthur. Who was to be the replacement for Admiral Stark? Would it be Admiral Rozhdestvensky, who so impressed the Tsar with his aggressive show of discipline and cannonry display? On the other hand, would it be the scientific and studious Admiral Makarov? The answer was not long in coming. The Tsar sent word from the Winter Palace to the naval base at Kronstadt for an emergency meeting with Admiral Makarov. On the 14th of January 1904, Tsar Nicholas went to Kronstadt and announced that Viceroy Alexeev had informed him of Admiral Stark's incompetence. The Tsar then said that he had chosen Makarov to leave at once to take over command of Russia's First Pacific Squadron. Makarov had already assessed the Japanese attack on the fleet anchored at the Port Arthur roadstead and wondered why the ships were not anchored in the safety of the harbour. Makarov for some time had felt that the squadron at Port Arthur should be bolstered with at least two or three more battleships. He had been pleased that a month earlier the battleship Oslyabya and two cruisers were on their way to Port Arthur. However, a short time later to his surprise the Tsar for some unknown reason had recalled them just before they reached the Suez Canal.

Upon receiving the news of his new appointment Makarov first asked that forty torpedo boats be disassembled, loaded on freight cars and be taken along with him to Port Arthur via the Trans-Siberian Railway. However, the Tsar on advice from his relatives and uninformed bureaucrats refused his request. Disappointed, but anxious to get on with taking over his new post, Makarov assembled his staff and ordered them to gather the equipment that he felt was necessary for their wartime duties at the now besieged Port Arthur. He knew that it was a dire necessity that the three wounded warships at Port Arthur be repaired as soon as possible, so that he would have at least a minimum of naval firepower to counter the aggressive and recently expanded Japanese navy. Since Port Arthur did not have a dry docking facility, he recruited 200 shipwrights from the Kronstadt base to accompany him to Port Arthur in the hope that cofferdams could be constructed to repair the ships damaged in the Japanese torpedo attack. With his staff, as well as the 200 shipwrights and their necessary equipment, seven freight cars were required. The Makaraov contingent then began their long railroad trek across the vast eastern expanse of Russia. They arrived at Port Arthur on the 24th of February 1904. As soon as Makarov set foot on the Port Arthur dock, he met with the three captains of the damaged ships. When Makarov boarded the Tsesarevich he greeted Grigorovich warmly and as Friedrich and Radomski were standing close by he shook hands with them and spoke of the time that he came to the Mikhailovich battleship at Kronstadt in April of 1903, to present Friedrich and Radomski with their earlier promotions.

The shipwrights and the crew of each ship were immediately set to work to design and build cofferdams to fit on the sides of the Tsesarevich, the Retvisan and the Pallada. Friedrich and Radomski watched studiously as the cofferdams were being built. The newly arrived shipwrights deftly spliced the planking together to make a waterproof wall. Once the cofferdams were built and placed against the ship there was the problem of sealing the cofferdam against the ship. Friedrich pointed out to the head shipwright how they had sealed the planks against the interior of the ship with hot tar and suggested they could do the same on the interior edge of the cofferdam where it rested against the ship. As they pumped the water out of the cofferdam, Friedrich and his stokers sealed the interior contacts with hot tar. Once the damaged plates were exposed Radomski and the other stokers removed the bent plates and sent them up to Friedrich who worked several days straightening and patching the thick plates.    When they were finished and the cofferdam was removed, Grigorovich took the Tsesarevich through the channel and out into the Bohai Gulf to test the ship's seaworthiness.  The armour plating held fast and he congratulated Friedrich and the stokers for a job well done.  It was not long before both the Pallada and Retvisan were also ready to put to sea.

Makarov wasted no time in making his squadron into a battle ready force.  He immediately saw that much work had to be done and during his briefings with Admiral Stark he realized what a monumental task it was going to be, not only to get the ships in shape but the coastal defenders had to be properly trained and equipped.  In a short time, he had them do routine target practice much like what Rozhdestvensky had the shore batteries do in the Baltic defences.  Makarov also required them to maintain a 24-hour watch for any enemy encroachment.  In addition, he was amazed that Stark had not put some sort of barriers on the approaches to the roadstead and the narrow outlet of the entry to the harbour.  He immediately had two rusted old tankers taken out of the harbour and scuttled them at staggered points on the approaches to the roadstead, this would force any approaching vessel to turn broadside to the Russian coastal batteries.  This soon paid dividends when two Japanese battleships approached the roadstead, obviously to shell the harbour.  As they wove their way into cannon range one of the battleships was hit broadside by shells from the shore batteries and had to be towed back to Japan for repairs.  Makarov scoffed at Stark's method of using tugs to guide the warships out through the narrow channel approach.  When he heard of Grigorovich refusing to have the Tsesarevich helped through this narrow harbour entry he enlisted him to show all of the other captains the route and had the Tsesarevich lead the fleet out to the roadstead and beyond every day for a whole week.  In addition, each time they went out to the open sea Makarov would train them in minor skirmishes.  With the practice of going through the channel every day, it now took the whole fleet less than three hours to get out of the harbour.  Having accomplished so much in the short time that he had been at Port Arthur, he also laid plans to take some of his fleet to Vladivostok, which had a much more secure harbour. From Vladivostok, he would be able to counter Japanese forays from both directions. He also felt that Russia's ground forces in Manchuria were being held at bay by the Japanese land army. Consequently, with two Russian fleets keeping the Japanese Navy at bay it would divert their attention away from making surprise ground landings anywhere on the Korean mainland adjacent to Port Arthur. However, these plans would never come to fruition.

On the night of March 30th, 1904, several Japanese destroyers passed by the entrance to the Port Arthur harbour just out of range of the shore batteries. Hidden among the destroyers was the Japanese minelayer Koryu Maru, which was not seen by the shore lookouts. One of Makarov's prime objectives had always been to familiarize himself with the territory he was to protect. Consequently, either he would go out himself on his flagship the Petropavlovsk, or he would send another ship out to do some reconnaissance. Earlier in the day, he had sent out the destroyer Strashnyi to monitor the coastline to the east. As the Strashnyi rounded a promontory, a flotilla of Japanese cruisers was steaming toward the lone Russian ship. They immediately began shelling the little destroyer. The Strashnyi, completely outgunned turned and started back to Port Arthur. Makarov was informed by the battery lookouts of the distress of the Strashnyi and sent the armoured cruisers Bayan and Diana to help the lone destroyer. Captain Wiren had his stokers push the Bayan over its base speed of 21 knots and arrived just as the Japanese were closing in on the Strashnyi, which by this time was badly damaged and beginning to sink. Wiren braved the Japanese shelling, brought the Bayan alongside the stricken Strashnyi and was able to rescue all of the crew. In the meantime, the Diana arrived and between them, they continued to shell the Japanese ships, which far outnumbered the two Russian cruisers. To Wiren's surprise the Japanese began to retreat. However, they soon saw why the Japanese destroyers were pulling back, for in the background loomed six more Japanese armoured cruisers and behind them three Japanese battleships.

In the meantime, Makarov aware now that a full fleet of Japanese warships were approaching hurriedly made his way through the tortuous channel on the Petropavlovsk and had the battleship Poltava and two armoured cruisers, the Novik and the Askold, follow him. When the Japanese saw the four approaching Russian ships they circled to the south and west, which Makarov thought was a rather strange move however he was still unaware that the Japanese had just laid mines stretching seaward from the Port Arthur roadstead. Admiral Togo Heihachiro had deliberately moved to the southwest to lure the Russian fleet through the minefield. To the surprise of Admiral Togo, the Russian fleet steamed through the mines without incident.  Makarov saw that the Japanese fleet outnumbered the Russian warships nearly two to one, so before they reached cannon range Makarov decided that he would return to the Port Arthur roadstead were he had ordered the other battleships and cruisers to stand by and get them to enter the fray.

However, when he passed through the mined area again the Petropavlovsk struck not one, but two mines. The second mine exploded just below the ship's powder magazine.  Friedrich and Radomski were on the deck of the Tsesarevich about to go below and alert the stokers to fire their boilers and be ready to go to sea, when they saw the Petropavlovsk strike the first mine and saw some of the superstructure tumble onto the deck. When the flagship hit the second mine it exploded just below the ammunition magazine. The next thing Friedrich saw was a great pillar of smoke and fire as the ammunition was detonated in the magazine. The eruption blew apart the entire front of the ship.  Friedrich stood immobile as he recalled how he had been in awe of the practice bombardment he had witnessed when he was back in the Baltic on the battleship Mikhailovich during Rozhdestvensky's shelling demonstrations that were performed for the Tsar and his German cousin Kaiser Wilhelm. Everyone on the deck of the Tsesarevich was transfixed watching as the stern of the Petropavlovsk rose skyward and in a matter of only a few minutes, the whole ship slid silently into the sea. Grigorovich had lifted anchor and shouted at Friedrich to get down to his stokers to man the boilers.  When the Tsesarevich arrived where the Petropavlovsk had vanished, they lowered the lifeboats but they were able to find only 58 survivors of the crew of 738. Six hundred and eighty seamen on the Petropavlovsk had perished, including Admiral Makarov. Once the survivors were on board, Captain Grigorovich signalled the rest of the Russian ships to head for the roadstead and file into the harbour and let the shore batteries protect their retreat. The Japanese fleet was still a distance to the southwest giving the Russian ships enough time to get to the harbour entrance even though the fastest ships in the Japanese fleet, their cruisers got within cannon range the Russian shore batteries were able to drive them off.

Once in the shelter of the harbour word from Captain Grigorovich was sent to Viceroy Alexeev at his mansion on Quail Hill that the Petropavlovsk had been sunk with the loss of 90 per cent of its crew, including Admiral Makarov. Alexeev on the point of panic, announced he would personally take over duties as commander of the squadron—a mistake that he was soon to regret. Even though Alexeev had three other admirals at Port Arthur they were, nevertheless, recent arrivals and had somewhat limited backgrounds. Several of the captains of the battleships were much better qualified to command the squadron, which included both Captain Grigorovich and Captain Wiren. In assuming command of the fleet Alexeev hoisted his flag on the battleship Sevastopol on the 4th of April 1904. His first encounter as commander of the squadron was on the night of 20th of April when the Japanese tried to block the harbour and attempted to blow up an old warship at its entrance. Alexeev thwarted the plan by anchoring his flagship at the roadstead and waited there until the Japanese gave up and left. However, while he was attending to his duties as Commander of the Fleet word had been received at his Quail Hill headquarters of an even more critical situation. The Japanese ground forces had taken the high lands immediately east of Port Arthur. This gave them a commanding view of the inner harbour at Port Arthur. Had the Viceroy been at his post at Quail Hill he could possibly have had the invasion challenged by calling on Russian land troops from the Russian Army to the north at Mukden that were under the command of General Kuropatkin.

While Alexeev was agonizing over the loss of Makarov, who not only had brought the First Pacific Squadron to fighting trim in the short two months that he had been at Port Arthur, but he had also charted the possibilities of a Japanese threat by land. He had told Alexeev that once the Japanese gained access to the hills surrounding Port Arthur it would be worse than an attack from the Yellow Sea. When word was received in St. Petersburg of the sinking of the Petropavlovsk with the loss of most of the crew including Makarov the wheels were immediately set in motion to recruit a competent admiral to command the Port Arthur squadron. Surprisingly, the Viceroy had made no request. Admiral O.V. Witgeft, who was a classmate of Zinoviev Rozhdestvensky, was chosen by the Tsar to take command of the First Pacific Squadron. Witgeft was a quiet and thoughtful seaman who had risen through the ranks by carefully avoiding confrontations with the Russian royalty, however, he had definite naval strategies of his own that he would quietly put into action. Back in early January of 1904, he had been appointed as chief of staff to Viceroy Alexeev. He was uneasy in this new post since he soon became aware of Alexeev's egotistical incompetence. Therefore, he was quite pleased when a fellow Naval Academy graduate Admiral Makarov was selected to command the Port Arthur fleet.

When the Tsar declared war on Japan Witgeft had informed his royal highness of his disagreement with Alexeev's performance, especially on naval tactics. Consequently, it was surprising that Alexeev had bowed so easily to the Tsar's selection of Witgeft as Commander of the Fleet at Port Arthur. However, as it turned out, Alexeev had become very preoccupied with a more critical matter, the Japanese land forces were established on the hills immediately to the east of Port Arthur and now had an unobstructed view into the harbour. Feeling that it was only a matter of time before Port Arthur fell to the Japanese Alexeev probably fearing for his own safety announced that he would have to conduct the defence of Port Arthur from the Russian army stronghold at Mukden. He said that he could stay at Port Arthur as an admiral, but as Viceroy he was obligated to leave and command the Russian defence of Port Arthur with the support of Russian ground forces. Alexeev left Port Arthur on his special train on the 22nd of April 1904, and by displaying a Red Cross flag cautiously made his way through the advancing Japanese ground army.    Once established at Mukden he again created dissension by overruling General Kuropatkin, the Military Commander of the Russian army in the Far East, by demanding that the General send his troops to the south to maintain contact with Port Arthur.  Kuropatkin on the other hand, wanted to wait since reinforcements were soon to arrive via the Trans-Siberian Railway. An intense argument followed and Alexeev insisted that the decision must rest with the Tsar himself.  Several days went by before the word came from the Winter Palace.  The Tsar of course, favoured the plan of Alexeev who still appeared to be an implicitly trusted Romanov in the eyes of Nicholas II, despite the fact that he was only a bastard nephew.  Kuropatkin unobtrusively saw to it that only a token offensive took place, which soon ended at the Battle of Telissu on the 2nd of June 1904, with the defeat of the Russian forces.  This now left the fate of Port Arthur in an even more precarious position.

Meanwhile, since the Japanese now controlled the telegraph lines in all of Korea, Viceroy Alexeev was sending continuous messages from Mukden to Witgeft by Chinese sloops, which were able to travel undetected along the coastline telling Witgeft to break out and leave Port Arthur immediately for Vladivostok. Witgeft, however, ignored the orders and pursued his own way of dealing with the defence of Port Arthur.  He felt that he still had enough warship firepower to win a battle against the Japanese in a naval confrontation.  Witgeft had selected the Tsesarevich as his flagship and kept it in the most protected corner of the harbour, since the Japanese ground forces on the hills to the east kept up a regular cannon bombardment.  Even though they were at long range some damage was done, in fact the mansion on Quail Hill was riddled with shell holes.  Witgeft's plan was to keep the fleet in the harbour and bombard the Japanese emplacements by taking the heaviest artillery from the battleships part way up the slopes to the east to counter the Japanese bombardment.  In the meantime, the Japanese navy was patrolling just out of reach of the Russian shore batteries waiting for the Russian fleet to emerge.  Still ignoring Alexeev's messages, Witgeft was casting about for ways to counter the ubiquitous Japanese patrols just outside the Port Arthur roadstead. Since there was still plenty of ammunition stored at Port Arthur, Admiral Wiren had the mine-laying cruiser Amur, which had been at anchor along with most of the rest of the fleet, stocked with explosives. After conferring with the captain of the Amur, the cruiser was sent out in the dark of night for several nights and fifty mines were planted just outside of the roadstead. A few days later, on May 1st, 1904, as the Japanese patrolled by the entrance to the port the battleships Hatsuse and Yashima and three cruisers struck mines; two Japanese ships were sunk and the other three were severely damaged. Now that the Japanese had lost nearly a third of their battle fleet Admiral Witgeft was sure that he could win a battle at sea. He and his captains immediately began to ready their vessels for a major confrontation. On June 10th, 1904, the shore batteries spotted the Japanese fleet approaching: six battleships: five cruisers and eight destroyers. Admiral Witgeft had been waiting for this moment. He now had his fleet trim and ready for battle: four battleships, ten cruisers and thirty destroyers. The First Pacific Squadron filed out of the narrow harbour channel and headed directly for the Japanese fleet. The Japanese were astonished to see that the three battleships torpedoed earlier by the Japanese at the Port Arthur roadstead: the Tsesarevich, Retvisan and Pobieda were leading the Russian fleet. It now was obvious to Admiral Togo that these three ships gave the Russians a distinct advantage in heavy guns. Consequently, the Japanese admiral decided not to attack and signalled his fleet to return to the safety of their home harbour. Witgeft's fleet was well beyond cannon range from the Japanese ships and he decided that it would be futile to pursue them so he had the Russian squadron return to Port Arthur.

Upon the return of the Russian squadron to their home port, Witgeft was greeted by yet another message from Alexeev. This one was couched in no uncertain terms. In addition to the Viceroy's stern message, there was a copy of a directive that had been telegraphed to Alexeev by Tsar Nicholas II. It directly ordered Witgeft to immediately take the squadron to Vladivostok. The Tsar's order also stated that if Witgeft refused to take the Russian squadron to Vladivostok he would be court-martiallled.  Witgeft now had no choice.  The Russian fleet was fully prepared for a head on confrontation with Admiral Togo, and Witgeft knew that he could more than hold his own in a face-to-face battle.  However, he would be at a disadvantage if he chose to flee to Vladivostok for he would have to deal not only with the Japanese attacking him from the rear but would risk running into a frontal attack from other Japanese warships, since he would be steaming directly toward the Japanese naval base at Sasebo.  As a further complication he would then have to brave the narrow passage between Japan and Korea at Tsushima; both sides of the passage would be guarded by Japanese gunboats.

# Chapter 7

# The Battle of the Yellow Sea

Witgeft, now having no choice and regardless of the hazards had to do his best to get the Russian fleet to Vladivostok.  In the early morning dawn of the 28th of July 1904, Russia's First Pacific Squadron left their home harbour with Admiral Witgeft in the lead on his flagship, the Tsesarevich.  Admiral Togo after he had left his post outside of the Port Arthur roadstead on June 10th had returned to the Japanese naval base of Sasebo and had since supplemented his fleet with four armoured cruisers, nine destroyers and four coastal gun ships.  This time he was sure Witgeft would challenge him in a frontal attack so the Japanese Commander placed his flagship, the Mikasa, at the head of his warships at a point somewhat to the southwest of Port Arthur where he had a good view of the entrance to the Russian port.  To his surprise, when the Russian fleet emerged the lead ship of the fleet, the Tsesarevich, veered immediately to the northeast leading the Russian squadron directly toward the narrow passage between Korea and Japan.  It was instantly apparent to Togo that Witgeft was on his way to Vladivostok and a direct confrontation was now out of the question.  Therefore, it was imperative that he overtake the Russian fleet.  To let the Port Arthur squadron join forces with the Vladivostok garrison would mean a strong Russian joint naval force would be a double threat to the northern part of Japan.

Witgeft could see he had a substantial lead on the Japanese fleet and they would avoid being caught if they could maintain a speed of at least 18 knots.  With him he had the battleships Retvisan,

Peresviet, Pobieda and Sevastopol. Bringing up the rear was the battleship Poltava. In a line between the four front running battleships and the Poltava were the cruisers Pallada, Diana, Askold and Novik plus eight destroyers. Witgeft had left several cruisers and destroyers at Port Arthur to hold the port as long as they could; one of the cruisers that remained was the Bayan. Witgeft had put its captain, Robert Nikolayevich Wiren, in command of the skeleton fleet that stayed to hold Port Arthur as long as possible.

As the Russian squadron steamed full ahead toward the bottleneck at the Korean Strait Witgeft felt that his ships could easily stay well ahead of the Japanese fleet. Suddenly, there came a signal from the Pobieda the third battleship in line. Two of their boilers had blown and they needed to cut their speed to 12 knots until repairs were made. Witgeft had to make the choice of leaving the Pobieda behind until repairs were made leaving her fate to the Japanese, or he could slow the whole squadron until the repairs were done. Friedrich had warned the Chief Engineer of the Pobieda to double check his boilers before they left Port Arthur. The Chief Engineer of the Pobieda had refused to take part in a ritual that had been instigated by Friedrich for the stoker contingent of each ship to check each other's boilers regularly. Now that the boilers of the Pobieda had been running under full steam for some time, two had failed at this critical time. Witgeft felt they could still stay ahead of the Japanese, so he signalled the other ships to slow to 12 knots. The squadron proceeded at this agonizingly slow pace for the next two hours, with everyone watching the Japanese fleet moving ever closer. Finally, the signal came from the flagship to increase speed, with great cheers from the anxious sailors on the decks. However, they were ordered not to exceed 15 knots. The disappointed Russian crews soon saw that at this rate the Japanese were still closing the distance between them. Even the helmsman on the Tsesarevich could not restrain his frustration and said, "Here we are moving at a snails pace and the Viceroy kept telling us we were the pride of the Russian Navy!"

By noon, the Japanese fleet was completely abreast of the Russian ships and organized into battle ready positions. When the range between the two fleets had fallen to 8,000 yards, all seven of the Japanese armoured cruisers opened fire. In a short time, the Japanese flagship Mikasa and the battleships abreast of it also came into range and started firing with their heavier artillery. Their main target of course, was the Russian flagship the Tsesarevich as well as the other four Russian battleships. The ordinary seamen on the Russian ships were shocked by the fire and smoke created by the strikes the Japanese shells made on the Russian ships. However, the Japanese shells were able to start fires but did not have good penetrating ability. On the other hand, the Russian shells were relatively smokeless but had better penetration force. This gave the impression to the Russian sailors that the Japanese were creating havoc with the Russian fleet with little apparent damage being inflicted on the Japanese ships.

At that range, Admiral Witgeft saw that most of the Japanese shells fell short of their targets so he waited until the Japanese ships closed to 6,000 yards before he signalled his battleships to return fire. As the shells streamed toward the Japanese ships the Russian crews on deck were finally able to cheer as they witnessed several of the Russian shells hit the Japanese ships and were able to see holes appear in Admiral Togo's flagship. Suddenly, the Tsesarevich turned sharply to the east and the rest of the fleet followed accordingly. What they were to discover later was that the speedier Japanese destroyers had gone ahead and thrown out drift mines (with no anchors). Captain Grigorovich without waiting to confer with Witgeft had immediately altered course to avoid the mines. The semaphore that soon came from the flagship was for the Russian fleet to alter course to the east to avoid the floating mines. As the cruisers, destroyers and the battleship Poltava, which was bringing up the rear passed the mined area they could see the mines bobbing harmlessly in the waters on their port side. At this point, the Japanese were still to the east of the Russians but had fallen back and now were closer to the central part of the Russian fleet where they concentrated their firepower on the cruisers and destroyers.

The armoured cruisers Pallada, Askold, Diana and Novik steamed directly toward the Japanese battleships so they could get closer with their shorter-range guns. They were successful in several strikes on the Japanese flagship; one of the shells from the Diana struck the turret of one of the Mikasa's heavy 12-inch gun turrets that not only disabled the gun but also killed the crew. In the melee, the Russian cruisers each suffered minor damage to their superstructures and funnels but there was no loss of life. The Japanese fleet then drew away to the southeast and kept apart from the Russian squadron at a range of 10,000 feet or more. At this range, their battleships were the only ships with firepower enough even to come close to the Russians and even then, nearly all of their shells only sent up sprays of water as they landed short of their targets. By 3 o'clock p.m., Togo withdrew even further allowing Witgeft again to set course for the Korean Strait. However, why did Togo withdraw? Perhaps they were assessing and repairing their damaged ships. Nevertheless, Witgeft felt Togo was falling back only to advance from behind and on the port or western side of the Russian fleet.

Consequently, Witgeft ordered the Russian cruisers and destroyers to pull alongside the battleships on his port side and maintain a distance of 4,000 feet. To Witgeft's surprise rather than coming behind the Russian squadron, Togo's fleet advanced directly toward the now unprotected eastern side of the Russian ships. The Japanese ships with their flagship Mikasa in the lead, approached and began shelling the Russian battleships. Witgeft trained all of his battleship's heavy artillery on any Japanese ship within range and scored as many hits as the Japanese. Now that the Russian armour-clad cruisers were making their way rapidly into the battle, Witgeft felt they would be able to gain the upper hand. Suddenly, a shell struck the hull of the Tsesarevich just above the armour plating. The fiery Japanese shell penetrated directly into one of the coalbunkers. Captain Grigorovich called the main boiler room and told Friedrich to go quickly and assess the damage. As Friedrich approached the stricken area, he was faced with fire coming from the coalbunker. The stokers from that boiler were already setting up pumps and laying hoses to fight the blaze. As he rushed to get on deck to alert the captain, he called for more of the stokers to get down and help with the fire. When Friedrich arrived on deck and up to the bridge,

Admiral Witgeft with his Chief of Staff, Rear Admiral Matusevich and two of his officers were in conference along the railing. Witgeft asked Friedrich as to what damage there was below and Friedrich explained the fire was spreading rapidly so he came to ask the captain for more help. Just as he turned to go into the conning tower to speak to Grigorovich there was a violent explosion when another shell struck the top of the conning tower sending shards of metal and glass flying across the bridge. When Friedrich looked back from the door of the conning tower, he saw Admiral Witgeft's headless body lying twitching on the floor of the bridge. His two officers lay motionless in a pool of blood beside him, and Chief of Staff Matusevich was clutching his shoulder that was bleeding profusely. Captain Grigorovich had come to the door just as the shell struck and was standing awestricken along with Friedrich. Finally, Grigorovich told Friedrich he must get down and see to the fires in the bunkers and that he would get the ships doctor to look after the carnage on the bridge. Just as Friedrich was starting to go below another jolt hit the Tsesarevich. A high-explosive shell again struck, this time at the top of the conning tower; it shattered the helm and Friedrich could see parts of the helmsman's body flying through the air.

Other shells had hit the funnels of the Tsesarevich and Friedrich saw the smoke from the boilers pouring from the holes rather than the top of the funnels. As he ran to get to his post at the boilers and bunkers, he was hailed by a deck hand that he must return to the bridge immediately to see the captain. Friedrich shouted back to the deck hand to go down to the boiler rooms and get Radomski to come on deck to assemble more help to fight the fires. Friedrich hurried back to the bridge to see the captain who was desperately trying to re-attach the wheel to get the ship righted and on course, but he was having little success. Friedrich examined the damage and quickly went to the nearest tool storage and got two iron rods some bolts and wrenches and rushed back to the helm to stabilize the shaft below the wheel. When the steering was disabled, the flagship had turned suddenly to port, so much so that everyone on the ship feared she would capsize. With the Tsesarevich now continuing to circle the whole squadron waited for a signal from the flagship as to why they were making this sudden turn to the west and then circling back toward the east. Some of the ships close to the Tsesarevich saw that something was wrong and took it upon themselves to slow down, stop or some even proceeded on a course toward the Korean Strait. The ones further away were not aware the flagship was in distress and, as was required in naval exercises, followed the sharply turning flagship but this just added more confusion in the ranks of the squadron. As the Tsesarevich was now out of control, the first priority of Grigorovich was to stabilize the steering that Friedrich had temporarily remedied. Now that they were able to proceed on a relatively straight line, Grigorovich called in his chief petty officer to man the helm. He then hurried to send a semaphore to Rear Admiral Prince Pavel Ukhtomsky, who was second in command to Admiral Witgeft and was stationed aboard the battleship Peresviet. By this time, the Tsesarevich had turned a complete circle and was headed directly toward the Japanese fleet. Since the Peresviet was fourth in the line of battleships its captain assumed the Tsesarevich was intending to ram the Japanese flagship so he also turned to face the Japanese. At the last moment, they saw the semaphore message: "6:10 p.m. August 28th, 1904—attention battleship Peresviet, Admiral Witgeft hands over command to Admiral Ukhtomsky."

Grigorovich expected an immediate response, but there was none and no admiral's flag went up on the Peresviet. It is true that the top masts of the Peresviet had been shattered by Japanese fire but any sort of line could have been hoisted to carry the admiral's flag that would have informed the fleet of the transfer of command. No flag was ever raised and as the Peresviet now made a complete turn to the west most of the rest of the fleet ignored it's change of direction. However, the four ships that had seen the semaphore message from the Tsesarevich, signalling that the Peresviet was now the official flagship, dutifully turned to follow the now official flagship, rightfully assuming this was their new leader. Panic-stricken Prince Ukhtomsky, who had only limited training as a royally appointed admiral chose to flee back to Port Arthur. A move that at this stage was suicidal. This should have been obvious to Ukhtomski as it was to all of the senior Russian officers in the squadron. They had left their besieged home port knowing Port Arthur would soon fall to the Japanese, since the Japanese had taken much of the high ground surrounding the port. Ukhtomsky would have been fully aware that Captain Wiren was left to hold the port only as long as his ammunition lasted. The five ships closest to the Tsesarevich who had seen the semaphore were the battleships Retvisan, Pobieda, Sevastopol, Poltava and the cruiser Pallada. All five of them turned and followed their new unmarked flagship. By this time, Admiral Togo seeing that the Russian flagship was in distress and the rest of the fleet was in total disarray moved in for the kill. The Japanese ships were ordered to encircle the Russian squadron.

Meanwhile, what was happening on the Tsesarevich? After helping Grigorovich restore the steering of the ship Friedrich returned to his post in the boiler rooms. On his way, he passed through what had always been designated as the sick bay, however, it had now been extended until it covered most of the quarter deck; in many places the floor was slippery from the blood of so many seamen wounded by flying shrapnel as the Japanese shelling shattered the ship's superstructure. Many of the injured were lying on temporary cots with bleeding wounds and severed limbs, with most of the injuries having been caused by flying shrapnel. When Friedrich got down to the boiler rooms Radomski and the stokers had the fires put out in the first two bunkers but by this time fire had spread to three adjoining bunkers and as the heat was increasing in the enclosed hold the fires were becoming more and more intense. Several of the stokers had passed out because of the heat and Radomski had them lying in the area where the fires had been put out. When Radomski went to rouse them, he found that two of them were no longer breathing. Friedrich hurried and got several men to carry the remaining unconscious fire fighters out of the heat and smoke in the bunkers knowing they would have a better chance of survival, or hopefully revival, in the fresh air on the open deck or in the sick bay. Friedrich kept only six men with him to fight the fires and sent Radomski to bring down as many blankets as they could muster from the sleeping quarters. This would give the fire fighters more protection for they could wrap themselves in wet blankets and perhaps get closer to the flames.  If just two more coalbunkers caught fire, the next one was directly under the ships ammunition magazine.  Needless to say, the Tsesarevich undoubtedly would then follow the same fate the Petropavlovsk had suffered three months earlier.  Friedrich told Radomski to tell the captain about the threat to the ammunition magazine and insist he send any able bodied men he could find to help in the sweltering boiler rooms.

When Radomski returned to the boiler rooms, the captain had conscripted twenty sailors some of whom had even been taken from the sick bay by Grigorovich who felt they were well enough to give a helping hand.  By this time, the fires had spread to yet another bunker and Friedrich sent several of the sailors to help man the pumps.  He then put two men on each of five hoses with each man soaked in a wet blanket.  He and Radomski led this complement of hoses right into the interior of the last burning bunker and as they sprayed the burning coal, now having greater pressure from the pumps, they were able to quell the flames.  As they were pulling the hoses out Radomski noticed there was still some coal burning in the far corner of the bunker and shouted to Friedrich that he would go in and put it out.  Friedrich noticed Radomski's blanket was dry and as Radomski got near the burning coal, his blanket burst into flames.  Friedrich quickly took another hose leaped into the bunker and sprayed water on the burning blanket.  By this time, Radomski had passed out so Friedrich and two of the other men lifted him out of the bunker.  During this time the other men had doused the last of the burning coal.  Friedrich had all of the stokers stay in the burned out boiler area to monitor any smouldering coals and to assess the damage done to each of their boilers.  Now that the fires were out Friedrich's concern was about Radomski who was conscious but in agonizing pain from the burns on his back.  Friedrich helped him up to the deck and took him to the sick bay portion of the deck where he got one of the medics, who had been dressing a wound on a man on the adjacent cot, to tend to Radomski.  Friedrich's next task was to find the captain who would now be relieved that the ammunition magazine was no longer in danger.  Friedrich climbed to the bridge where he found Grigorovich talking to the other officers and when they saw Friedrich, they all wanted to know how far the bunker fires had advanced.     When Friedrich said the fires were now out Grigorovich breathed a sigh of relief and said they had been making plans to open the seacocks to scuttle the ship before the fire reached the bunker below the magazine.     However, Friedrich told Grigorovich at least ten or more of the boilers were out of commission and he would have to see what repairs would have to be made to get at least some of them back into operation.  Grigorovich told Friedrich he would get him whatever help he needed to get as many boilers as possible into operation.

It was now 9 o'clock p.m., nearly three hours since the two devastating Japanese strikes on the conning tower had killed Admiral Witgeft, two of his staff, and the helmsman.  Darkness was now rapidly falling, but the Japanese warships had been moving in from all sides.  The three cruisers, Diana and Novik led by the cruiser flagship Askold had surrounded the crippled Tsesarevich and diverted much of the fire from the Japanese battleships.  Admiral Togo's flagship, the Mikasa, also had suffered substantial damage and since most of its guns had been disabled, had not fired a shot for some time.  It was later established that during the Battle of the Yellow Sea the Tsesarevich was hit nearly exclusively by the heavy shells from the Japanese battleships.  One of the heavy 12-inch shells was the one that killed Admiral Witgeft and his officers and another disabled the helm and killed the helmsman.  Both of these hits were only inches from over-shooting the Tsesarevich entirely.  It was also a heavy shell that hit the hull just above the ships armour belt penetrated into the bunker and started the fire.  In total, fifteen heavy shells struck the Tsesarevich and only one lighter eight-inch shell pierced the relatively thin armour of one of the gun turrets.  The Japanese flagship Mikasa was struck even more times than the Tsesarevich.  Thirty-one hits were made on Admiral Togo's flagship although most of the strikes were made by the smaller guns of the Russian cruisers they inflicted severe damage to the big guns of the Japanese flagship.  By the time total darkness fell, the Mikasa had lost nearly all of its firepower.  In addition to the loss of its heavy artillery, eighty-two crew members aboard the Mikasa were killed.

What had happened to the rest of the Russian squadron during the crisis aboard the Tsesarevich? As mentioned previously, shortly after 6 p.m., Admiral Prince Ukhtomski on his unmarked flagship the Peresviet had fled leading the other four battleships: Retvisan, Pobieda, Sevastopol, Poltava and the cruiser Pallada back to Port Arthur. Following the departure of the six warships the remaining Russian cruisers and destroyers mounted a surprising barrage of cannon fire on the Japanese fleet as it began to encircle the remnants of the Russian squadron. All of the remaining Russian fleet by now realized the desperate straits of the Tsesarevich. The three armoured cruisers led by the cruiser flagship Askold and two of the destroyers diverted the Japanese fire away from their crippled flagship, which gave Captain Grigorovich and his crewmen time to repair some of the damage to their ship. Even though many of the sailors on the Tsesarevich were engrossed in battling the fires and coping with the loss of Admiral Witgeft, the rest of the crew of the flagship trained their big twelve-inch guns on the encroaching circle of Japanese warships. Had darkness not fallen on this naval conflict in the Yellow Sea the Japanese undoubtedly would have sunk or captured the remnants of the Russian fleet. When Admiral Prince Ukhtomski fled to Port Arthur, the only battleship left was the crippled Tsesarevich. It was left alone with three armoured cruisers and eight destroyers. At this point in the battle, only twelve Russian warships were pitted against thirty-two Japanese vessels consisting of: four battleships, seven cruisers, four coastal defence ships and seventeen destroyers.

Fortunately, July 28th, 1904, was a moonless night and Captain Grigorovich desperately waited for darkness to fall, for he could see the Tsesarevich now was completely encircled by the Japanese and their only hope would be to slip through the Japanese line under cover of darkness. What complicated the matter however was that the Tsesarevich had lost much of its steam power, which limited its speed and maneuverability. To attempt to get through the Japanese line to the northeast would be the most risky since Togo would be expecting him to head toward the Korean Strait and Vladivostok.

Considering the state of damage to the ship, he knew his only avenue of escape would be to head for any nearby port that was not held by the Japanese. Port Arthur was out of the question for he felt it would soon be in Japanese hands. The closest port that did not have political ties to either Japan or Britain was the neutral Chinese port of Tsintao to the southwest, which was a German protectorate. However, his main concern was the fact so many of the ship's boilers were out of commission. He was counting on Friedrich to get as many of them operational as possible now that near total darkness began to protect them.

Even though several of the ships generators were disabled in the battle, one was still operable so Grigorovich ordered the few lights that were on to be put out. Friedrich reported to the captain that two of the burned out boilers were now operational and he had stokers' helpers taking coal from other bunkers to fire the repaired boilers. With twelve boilers now in operation, the Tsesarevich crept slowly and silently in a general southwest direction. Lookouts had to be posted at the bow and on the bridge, since the shells that hit the conning tower had disabled much of the navigational equipment. To Friedrich their progress seemed to be agonizingly slow, even though he had all twelve boilers burning at their maximum, and they were moving at a steady eleven knots. As midnight approached they had encountered no Japanese ships, however, all through the night Grigorovich kept all lights out so the lookouts could keep their eyes accustomed to the darkness to be better able to see ships, reefs or land. He had no way of knowing their exact position and steered mainly by the stars and the reports of his lookouts.

As dawn broke, they could see land directly ahead of them and the broad indentation of a harbour far to the south. As they drew nearer to the shoreline, one of the lookouts shouted he thought it was the port of Tsintao. He recognized it from the previous October when they passed by on their way to Port Arthur. Grigorovich was pleased that their estimate of the distance and direction had proven to be relatively accurate. As dawn broke behind them and as they slowly approached the interior of the harbour, they saw a craft approaching them. A small launch hailed them and signalled them to stop. Grigorovich noted that among the Chinese crew the man holding a megaphone was a tall Caucasian. When the man called for the captain, Grigorovich noted he was speaking in German and being aware of Friedrich's background he sent a deckhand down to the boiler rooms to get him to come up and translate. Friedrich found that the man was the Harbour Master and he was warning them that if the Tsesarevich had been involved in the Russian war with Japan and if they were to enter this port their ship would have to be disarmed and interned until the war was over. Grigorovich had no alternative. He formally asked for privileges to dock at the port of Tsintao not knowing this was going to be their home for the next year and a half.

In the meantime, what had happened to the rest of Russia's First Pacific Squadron? Midway through the Battle of the Yellow Sea on July 28th 1904, just after 6 o'clock p.m., the newly designated "flagship" Peresviet under the command of Admiral Ukhtomski along with the battleships Retvisan, Pobieda, Sevastopol, Poltava and the cruiser Pallada had turned and fled back to Port Arthur. This was a move that every captain at Port Arthur would have known was contrary to Admiral Witgeft's orders. When the Admiralty at St. Petersburg got word that Admiral Witgeft had left Captain Wiren in command of the skeleton fleet at Port Arthur the news of Witgeft's departure to Vladivostok was passed on to the Tsar. The Tsar then insisted that anyone in charge of Russia's stronghold in the Far East would have to be an admiral. The news of Wiren's promotion to Rear Admiral never reached Witgeft, for by this time he had already been killed in the Battle of the Yellow Sea. Admiral Wiren at first was pleased to see the five battleships and one cruiser arrive the morning after the Yellow Sea encounter; however, he was now even more apprehensive of the fate of Port Arthur when he heard the report of what happened to Witgeft and the loss of the Tsesarevich. As a small consolation, he now had more firepower from the six warships to fend off the Japanese land attacks. To this point Admiral Wiren had been able to stem the Japanese shelling of the ships in the harbour from the surrounding hillsides by taking the smaller armament from the ships part way up the hillsides. Wiren decided any sort of sea battle would be hopeless and since he was well versed in explosives and the laying of mines, nearly every night he would have his ships place mines on the outer roadstead and well beyond, to stall the Japanese from invading by sea. In the process, his mining paid off and resulted in the sinking of a Japanese cruiser, one destroyer and two coastal vessels.

On September 19th the Japanese ground forces were able to move down-slope and nearly into the harbour with their heavy artillery. They were now able to fire more accurately at the trapped battleships. However, despite the heavier bombardment Admiral Wiren, with the added artillery on the ships in the harbour, returned the fire and held the port for an unbelievable 75 days. Then on November 22nd, a Japanese shell detonated the ammunition magazine on the battleship Poltava and the resulting explosion shattered the conning tower and turrets of the Pobieda, which was moored adjacent to the Poltava. The stern of the Poltava was completely demolished; the bow rose skyward and what remained of the ship sank in minutes. The Pobieda listed precariously on its starboard side and had to be scuttled. In the next four days the remaining two battleships, Retvisan and Peresviet and the cruisers Bayan and Pallada, also were sunk by heavy shells that penetrated their armoured hulls. Admiral Wiren then ordered the only remaining battleship, the Sevastopol, and several destroyers to go out to the roadstead to make a last stand facing the Japanese Navy. For the next six days, the Sevastopol and the destroyers held the Japanese gunboats at bay until finally the Sevastopol ran out of ammunition. Her captain then had the seamen open the seacocks and scuttled the shell-riddled Sevastopol before the Japanese could board and confiscate the ship. On the 20th of December 1904, Port Arthur was surrendered to the Japanese. Admiral Wiren was taken prisoner and spent the rest of the war imprisoned in Japan.

When the Tsesarevich slipped through the Japanese circle of warships in the darkness on the night of July 8th, three of the Russian destroyers also made it through the southern alignment of Japanese warships. They too, arrived at Tsintao shortly after the Tsesarevich and were disarmed and interned along with their flagship. The cruisers Askold and Diana also were able to pass unheeded through the southeastern alignment of Japanese warships; they went further south than the Tsesarevich and were both disarmed and interned at the port of Saigon.    The cruiser Novik broke through the northeastern barrier of Japanese warships and took a direct course to Vladivostok.    However, in the morning of July 29th she was observed by several Japanese coastal vessels who then alerted Japanese warships.    They gave chase and surrounded the Novik in the northern part of the Sea of Japan just as the Novik was within sight of Vladivostok.    The Novik fought an uneven battle with several Japanese cruisers and finally when her gunners ran out of ammunition the Russian crew scuttled her.

## Chapter 8

## Rozhdestvensky and the Second Pacific Squadron

Back at St. Petersburg in the early summer of 1904, Admiral Rozhdestvensky was uneasy in his role as Head of the Naval General Staff. Here he was not at the helm of a ship where he would be in total charge of everyone on board. At the Naval Department in St. Petersburg even though he was now a top dignitary there were only two positions in the navy higher, and they were posts that could be held only by a Romanov—he yearned to be in full charge of his destiny at the helm of a ship. Social diplomacy was not one of Rozhdestvensky's high points and being that he was ill at ease in this new lifestyle, what irritated him most was that the elite of St. Petersburg spent their time climbing the social ladder by fawning over those who had wheedled their way into the Tsar's inner circle. Therefore, it was with some relief to Rozhdestvensky that when war was declared against Japan it became his main preoccupation, and he made it be known to everyone that Viceroy Alexeev was unfit to be in charge of both the navy and army in the Far East regardless of the fact he was a favourite of Tsar Nicholas. Rozhdestvensky was becoming increasingly more apprehensive about Russia's expansion beyond Manchuria. He soon saw that the Tsar was so obsessed with trying to please everyone that he did not attempt to comprehend the basic factors of warfare, such as transporting troops and artillery and sending ships nearly half way around the world to combat the Japanese in their own back yard.

The advisors to the easily influenced Tsar were the usual egotistical grand dukes, his cousin Kaiser Wilhelm, his bastard nephew Viceroy Alexeev and even his grandmother Denmark's

Dowager Empress, Maria Federovna. Rozhdestvensky's pleas to the Tsar about logistical problems went unheeded, which drove the Head of the Naval General Staff into fits of anger and with no field glasses to throw overboard he would vent his irritation by smashing furniture. To add to his frustration the admiral felt Port Arthur was a poor choice as a naval base and the entire Far Eastern adventure would turn out to be a disaster. From the time of the sinking of the Petropavlovsk and the death of Admiral Makarov, the Tsar had Rozhdestvensky begin to assemble a Second Pacific Squadron, which was something the admiral emphatically disagreed with. However, being that his disenchantment was increasing daily with all of the bureaucratic bickering, action at the head of a fleet of Russian battleships became increasingly more attractive to him.

By the 30th of July 1904, most of the information about the Battle of the Yellow Sea had been transmitted to St. Petersburg. On August 11th, the Tsar called a meeting at his summer residence Peterhof. This was the opulent residence created by Italian architects that was surrounded by golden statues set amidst babbling brooks that wound their way down to the Baltic Sea. The meeting hosted the elite of the Russian navy. It included several Grand Dukes, the Minister of the Navy, the Minister of War, the Minister of Foreign Affairs and of course the Head of the Naval General Staff—Admiral Zinoviev Rozhdestvensky. The admiral, who had risen through the ranks by sheer determination and to the dismay of many in the naval hierarchy, had acquired the blessing of Tsar Nicholas II. Here he was now facing the prime of the Russian Empire.

The Tsar's first item on the agenda was to let those present know that he had chosen Admiral Rozhdestvensky as the Commander-in-Chief of Russia's Second Pacific Squadron; in addition Rozhdestvensky would keep his post as Head of the Naval General Staff. Rozhdestvensky made no gesture of acknowledgement, but immediately launched into a pointed account of what was not going right in the Far East. As was his nature he of course had his own definite ideas about the war and did not hesitate in letting his august company know his views. Firstly, he announced that he disagreed with the Tsar about the long and arduous trip a second squadron would have to make just to get to Port Arthur even before a ship's cannon could be fired.  However, he said that even though sending a Second Pacific Squadron to the Far East was against his own better judgement, if the Tsar insisted he would assemble several ships as the nucleus of what he felt could be a squadron.  However, he stated that a hastily assembled squadron would be doomed to suffer the same fate as the First Pacific Squadron.  He carried on by scoffing at his classmate, Admiral Witgeft, condemning his performance in the Battle of the Yellow Sea and labelled him as being too timid, and the hesitation in slowing the fleet to wait for one ship cost him his life and the battle.  However, considering all facts, Witgeft had graduated from the Naval Academy second only to Rozhdestvensky himself and even though he was not blunt and aggressive like his classmate, he had maintained an unblemished record throughout his naval career.  In reality, his death was solely the result of a chance shot by the Japanese.  Witgeft, who by the time the Japanese surrounded the Russian fleet, was already dead, therefore, could not have lost the ensuing battle.  Actually, the Battle of the Yellow Sea was lost by the second-in-command, Admiral Ukhtomski, who took five warships, abandoned the squadron and fled back to Port Arthur.  When Rozhdestvensky unleashed his blunt opinions to the cream of the Russian Navy, the naval bigwigs all immediately looked at the Tsar to see what his reaction would be to the admiral's cutting statements about the way the war was being handled.  Undoubtedly, they were certain Rozhdestvensky would immediately be demoted, fired or even be banished from the kingdom.  Surprisingly, however, the Tsar quietly said that Rozhdestvensky should immediately get on with assembling the Second Pacific Squadron.

After the meeting at Peterhof Rozhdestvensky did as he promised and went directly to Kronstadt, all the while agonizing over the fact that many of the best warships had already been dispatched to the Far East.  There were only five relatively new battleships, from which Rozhdestvensky selected his flagship, the newest ironclad, the Prince Suvorov.  Of the remaining warships there were only two other twenty-year-old battleships, and four of seven cruisers were new and well armed.  The other three were without armour or proper cannonry and had been pleasure craft that were modified toys of the Grand Dukes. This left just nine torpedo boats and a multitude of old transports and coastal vessels. When Rozhdestvensky assessed the fleet at Kronstadt, the number of ships was impressive but their quality as warships was appalling. To get them repaired and fitted to be able to steam the 18,000 miles to the Far East would require months of repair and preparation. After surveying what was available to constitute a squadron, he immediately sent a request to the Tsar that he needed the seven sleek new cruisers that had just been built for the Russian Navy by Argentina. Some of the Tsar's ministers agreed with Rozhdestvensky but the Tsar was adamant the squadron must be ready to sail within weeks and it would take too much time to wait for the Argentinian craft to be delivered. The Tsar, and of course most of his naval bureaucracy, felt as many ships as possible should be mustered with little thought being given to their seaworthiness or battle capabilities. The Tsar informed Rozhdestvensky that since there were at least sixty Russian ships at Kronstadt he and his naval hierarchy had decided the Second Pacific Squadron should consist of at least forty ships. This left the admiral in a state of total exasperation; he felt like telling the Tsar to go to hell but his diplomatic experience held him to saying only that it would take several months to train the crews, arm and repair seventeen of the best dilapidated old tubs stationed at Kronstadt.

During his service in the Baltic and elsewhere Rozhdestvensky had become familiar with the captains of the twenty-three warships as well as many of their seamen. However, he had to utilize his power as Head of the Naval General Staff to commandeer the other seventeen ships requested by the Tsar. Of these, he chose icebreakers, transports, coastal patrol boats and even several vulnerable but speedy pleasure craft that had been reserved for the Tsar's hangers-on. He had no idea of the sea-going experience of any of the seventeen newcomers so he set about having regular training exercises on a daily basis, but was appalled at their incompetence. Two of the newly conscripted ships collided while making a routine turn, another was boldly trying to outdistance the admiral's flagship and did not respond to signals—Rozhdestvensky had to fire a salvo across her hull to subdue the foolhardy captain. It now had become commonplace that binoculars regularly were flung overboard, accompanied by outbursts of profanity by the admiral. The newer battleships were capable of doing 18 to 20 knots, the older battleships could do no more than 15 knots and some of the clunkers could only lumber along at 12 knots. During most of the training periods Rozhdestvensky paced along the bridge shouting insults at errant captains. How could he possibly guide this motley conglomeration of ships half-way around the world? It was obvious they could easily be sabotaged by the naval forces of Japanese allies before they even got to face the Japanese Navy; a naval force that had already sunk nearly all of Russia's First Pacific Squadron. To add to Zinoviev's apprehension the Russian Admiralty was getting information from various sources about Japanese torpedo boats lurking in wait at specific places along the route; a route now guarded by Japan's ally—the British Navy. Coaling was an absolute necessity and the British Empire controlled most of the ports along the route. Rozhdestvensky's only hope was that Kaiser Wilhelm's colliers could be in the right place at the right time. To make matters even worse it would be impossible for the Second Pacific Squadron to pass through the Suez Canal, which was totally controlled by the British so the armada would have to take the much longer route around the southern tip of Africa.

On September 26th, 1904, less than six weeks after Rozhdestvensky's meeting with the naval elite at Peterhof, the Tsar arrived at the harbour at Reval basking in high spirits for what turned out to be his final farewell to the Second Pacific Squadron. He was certain these forty warships would bring the Japanese Navy to heel. With him, he brought his wife Empress Alexandra, their young son Alexei and other Romanov royalty including the Dowager Empress of Greece, several Grand Dukes and his sister Xenia. Rozhdestvensky of course had the flagship in fine form for the arrival of the royal entourage. All of his officers and men were in full uniform and stood at attention on deck. The Commander-in-Chief himself was at the forefront in a smartly tailored uniform, which was adorned with his Cross of St. George, the Cross of St. Vladimir, the scarlet ribbon of the Order of St. Anne and the silver chords of a Senior Staff Officer. The Tsar made a point of visiting all the warships and closed the day by holding a lavish dinner for all the captains and their officers on his yacht the Standart. Before the Tsar and his royal entourage left the new ironclad Suvorov to board the Standart to go back to St. Petersburg, touching farewells took place on the flagship. The Tsar assured the squadron's Commander-in-Chief that undoubtedly victory would be forthcoming. However, Rozhdestvensky replied that with all the hurdles that confronted him the fleet would probably perish before it even reached the Far East and if they were fortunate enough to get to Korea, Port Arthur by that time would probably be overrun by the Japanese. Unfortunately, this dire prediction in many ways would come true, for this was the last time that the Tsar would see his beloved Second Pacific Squadron.

As the fleet steamed out of port, Rozhdestvensky was relieved that he could concentrate solely on keeping the ships at arms length from one another to avoid collisions or any other disaster. At this early point in their voyage, the commander of the squadron was certain they would be safe from any Japanese threat as long as they were in the friendly waters of the Baltic Sea. Rozhdestvensky was keeping a close eye on one vessel in particular the Orel, which was the squadron's hospital ship. In the interests of all of the sailors including the Commander himself, it housed a bevy of young nurses. The matron in charge was an attractive nurse named Natalia Sivers whom Rozhdestvensky had entertained earlier on the Suvorov. As their long voyage progressed, a firm relationship developed between them. This, however, became somewhat of a problem with the other sailors, especially the officers since they too would periodically cast their eyes longingly at the Orel and it took all of Rozhdestvensky's disciplinary acumen to keep his seamen in line. This now established Rozhdestvensky not only as a dedicated senior admiral commanding Russia's Second Pacific Squadron but also as an expert in ships cannonry, as a naval diplomat and most recently as an ardent lover. He now was faced with managing these juggling acts all at the same time. This included: guiding his hastily assembled armada half-way around the world, taking this huge fleet through hostile waters, avoiding Japanese torpedo boats, entering hostile ports to load coal and accommodating three lovers: his wife; his grieving mistress, widow Capitolina Makarova and his latest paramour on the squadron's hospital ship—Natalia Sivers.

Their first coaling station was at the safe harbour at Skagen, Denmark; here they were able to load coal without interference since they had the blessing of the Tsar's Romanov grandfather Danish King Christian IX. From here on, however, the squadron had to venture into alien British territorial waters—the North Sea. What made Rozhdestvensky increasingly uneasy was that he had received several reports warning him of the presence of Japanese torpedo boats in the North Sea. He called a meeting of the captains before leaving Skagen to warn them of the possibility of encountering Japanese gunboats after leaving the safe waters of the Baltic. Rozhdestvensky scheduled their departure so they would get through the main part of the North Sea under cover of darkness. This of course, made the crew of every ship nervous and, as the trigger-happy armada ventured forth into hostile waters, the eyes of all the deck hands were straining in the darkness to detect any sign of enemy torpedo boats. Suddenly, the flagship got a message from one of the plodding old coastal patrol ships that two torpedo boats were spotted, followed immediately by another message that seven unidentified craft were approaching. Without asking permission of the flagship, the captain panicked and opened fire. Hearing the barrage of gunfire several of the other edgy captains also began a cannon barrage regardless of whether they even saw what they thought was a torpedo boat. Rozhdestvensky ordered the fleet to steam ahead at full speed, which in fact was a speed of about 15 knots. Rather than circumventing the British Isles on the Atlantic side as was his original plan he chose a route directly through the English Channel damning the consequences of encountering British or Japanese resistance. As the Russian squadron moved into the English Channel, they passed several coastal patrol craft, which suspiciously followed them until they were nearly abreast of London. It was here where Rozhdestvensky received his first message from St.

Petersburg, a communication that came directly from the Tsar asking why Russia's Second Pacific Squadron had made an unprovoked attack on British fishing vessels, several of which were sunk and the squadron did not even stop to rescue survivors.

What followed became an international incident, the Tsar's uncle Edward VII the King of England, was incensed and told the Tsar he had the Royal Navy on full alert—His Majesty was ready for war. By the time Rozhdestvensky's fleet steamed into the Bay of Biscay the British Admiralty had their imposing Channel Fleet consisting of nineteen heavily armed warships including six armour-clad battleships, thirteen armoured cruisers and an array of torpedo boats made ready to intercept the Russians at Gibraltar. To supplement the Channel Fleet England's powerful Mediterranean Naval contingent was notified to meet the Channel fleet at Gibralter. The Mediterranean Naval contingent alone had considerably more firepower than Rozhdestvensky's squadron. The British Admiralty warned its two major squadrons as they approached Gibraltar to be mindful of how the Japanese had launched an unprovoked attack on the ships anchored at the Port Arthur roadstead, and now Russia's blatant attack on British fishing vessels made it mandatory to respond at a moments notice. It was emphasized that both of these incidents occurred without a formal declaration of war and for them to be ready to fire on any suspicious move by the Russian fleet. They further labelled Rozhdestvensky as the Mad Dog of the Russian Navy because of his attack on defenceless British fishing trawlers followed by his bold passage through their own sacred waterway—the English Channel.

Rozhdestvensky's armada now, in dire need of coal was obliged to seek replenishment at some neutral port. Spain was his only hope of obtaining coal. Therefore, he cautiously entered the port of Vigo on Spain's western coast. The fleet was no sooner in the harbour when several British cruisers steamed into the port. The lead cruiser formally signalled asking the Spanish harbour master permission to dock and surprisingly also saluted the Russian flagship. Rozhdestvensky immediately acknowledged the compliment and in a gesture of naval etiquette sent a launch to the cruiser inviting the admiral of the British flagship to join him on the Suvorov. Rozhdestvensky greeted the admiral in eloquent French and then asked him very formally if he could speak to him in what he said was broken English. Knowing of course, that he was more proficient in English than in French. He began by apologizing for the terrible mistake he had made shelling the British fishing fleet in the North Sea. He added that as soon as possible he would see to it that reparations would be made. Little did the British admiral know that Rozhdestvensky could draw upon his diplomatic charm in practically any crisis. The British admiral was so impressed with Rozhdestvensky's sincerity that he sent word to the British Admiralty that the North Sea encounter was nothing but a terrible accident.

After the British cruisers left, and coaling had been completed, the Russian squadron steamed out into the Atlantic and headed south not knowing what to expect when they reached their next coaling stop at the French port of Tangier in Morocco. In the interim, the Tsar having been advised that war was imminent with Britain because of Rozhdestvensky's attack on defenceless British fishing vessels, cabled his uncle King Edward VII with a heartfelt apology and as well offered reparations of substantial monetary compensation. The King discussed the offer with his British naval hierarchy and it was decided that they would investigate whether or not there actually were Japanese torpedo boats in the area that may have triggered the Russian shelling of British fishing vessels. A message was sent to the two British naval squadrons, now on high alert at Gibraltar, not to confront the Russian fleet but closely monitor their movements. In Germany, the Tsar's cousin, Kaiser Wilhelm was ecstatic. He had little respect for his English relatives and now that controversy had erupted between Russia and England, it was an opportunity for him to embellish the situation to his own advantage. He immediately contacted the Tsar and told him this was a dastardly trick by the British to have Japanese torpedo boats hidden in the North Sea just to provoke the Russian armada. The Kaiser assured the Tsar he would support Rozhdestvensky's passage to Port Arthur by having his colliers ready wherever he could find ports friendly to Germany anywhere along the entire route, to provide the Second Pacific

Squadron with coal. By the time the Russian squadron reached Gibraltar Rozhdestvensky was braced for battle with the mightiest navy in the world, against not one but two powerful fleets of the British Navy. As the motley and disorganized collection of ships in Russia's Second Pacific Squadron reached Gibraltar, to Rozhdestvensky's surprise the British flagship signalled them to pass. Two British cruisers broke formation and followed at a measured distance of 5,000 feet.

The Admiral on the flagship of the British Mediterranean Squadron, watched closely as the Russian ships passed slowly by and commented to his junior officer that the Russian sailors appeared well fed and healthy but most of the ships were poorly tended and filthy. Although he said, that the hands on the battleships appeared to be of a better class but the lower ranks appeared rather common. Even though Rozhdestvensky was flooded with relief that they were allowed to carry on without confrontation, he could not help being impressed by the perfect and carefully orchestrated manoeuvres of the British cruisers and the neatly aligned battleships. He dreaded the thought of meeting them in battle. Now that he had at this particular point avoided being attacked by the British, he had even more reservations about herding this cumbersome collection of ships at an agonizing speed of no more than 12 knots all the way to the Far East. He knew the British cruisers would follow them for the rest of the voyage and would seize any opportunity to call in the heavy artillery. On October 21, 1904, they reached Tangier on the northwest coast of Morocco. By this time, Rozhdestvensky was fraught with doubts about guiding his collection of warships that ranged from pleasure yachts to coastal patrol vessels to fishing trawlers to ironclad cruisers and battleships, around the Cape of Good Hope at the southern tip of Africa. He knew that there the weather was an even more threatening adversary than British cruisers or Japanese torpedo boats. During the earlier days of sail-propelled ships, ship's captains dreaded sailing around the Cape of Good Hope. The strength of the prevailing westerly winds often drove some hapless sailing ships as far east as the rocky and reef-ridden west coast of Australia where the wrecked hulls of many ships are still found today.

Rozhdestvensky foresaw the possibility of losing half the ill-prepared ships of his squadron, many of which were not built to face the heavy open-ocean seas let alone doing battle with enemy warships. The treacherous waters of the Cape of Good Hope could sweep them off course to the east and well beyond the south coast of Africa. He feared for the frail converted pleasure yachts, the old fishing trawlers, the top-heavy transports and even the older battleships. Now that the furor over the fishing vessel encounter in the North Sea had subsided, Rozhdestvensky pondered that the South African route would be made less hazardous if he could somehow send the old and most vulnerable ships through the Suez Canal. This would allow him to negotiate the stormy passage around the Cape of Good Hope with the more seaworthy ships and rendezvous with the Suez contingent at Madagascar. However, this would have to be sanctioned by the controlling interests of the Suez Canal – the British Navy.

The admiral spent hours churning out short and eloquent cables. The first went to St. Petersburg, then one to every Russian ally he could think of, the French, the Danes, the Greeks, the Portuguese and even Kaiser Wilhelm of Germany, anyone that he thought could in some way influence the British. The gist of his messages in effect was how could the British not allow peaceful Russian trade vessels to pass through their canal? After all, many other countries were allowed to run trade vessels through this international waterway so why could a peaceful Russian vessel not pass through. Now that apologies and cash had resolved the Mad Dog's attack on British fishing boats in the North Sea, as well as with pressure from other countries, Britain finally relented and agreed to allow non-combative Russian ships through the Suez Canal. Rozhdestvensky immediately conferred with the two admirals who were second-in-command of the Second Pacific Squadron, Rear Admirals Dmitri Felkersam and Oskar Enkvist, to select which of them would command the squadron's fleet of "trade vessels" to Madagascar. Of course, the meeting was merely a formality since Rozhdestvensky had already decided to put Felkersam in charge of the Suez contingent. In his mind, he had previously labelled Enkvist as being incompetent and indecisive and rejected him as a candidate. He knew this would not sit well with the Admiralty or the Tsar since Enkvist was a favourite with the naval elite, for he had royal ties and as well was a relative of Russia's weak-willed Naval Minister Vice Admiral Fedor Avelan. On October 22$^{nd}$, Felkersam departed in command of his flotilla of derelict warships and left from Gibraltar to head across the Mediterranean Sea through the Suez Canal and then on to Madagascar.

During their three-day stop at Tangier, Rozhdestvensky worked at his usual feverish pace. Firstly, he supervised the purchase and loading of coal. Secondly, he was sending non-stop cables in hopes he could embellish the passage of his "trade vessels" through the Suez Canal. Thirdly, he had to organize the travel routes for both factions of his squadron. Despite this hectic schedule, he found time for a bit of rest and relaxation by paying a visit to the hospital ship Orel. After all, it had been nearly a month since he had last had intimate contact with the matron of the hospital ship, the attractive Natalia Sivers. He apologized to her for his long absence in the voyage so far, but assured her he would visit the Orel again at their next coaling stop. The affair had become common knowledge among the sailors on the squadron's warships. The admiral's close attention to the hospital ship resulted in a great variety of action among the sailors of the other ships who sought any excuse, sometimes even illness, to make a trip to the Orel. However, Rozhdestvensky made it clear that any excursion to the hospital ship had to be authorized by the Commander of the Squadron. If any craft was discovered making an unauthorized trip to the Orel, especially after dark, all the occupants would be charged and the culprits would be duly escorted ashore at whatever port they happened to be, to find their own way back to Russia and as well face punishment from local authorities.

Early on the morning of October 23rd, 1904, the actual warships of the squadron departed on their way around the southern extremity of Africa and on to Madagascar. When they left Tangier, Rozhdestvensky was looking forward to their next coaling stop at Dakar a port on the west coast of the French colony of Senegal.

While in Tangier he had cabled Russia's German ally, Kaiser Wilhelm to have colliers meet the squadron at Dakar. Before they left Kronstadt, he had made tentative arrangements with the French to coal at Dakar, but with the events that occurred in the North Sea he was unsure what the squadron's reception would be when they would arrive at the French port. As they steamed southward, the warmer temperatures as they approached the equator began to take its toll on the seamen most of whom had experienced only the cold and stormy waters of the northern Baltic Sea. It took the squadron only seven days to reach Dakar now that the derelicts were no longer with them. Thankfully, Felkersam had the dubious honour of herding them through the Suez Canal and beyond.

As Rozhdestvensky approached the harbour at Dakar, they were hailed by a launch, which signalled them to stand by, for the French governor wished to speak to the Commander of the Fleet. When the governor boarded Rozhdestvensky greeted him like an old friend in the most eloquent French he could muster. However, the governor was adamant that no coaling could take place in his harbour. He was made aware that German colliers would be arriving shortly, but he insisted coaling would have to take place outside of French territorial waters. Rozhdestvensky was now faced with the same dilemma the Tsesarevich and Bayan had to deal with at Djibouti—coaling on the heaving waters of the open ocean in the stifling equatorial heat. However, compared to the Djibouti coaling Rozhdestvensky had twenty-three ships rather than the two ships the Grigorovich and Wiren stokers had to deal with.

The next morning, the captains of the Russian fleet were relieved to see that six German colliers had arrived during the night and coaling began immediately. By mid-morning, the sky was filled with so much coal dust that to the sailors in the midst of the thirty ships would have thought night had fallen. Everyone, including the Commander dreaded the thought of steaming on to their next stop that lay right on the equator and was another French controlled port near Libreville on the west coast of Gabon. The next day, as they proceeded southward and got ever closer to the equator the ships crews suffered more and more from the heat especially the stokers, several of whom perished from heat stroke or exhaustion and their bodies had to be quickly cast into the sea. When they arrived at Gabon there were German colliers waiting for them, but here again the squadron would have to coal on the open ocean. The intense heat became overpowering especially for the stokers and their helpers who were responsible for getting the coal to the bunkers deep in the ship's hold. With so many of the coaling contingent collapsing from the dust and heat as mid-day approached a general strike was brewing, but it was quickly averted when the ever observant admiral let the coaling crews rest from 10 a.m. to 4 p.m.

Thankfully, on December 6, 1904, the Russian squadron was able to depart from Gabon. All the crews dreamt of cooler temperatures as they steamed southward away from the heat of the equator. Everyone, especially Rozhdestvensky, was looking forward to their next stop, which would obviously be cooler and was not a French port, the Portuguese port of Great Fish Bay. The admiral already had word from the German Admiralty that colliers would be waiting there for them—trusty old Kaiser Wilhelm. However, when they arrived at Great Fish Bay they were again treated with suspicion. Their reputation had preceded them. The British had alerted the Commandant at the Portuguese colony that if the Russian squadron tried to use their sheltered bay to load coal, for the port authorities immediately to notify the British naval units stationed nearby. As the Russian ironclads dropped anchor in the calm waters of Great Fish Bay, a little gunboat officiously came alongside the Suvorov. When the captain came bustling aboard, Rozhdestvensky was there to greet him in his usual charming manner, but was instantly rebuffed. The captain informed Rozhdestvensky the Russian ships must leave at once or he would have to take military action. Rozhdestvensky noticed coaling had already begun on several of the squadron's ships and as far as Rozhdestvensky could see, the only gun in the vicinity was a single three-pounder on the diminutive gunboat. He then tilted his head toward one of the 12-pound turret guns on the Suvorov and said to the captain of the gunboat to fire at will. The captain took one look at the big gun and left immediately. The admiral said quietly to the officers around him that by the time any British ships arrived there would be no Russian ships at Great Fish Bay. Their next coaling would be at the relatively nearby friendly port of Angra Pequena and he said that in only a few hours they would load just enough coal to get them to the Angra Pequena. This would allow them to be gone by daybreak.

By the next day, December 7th, they were well out in the Atlantic and headed not only into cooler weather but finally to a friendly port the German held port of Angra Pequena. To the irritation of the British cruisers that were shadowing the Russian squadron, Angra Pequena was no longer a British protectorate and had been taken over by Germany some years earlier. The German Governor, under orders directly from Kaiser Wilhelm, sent out several harbour gunboats to make it clear to the British cruisers they were not to enter German territorial waters. Since the fleet's reserve of coal was nearly depleted, the bunkers would have to be filled to capacity. However, since they were still some 3,000 miles from their destination at Madagascar, and there were no friendly ports on the way for them to replenish their fuel supply they would have to load coal in every available nook and cranny on the ships. The coaling went relatively well even though the waters of the port were choppy and the launches ferrying the coal from the colliers often bounced dangerously against the ironclad warships. Sacks of coal were stored in passageways and on deck. In fact, the extra weight of coal in the passageways and on the decks made the ships somewhat unbalanced and the captains wondered how the ships would perform on rough seas with such a high centre of gravity. The admiral held a lavish banquet on the Suvorov on their last day at Angra Pequena. He knew this would be the last friendly port they would encounter on their voyage to the Far East. The Governor, his wife and several officers of the German battalion posted at Angra Pequena were invited. A special boat was sent to the Orel on the pretext of bringing several of the nurses to entertain the company of German officers, but the main reason was to bring Natalia Sivers along as a chaperone.

# Chapter 9

## From South Africa to the Battle of Tsushima

The next morning after the squadron left the shelter of the Angra Pequena harbour, Rozhdestvensky informed his officers of a cable he had received from St. Petersburg just before leaving Angra Pequena. The message warned that German intelligence had informed them that British fishing vessels at Durban were being fitted with torpedoes and could be lying in wait for the Mad Dog of North Sea fame. Obviously, the British were now more anxious than ever to delay or decimate Russia's Second Pacific Squadron. As the fleet rounded the Cape of Good Hope, they were assailed by high winds and swells that rocked even the larger ships. The cruisers suffered the most with waves washing as high as the upper decks and conning towers. With the high winds, it was not long before coal dust was everywhere and the sailors coughed constantly. The black grime was in their food, in their bedding and in their clothes. With the threat of torpedo attacks and the battering the fleet was taking from the pounding seas the admiral was having progressively more doubts about the armada ever getting to Port Arthur. To further add to his concerns, several of the ships had signalled the flagship they were falling out of line to stop and make repairs, ranging from blown boilers to flooded bunkers to bent and twisted drive shafts to say nothing of the thick layers of coal dust and mud that covered the decks and passageways. During the storm, they passed Durban without incident; the waves were so high that no fishing boat would have even been able to stay afloat in the heavy seas. In a moment of despair, the admiral wrote a letter to his wife. In it, he said that he felt it would be a miracle to even get to the Far East with this convoy of ill-trained and undisciplined crews, let alone organize them into a battle-ready unit to confront the Japanese Navy. He even doubted they had enough ammunition to do target practice.

The only positive aspect of the passage around South Africa was that the winds and mountainous waves swept them along at such a pace that they sighted Madagascar sooner than Rozhdestvensky had expected. The fleet steamed to the east side of the Madagascar mainland and set course directly for the coaling stop at Sainte Marie, an island just off the east coast of Madagascar. The admiral was optimistic that word of Felkersam's fleet would be waiting for him at Sainte Marie, but there was no sign of an emissary from the second contingent. Where could Felkersam be? Surely, he should have been at their meeting point at Diego Suarez long ago, since he had a much shorter distance to travel. Perhaps he had encountered Japanese gunboats and with the light armaments of the old ships at his command, the plodding fleet could have been fair game for even a small array of enemy warships. However, on December 23rd, the day after their arrival at Sainte Marie, a transport ship from the Felkersam contingent arrived at the Sainte Marie harbour. The message from Felkersam to Rozhdestvensky was that they were not at Diego Suarez, but were anchored at Nosi-Be, a port on the other side of Madagascar and some 500 miles from Sainte Marie. Felkersam further stated he would have to anchor at Nosi-Be for some time to make necessary repairs to some of the ships. This blatant change of meeting the main fleet at Nosi-Be was not only puzzling but downright irritating to the admiral even though he realized most of the ships that Felkersam had squired through the Suez Canal were in no condition for long sea voyages. However, as he read on there was even more disconcerting news for the squadron's Commander-in-Chief. The Admiralty at St. Petersburg, on the advice of the Tsar, had decided to launch a Third Pacific Squadron. Undoubtedly, the ships for this new fleet would have to be drawn from the miserable cast-off craft that were now at Kronstadt and would be the ones Rozhdesvensky had flatly refused to take into his squadron. In a fit of rage, the admiral shouted a string of curses and flung yet another set of binoculars into the sea. Surely, the Admiralty was not so naive as to send even more cannon fodder to the Far East. In a downcast mood, he confided to his second-in-command that Admiral Togo had already had enough target practice on Russia's First Pacific Squadron without the Tsar sending yet another fleet, this time consisting of nothing more than floating washtubs half way around the world to amuse the Japanese Navy. Rozhdestvensky's last hope was that Port Arthur would hold out long enough for him to salvage what he could from what was left of Russia's First Pacific Squadron when Rozhdestvensky's fleet arrived at Port Arthur. Little did he know, however, that Port Arthur had already fallen to the Japanese. The Tsar's prized ice-free Far East Russian port had capitulated nearly a week previously, on December 20th, 1904.

Rozhdestvensky was completely exasperated with Felkersam's decision to proceed to Nosi-Be without permission from the flagship. In his frustration, he decided to bypass Diego Suarez and go directly to Nosi-Be, allow only the bare necessity of repairs to Felkersam's ships and set sail immediately for Port Arthur. However, shortly after the squadron left Sainte Marie they were met by a coastal patrol boat from the Nosi-Be contingent carrying a cable that had just been received by Felkersam from the Admiralty. It read that Port Arthur had fallen to the Japanese and since there were no telegraph facilities on the island of Sainte Marie, they could not get in touch with the Suvorov. Consequently, when the Tsar was notified Port Arthur had fallen the Russian Admiralty was only able to contact Felkersam's fleet. In the light of the fall of Port Arthur they ordered Felkersam to proceed to Nosi-Be and wait there with Rozhdestvensky, then it would only be a few weeks until they would be joined by the Third Pacific Squadron. However, Rozhdestvensky knew it would take longer than just a few weeks before this new squadron could be assembled, organized, trained and even put to sea. The admiral scoffed at the message from the Admiralty and told his captains it would take not just weeks but several months for this decrepit fleet to be fitted and sent to join the rest of the Second Pacific Squadron at Nosi-Be. Rozhdestvensky, now completely beside himself pondered the dilemma he now faced. Here he was half-way around the world from Kronstadt and would have to wait for yet more old ships piloted by inexperienced seamen that would be even more of a headache for him than the motley array of craft he already had. So far, he had nursed his armada through the British naval net and constantly had to anchor in hostile ports. He had to face the threat of confrontation by Japanese torpedo boats and during this time had to keep discipline among nearly 10,000 sailors that made up the crews of 40 ships some of which were commanded by captains who had little or no open sea-going experience, and had never fired a cannon—even in practice. Now saddled with these overwhelming odds he still had to travel through even more hostile waters and would have to bypass their destination that had been captured by their enemy. Then they had to face the Japanese Navy. In view of these developments, Rozhdestvensky would somehow have to try to squeeze his travel weary fleet of uncoordinated ships through the Korean Strait and the narrow channel between Japan and Korea. Since they would have to pass through the Korean Strait, they would undoubtedly be observed, and likely be attacked, by the Japanese Navy. Then they still would have to find their way across the Sea of Japan to the safety of Vladivostok. This route would be infested with Japanese coastal patrol boats, fishing vessels and an unknown number of warships. In addition, the man guiding this network of Japanese vessels, as Russia's Second Pacific Squadron would be wending its way through the Sea of Japan, would be none other than Admiral Togo Heihachiro who had just defeated Russia's First Pacific Squadron.

By this time, the crew of every ship in the squadron was aware of the fall of Port Arthur and an aura of gloom permeated the whole squadron. It did not help the mood of the ordinary sailors who now more than ever were exposed to the Commander's outbursts. They often thought of their homes and families and wondered if they would ever see them again. As the squadron approached Nosi-Be, Rozhdestvensky decided he would be damned if he would bother to wait for this unmanageable Third Pacific Squadron. He would take on as much coal as he could and carry on to whatever battles he might have to face when he got to the Far East. On December 27th, 1904, as the fleet steamed into the harbour at Nosi-Be, all hands were on deck to see if they could spot their comrades who they had not seen since the squadron had separated at Tangier; this gave them all a feeling of greeting someone from home. As soon as the ships were docked boats rowed back and forth between the ships and old acquaintances were renewed. Another cable from St. Petersburg again drove the admiral into even greater despair. It informed him that in no way was he to leave Nosi-Be, since the first contingent of the Third Pacific Squadron was well on it's way under the command of Admiral Dobrotvorsky and would be arriving at Nosi-Be in early February. To Rozhdestvensky's dismay, he was informed this fleet consisted of just one adequate armoured cruiser with the rest comprising mainly of useless military patrol vessels. The cable read further that the remainder of the Third Pacific Squadron would be under the command of Admiral Nebogatov and would arrive at Madagascar sometime in early May. This meant nearly a four month wait in the French port where they were not particularly welcome. As time dragged on and the fleet waited at Nosi-Be the admiral was confronted by yet another set of problems, not only among the crew of his own ship but also among crews throughout the whole squadron. The sailors of the fleet had been at sea for nearly four months and had been closeted cheek to jowl with their shipmates on deck and in the steaming hot holds of each craft. By this time, they all knew this was not just a quick coaling stop and that they probably would be anchored here for some time.

With diversions ashore constantly beckoning any semblance of order was easily broken and shore excursions were commonplace—at first these were approved by the captains, but later curfews had to be established. Commonly, these were ignored despite the fact severe consequences would eventually be suffered. Once on shore the freedom starved sailors first sought out the nearest drinking establishments, followed by frequenting anything that resembled a bawdy house; it wasn't long before word spread over the island and prostitutes from all parts arrived to cash in on this influx of sex-starved seamen. Many of the sailors made excursions into the interior to hunt, or just to observe wildlife that they had never seen before: water buffalo, crocodiles, parrots, frogs, wild dogs, monkeys and snakes, many of which were smuggled aboard the sailor's respective ships. The flagship was not immune and several parrots and three monkeys joining the crew. The Commander-in-Chief was not amused, especially since he had always detested pets and was enraged when one of the monkeys climbed onto his shoulder. He yelled at the owner that he had enough monkeys on his back without the real thing breathing in his ear. It was now only mid-January and still two weeks or more before the arrival of the Dobrotvorsky contingent of the Third Pacific Squadron. To the dismay of many of the captains all hell was breaking loose among many of the less disciplined crews. In the oppressive equatorial heat and the fear of what the future held for them, the crews on some of the older ships were threatening mutiny, many felt that they in some way could find their way back to Russia rather than facing near certain death by Japanese cannon fire. Toward the end of January, out of frustration and as a diversion the Commander-in-Chief took the fleet out to the open ocean for target practice despite the fact that the squadron had only a limited amount of ammunition. As it turned out, the exercise was not too successful since from some fifty cannon blasts only one direct hit was made; a shell shattered the mast of the tug that was pulling the target.

Rozhdestvensky knew that all of this waiting was to Admiral Togo's advantage, which would allow him time to prepare his fleet to meet the exhausted and disorganized Russian armada. Without letting his plans be known Rozhdestvensky decided to have coal, water and food loaded on board each ship so that when Dobrotvorsky arrived in early February the squadron could depart immediately for the Far East. The admiral found that the time they spent waiting day after day was extremely demoralizing, not only for himself but also for all the crews; already deaths from equatorial illnesses, onshore brawls and suicides were becoming common. During this time, Rozhdestvensky was brought to near exhaustion fielding directives from the Admiralty, coaling, loading food and supplies, keeping discipline -- not only among the ships in the squadron, but also on the flagship. To sooth his frazzled nerves and to take his mind off the impending gloom and doom, he somehow regularly found time to visit the hospital ship, Orel. Here he was able to momentarily let his cares fade away and to languish in the comfort of the arms of lovely Natalia Sivers. On several other occasions, he also did not shirk his duty to his long-time mistress and sent cables to Capitolina Makarova in St. Petersburg in which he outlined the hazards he and his Second Pacific Squadron were now facing.

Fearing the trials and tribulations of coaling at hostile ports along the route to the Far East Rozhdestvensky sent many cables negotiating with the German Admiralty. He wanted to have German colliers waiting at specific points along the route where it would be possible to coal on the open sea; a task he did not relish, but felt would be less dangerous than entering hostile ports. On February 1st, 1905, Dobrotvorsky's first contingent of the Third Pacific Squadron arrived at Nosi-Be. Rozhdestvensky stoically greeted the fleet, and immediately had its ships begin coaling and loading supplies. He was appalled by the decrepit state of some of the recently arrived ships and grudgingly announced that major repair work had to be done before they could leave for the Far East. On the 10th of March, Rozhdestvensky notified all the captains that they were leaving within five days whether their ships were ready or not. By the night of the 15th of March, much excitement permeated the squadron as boilers were being fired and screws tested; great billows of black smoke hung over the harbour valley as each ship tested its propulsion system. Early the next morning, the signal for departure was given from the flagship. One by one, each of the squadron's forty ships steamed into the open ocean. Rozhdestvensky had seen to it that no cable advising the Russian Admiralty of their departure was sent; for the next three weeks the Tsar would have no idea where his Second Pacific Squadron was or even where it was going. The fate of Admiral Nebogatov and the rest of the Third Pacific Squadron were now in limbo. Where would they rendezvous with Rozhdestvensky? The route of the Second Pacific Squadron across the Indian Ocean was known to no one. As they steamed through the smothering equatorial heat they, and especially their stokers, suffered as much or more than was endured during the voyage of the Tsesarevich and Bayan, when Friedrich manned the boilers as these two Russian warships steamed their way along the same route some 18 months earlier. Consequently, from March 16th to April 8th, the Tsar and his Admiralty had no idea where their Second Pacific Squadron was or even where it was headed.

It took the old and decrepit barnacle encrusted ships of the Russian armada a good three weeks to cover the 3,500 miles from Madagascar to Singapore, at an exasperating speed of no more than 8 to 10 knots. Finally, on the early morning of April 8th, the port authorities at Singapore observed a large collection of ships approaching from the west led by a flagship with Russian colours flying. No pretence of entering the port was indicated and the fleet appeared to be heading directly past the Singapore harbour and continuing through the Mallacan Strait. As the fleet approached the entrance to the harbour, a launch flying Russian colours sped out carrying the Russian consul who was stationed at Singapore. The Suvorov was hailed by megaphone and the latest communications from St. Petersburg were passed to the flagship. All of the news was depressing for everyone except, of course, the Commander-in-chief. The Russian land forces in the Far East were retreating and Mukden had fallen to the Japanese. Consequently, General Kuropatkin had been dismissed and had been ordered back to St. Petersburg. The friction between Kuropatkin and Alexeev had been increasingly evident to the entire military, and now after the Japanese rout of the Russian Army at Mukden, it appeared that even the Tsar was becoming disgruntled with Alexeev's inane actions. The Tsar had Alexeev, his favourite hanger-on, recalled to St. Petersburg and the post of Viceroy of the Far East had been abolished.

Indeed, his royal highness had little time to be too concerned about satisfying his favourite cronies in the Romanov hierarchy, since the rumblings of revolution were escalating by the day. The Singapore consul also conveyed further instructions that had come directly from the Tsar that Rozhdestvensky was to rendezvous with Nebogatov's remainder of the Third Pacific Squadron at Kamranh Bay on the Vietnamese coast. Moreover, under no circumstances was that Rozhdestvensky was not to leave until Nebogatov's contingent arrived. To add even more indignation to the Commander-in-Chief, he was told to proceed directly to Vladivostok without engaging the Japanese Navy and upon his arrival at Vladivostok, he was to relinquish command of the squadron to Admiral Biriliov who already was on his way to the Far East via the Trans-Siberian Railway. Rozhdestvensky, in a fit of exasperation and disgust, immediately decided to confront Admiral Togo at the first opportunity. The admiral reasoned that this was the only opportunity for Russia's Second Pacific Squadron to redeem Russian superiority in the Far East. The Japanese had already wrought enough havoc. After all, the First Pacific Squadron had been defeated, Port Arthur was now fully in Japanese hands, Mukden had fallen and the ground forces in Manchuria were in full retreat. It was not long after the Russian armada had passed Singapore that the news spread worldwide; Russia was indeed poised to confront the Japanese Navy. It was now obvious Admiral Rozhdestvensky had not only guided his helter-skelter collection of ships on a tortuous 18,000 mile journey, he had out-negotiated not only the British Navy but also by shrewd diplomacy and delicate demands he had his fleet re-fitted and re-supplied at several openly hostile ports. Superimposed on the trying demands of sailing halfway around the world, he was able to counter the erratic commands of the Tsar and his fawning bureaucratic advisors, and in addition was able to keep discipline among a diverse crew of over 10,000 poorly trained seamen. As the word of Rozhdestvensky's accomplishments spread around the world, it aroused admiration and respect among his naval peers and he was now considered as somewhat of a naval genius— even within the Japanese naval hierarchy.

On the morning of April 28th, 1905, Nebogatov and his contingent finally joined the Second Pacific Squadron. The Russian Far Eastern Armada finally was complete. In total, there were now fifty Russian ships poised to face the Japanese, but in what condition? Many were old transformed sailing ships, others were ill-equipped as to fire-power and short of ammunition, the newer battleships and cruisers could travel at speeds of 18 to 20 knots but the top speed of most of the fleet was in the range of 10 to 15 knots. The ships of the squadron had now been at sea for nearly seven months and were coated in rust and encrusted with barnacles and other debris, slowing the whole fleet by 5 or 6 knots. In numbers, they exceeded Togo's fleet. However, could they challenge a fully equipped, rested and much more mobile naval force?

As the critical time at last approached, Rozhdestvensky had become reticent to discuss his battle plans with his subordinates. Whom could he trust among his junior officers? He had always regarded Admiral Enkvist as incompetent and indecisive. Admiral Nebogatov was a good seaman but was too hesitant, a critical flaw in any crisis. Admiral Felkersam was level headed and had done well in bringing his contingent through the Suez Canal to Madagascar, but now was very ill and on the verge of death. Without telling anyone, Rozhdestvensky decided whatever route he took he would try to avoid Togo and attempt to get through to Vladivostok. He could take to the open Pacific on the east of the Japanese mainland and approach Vladivostok from the north but would have to negotiate narrow channels at La Perouse or Tsugaru which were both dangerous, not only because they were narrow with a width of no more than 25 miles, but the passages also were relatively long and tortuous. On the other hand, the channel at Tsushima was equally narrow but shorter. The other factor the Mad Dog had to consider was that even though the Tsushima channel shorter it would be closely guarded by Togo. Once this shorter bottleneck was negotiated, the Russian armada would have just 600 miles to go to get to Vladivostok rather than the 1800 miles it would take to go the northern route. On the 1st of May, the Second Pacific Squadron, now supplemented by the Third Pacific Squadron, departed on their final lap to face whatever challenges would come from the Japanese.

The Russian squadron proceeded at a pace of only 9 or 10 knots with the destroyers and cruisers going in various directions to give the Japanese the impression that Rozhdestvensky was headed for the eastern coast of Japan. On May 12th, on the day they reached the Yellow Sea Admiral Felkersam died, Rozhdestvensky decided to keep the second-in-command flag on Felkersam's battleship the Oslyabya so as not to give the impression to Nebogatov that he would be taking charge if anything happened to Rozhdestvensky. This left the fleet with the knowledge that the Oslyabya was still second-in-command. As the squadron continued at a pace of 9 knots into the morning of May 13th, a welcome fog shrouded them as they approached the Tsushima channel. Nevertheless, Rozhdestvensky was sure Togo was aware of their presence. Unfortunately, by morning of May 14th, the fog began to dissipate and as the Russian fleet emerged from the Tsushima bottleneck, they faced the entire Japanese Navy and in the lead they saw the Japanese flagship, the Mikasa with Admiral Togo Heihachiro on the bridge. As the distance closed between the two squadrons the heavy artillery of four Japanese battleships immediately concentrated their fire solely on the Russian Flagship. Since the Russian fleet was travelling in two parallel lines the two lead Russian battleships Suvorov and Oslyabya blocked the other two Russian battleships and their powerful 12-inch cannons. It took nearly half an hour to get the fleet travelling in a single line but by this time, the heavy shelling had taken its toll on the two Russian flagships. Heavy shells had struck the conning tower of the Suvorov several times and even though it was heavily armoured splinters of metal flew through the narrow observation ports, killing the helmsman and injuring not only Rozhdestvensky but most of his officers.

In the meantime, the rest of the ship fared no better. The Suvorov's funnels, masts and halyards had all been blown off so no communications could be sent to the rest of the fleet. Rozhdestvensky's right side was paralyzed from a steel splinter lodged in his spine and he was delirious from other shrapnel that had struck his head and back. Those officers that were unhurt sought to get their admiral to one of the lower decks. This was difficult for they had to navigate through the narrow passageways that were clogged with dead and bleeding bodies. The Russian destroyer Buiny that had been assigned to protect one of the other ironclad battleships saw the plight of the flagship and came to help the stricken Suvorov. The surviving officers semaphored the Buiny to come alongside and take on the unconscious Commander-in-Chief.

The destroyer, ignoring the danger of collision in the turbulent water and the incessant shelling from Japanese warships, came adjacent to the flagship and as quickly as possible the unconscious Rozhdestvensky was safely aboard the Buiny. At 7 p.m. on May 14th, as the Buiny pulled away, four torpedoes hit the Suvorov simultaneously. It gently heeled over and slowly sank with most of its crew still on board. Ironically, Russian shells hit the Japanese Flagship Mikasa more times and 31 of its sailors were killed. However, even though the Suvorov had taken fewer cannon hits they struck vulnerable spots and therefore created more shipboard havoc. It was later determined that the Japanese shimosae shells were more telling, even though they were not too effective in penetrating armour they would burst into flames on impact starting fires on the paint, woodwork and coal bunkers of the Russian ships. Their effect was similar to what had transpired in the Battle of the Yellow Sea, when the fiery Japanese shells penetrated just above the unarmoured hull and ignited the coal in the bunkers of the Tsesarevich.

The Oslyabya was the first Russian battleship to sink and went under at 3 p.m. This was only one hour after the first salvo of the battle had been fired. She had suffered several direct hits that penetrated her hull just above the water line; she sank like a stone with the hands on board having little chance of survival. The remainder of the fleet fared no better. With relatively no commands from the flagship after the first two hours of the battle, the Russian fleet was in much disarray. Admiral Nebogatov's division that was bringing up the rear had lagged far behind, since it was difficult for his ships to maintain even the slow pace of the 9 knots that Rozhdestvensky had set for the whole squadron. Admiral Enkvist, true to Rozhdestvensky's prediction, collapsed under fire and not only abandoned his orders to protect the firing warships and had his division hide behind the very ships that he was to protect. In addition, in the confusion some of his ships collided with each other and one sank as a result. The Japanese found no problem with disposing of his unit. However, they probably would have been more successful by leaving Enkvist to orchestrate his own destruction. Fortunately, when night engulfed the battle scene

Enkvist took the only three of his remaining ships and fled to Manila.

By the time Nebogatov got through the Tsushima bottleneck the battle was nearly over with the Japanese ships spread across the Sea of Japan pursuing Russian targets. Once they saw the Nebogatov division, it was not long before several of Togo's craft took chase. When the Japanese caught up to Nebogatov, who had his flag on the old battleship Nicholas I, several shells struck the ship. Nebogatov, from either fright or self-preservation had his signalman run up a white flag. The Japanese could not believe that five unscarred warships were surrendering, nevertheless they cautiously approached and boarded Nebogatov's battleship. One of Nebogatov's cruisers the Izumrud ignored the surrender command and sped off heading north toward Vladivostok. Unfortunately, the speedy Izumrud as it steamed northward ran into reefs along the western coast and had to be scuttled by her crew. The only ships of Russia's Second and Third Pacific Squadrons to reach Vladivostok were a cruiser and two badly damaged destroyers.

The destroyer Buiny carrying the unconscious Commander-in-Chief, along with several other smaller craft of their squadron headed directly for Vladivostok. It was not long, however, before they were surrounded by a complement of Japanese cruisers making surrender inevitable. The Buiny was towed to the Japanese port of Sasebo. When they entered the harbour, it was fortunate Rozhdestvensky was still unconscious for there stood the four ironclad warships of Nebogatov's division—flying Japanese flags. This was the sad end to the Second and Third Pacific Squadrons. Not counting the loss of lives en route to the Far East, during the Battle of Tsushima on the 14/15 of May 1905, 5,015 Russian sailors lost their lives and 6,106 were taken prisoner. On the other side of the battle 700 Japanese sailors died and only 3 destroyers were sunk.

At Sasebo, the Mad Dog was hospitalized and despite his many injuries, his indomitable spirit carried him through to a relatively speedy recovery. During his time at Sasebo, he was sent honours by many seamen not only from Russia, but also from many other countries. He was even visited by Admiral Togo Heihachiro who congratulated him on his efforts to bring the Russian armada to the

Far East.  By the end of August, he was well enough to travel and the Japanese allowed him to be taken to Vladivostok.  From there he travelled on the Trans-Siberian Railway back home to St. Petersburg where his heroic effort in nursing the Second and Third Pacific Squadrons to the Far East to face certain defeat was hardly noticed or even acknowledged.  Most attention was being paid to the rumblings of discontent, which were now rampant among the peasants and discord was becoming apparent in the Romanov hierarchy as well as in the Tsar's bureaucratic maze.  On September 5th, 1905, a peace treaty was signed under the mediation of United States president Theodore Roosevelt at Portsmouth, New Hampshire.  Korea and the Liaotung Peninsula including Port Arthur as well as the southern half of Sakhalin Island were ceded to Japan.  Russia also agreed to turn southern Manchuria over to the Chinese.

# Chapter 10

## Tsintao to St. Petersburg

The Russo-Japanese War was now over and the flagship of Russia's First Pacific Squadron had been interned at Tsintao from July 29th, 1904, to September 5th, 1905. The Tsesarevich had now been detained at Tsintao for a period of some thirteen months. While at Tsintao, much repair work was done on the Tsesarevich. Friedrich and Radomski who both could speak freely with the Germans in charge of the harbour staff led the negotiations. Firstly, they had to seek permission to be allowed to work on their ship and, secondly, they somehow had to find a way to get the material necessary for all the things that needed attention. The shattered conning tower, the nerve centre of the ship, had to be completely rebuilt from navigation equipment to armour plating. Some of the turrets had to be overhauled; over half of the boilers needed to be replaced and the fires had scorched the passageway walls and burned flooring of the decks had to be replaced. Much of this work fell to Friedrich and his stokers since he had to supervise the ironwork. As they worked through the first six months of their stay, the time went relatively quickly but once the ship slowly became seaworthy there was more free time and, consequently, getting home became an obsession with nearly all the crew of the Tsesarevich. Friedrich would often pull out the tattered picture of his family and wonder what they all were doing back in Nataliendorf; he yearned to get back to his blacksmithing work in the community. Much of the spare time the crew now had was spent wondering and talking about what was happening in the war.

Finally, on Christmas Day, 1904, Captain Grigorovich heard from the German port authorities that Port Arthur had fallen to the

Japanese five days previously. Knowing that Port Arthur's surrender was inevitable this news immediately led everyone on the Tsesarevich to wonder how soon it would be before Russia would face a total defeat in the Far East. Grigorovich also was informed that a Second Pacific Squadron was on its way to the Far East, but there was no word of what ships were coming or who was commanding the new fleet. For the next five months, they heard nothing about the Second Pacific Squadron, the war or anything about what was going on at St. Petersburg, or for that matter anywhere in Russia. Then, at the end of May 1905, they were told of the defeat of the Second Pacific Squadron and that the hardened and battle-wise commander of the squadron, Admiral Rozhdestvensky, was severely injured and was now a prisoner in Japan. More waiting and wondering ensued. Three months later the news of the signing of the Peace Treaty at Portsmouth on September 5th, 1905, spread quickly throughout the Far Eastern countries and when the Russian detainees at Tsintao heard that the war at last was over they immediately started preparing for their homeward voyage. However, they still had to wait another agonizing three weeks until finally on the 1st of October 1905, they were allowed to leave Tsintao. With great relief, Captain Grigorovich informed his officers, Friedrich Fischbuch, Lubomir Radomski and the rest of the Russian sailors that they were now free to leave. The Tsesarevich immediately weighed anchor and left the Far East forever.

The voyage home was much different from the slow and somewhat cumbersome trip they had in the summer of 1903. Now the crew were all familiar with their duties and Friedrich made sure the stokers kept the ship at its top speed of 18 knots and the stokers worked at full capacity. In their eagerness to get home they all performed their duties religiously. Coaling was never a problem for the port authorities at Singapore, Djibouti, Toulon, Gibraltar, London and Skagen were all co-operative since they all had heard of what the Russian fleet had endured at Tsushima and were sympathetic to see the return of the only Russian battleship that survived the sea battles in the Far East. The Tsesarevich arrived at Kronstadt on the 5th of January 1906, and Tsar Nicholas II was waiting for their arrival on his royal yacht the Standart. He came aboard the Tsesarevich and requested a private meeting with Captain Grigorovich. When they emerged from the officers' quarters, the Tsar addressed the assembled crew and congratulated them on returning the only battleship that had survived the conflict with the Japanese. The Tsar also announced that he wanted the captain and all the officers of the Tsesarevich to appear at the Winter Palace on January 22nd. Friedrich wondered why they were requested to be at the Winter Palace. If it was a new assignment for the Tsesarevich this should have been done at The Admiralty or at Kronstadt. Why would they be summoned to the Winter Palace? For the next two weeks, the ship was thoroughly washed down and re-painted. Friedrich had the stokers check and repair each boiler; the propulsion system was examined and the barnacles were scraped from the hull. Early on the morning of January 22$^{nd}$, the Tsar's launch arrived to take Grigorovich, Friedrich and the other twenty-four officers directly to the Winter Palace. As they were squired into the main hall, the Tsar introduced them to Naval Minister Fedor Avelan, Minister of War Sakharov and Foreign Minister Count Lamsdorf. Among the other military elite Friedrich noted Admiral Alexeev was also present. Friedrich wondered why Alexeev was still part of the Tsar's inner group. After all, he had been terminated as Supreme Commander and Viceroy of the Far East. Friedrich recalled how Alexeev had presided at the occasion when Friedrich received his promotion to Engineer First Class at the mansion on Quail Hill when the Tsesarevich had arrived at Port Arthur.

The Tsar then announced that Grigorovich was now promoted to Admiral and would be the new Commander of the Baltic Fleet. He went on to say that after conferring with Grigorovich upon the arrival of the Tsesarevich he would like the Minister of War to present Engineer First Class Friedrich Fischbuch with the Cross of St. George in recognition of his bravery during the Battle of the Yellow Sea and for his role in helping to save the battleship Tsesarevich. The Tsar then gave Admiral Grigorovich medallions to present to each of the crew of the Tsesarevich for their service in the Russo-Japanese war. As Friedrich and the rest of the officers filed out of the Winter Palace he noticed Admiral Alexeev did not even acknowledge Friedrich's presence or even his award and just looked the other way.

When they all arrived back on board the Tsesarevich Grigorovich drew Friedrich aside and said that a new officer would be appointed as captain of the Tsesarevich. He explained that now that he was Commander of the Baltic Fleet his time would be spent at the Admiralty and at Kronstadt but more importantly he would like Friedrich to remain as Chief Engineer on the Tsesarevich. Friedrich said he would consider it but already he was thinking of his family and the comfortable life he had back at Nataliendorf. That night he agonized about leaving the Tsesarevich; this battleship had now become his second home and the kinship that had grown among the crew of nearly 800 men that by this time had infected them all. They had come from so many different backgrounds and yet through the guidance of their captain they had evolved as a unit to defend and save their ship.

1899, Fischbuch Family Photo Minus Friedrich.
Michel jr, Justina Gustel, Gustav, August
Olga, Justina, Michel, Eduard, Lydia, Johann
Emil, Albert, Zamel, Robert

That night he unfolded the tattered picture his family had sent him when he first arrived at Kronstadt and as he looked at his stoic and well-dressed family he noted the space between August and Gustav where he should have been standing. The next day, without hesitation Friedrich informed Admiral Grigorovich he had decided he would ask for a discharge and leave for home. Grigorovich replied if that was his wish, he could leave whenever he wished and grudgingly signed Friedrich's discharge papers. On January 23rd, 1906, Friedrich left the battleship that for he and his shipmates had been their home for the past 2 ½ years. They had collectively guided this battleship halfway around the world, fought an overpowering foe, nurtured it back to life after the conflict and brought it safely back to its home port. His last goodbye was to his long time friend and fellow stoker Lubomir Radomski. They both agreed to get together whenever Radomski got back to his home at Lutsk in Poland, a small city just across the Polish-Ukrainian border from Nataliendorf. The long lonely train trip of nearly 900 miles from St. Petersburg to Kiev took almost a week and gave Friedrich time to think of the futility of war and the senseless political motive of sending two ill-prepared armada's half way around the world to face a foe in its home territory.

When he arrived at Kiev, he tried to find someone who would take him to Nataliendorf by horse and buggy, however, he could find no one willing to make a journey of over 50 miles. Finally, he bought a sturdy buggy and a healthy horse with the idea that he could use this transportation when he got back into his work as the community blacksmith. It took him nearly two days of travel and both he and his horse were exhausted when he arrived at the tree-lined roads of Nataliendorf on February 3rd, 1906. When he drove into the yard of his parent's home, the quiet farmyard was bustling with activity. Teams of horses were tethered to wagons and buggies. His next youngest brothers, Michel Jr. and Emil had seen someone driving into the yard and wondered who this stranger could be and as soon as they realized it was Friedrich they came running out of the house. For the last four years, they had heard only that things were not going well for the Russian Navy in the Japanese conflict, and the whole family feared their brother and son had perished in the war. When the three brothers entered the house, there was a great celebration going on and Friedrich soon found this was the wedding celebration of his oldest sister Justina-Gustel. Her new husband was Dmitri Bolislav the Russian butcher from Novograd Volinskiy. Friedrich had met him just before he was called to the navy. Just before Friedrich left for Kronstadt, he and his friend Gustav Wendtland had delivered several head of cattle to the Novograd Volinskiy butcher shop. The whole family crowded around to hear the stories of Friedrich's naval experiences. However, he had to shorten his tales because he too wanted to know what had happened at home while he was away. Michel and Justina finally put the entire story-telling episode on hold since they insisted that even though the arrival of Friedrich was important the whole family must first deal with the wedding celebration. In the days that followed, Friedrich started telling of his experieces from the time of his arrival and training at Kronstadt. He explained what had transpired at Toulon and the tribulations on the voyage to the Far East, the Battle of the Yellow Sea, their internment at Tsintao, their voyage back to St. Petersburg and finally the Tsar's presentation to Friedrich with the Cross of St. George.

The younger brothers and sisters who now ranged in age from six to twenty-three-years-old listened intently to Friedrich's accounts and could not wait to spread the tales of their brother among their neighbours and friends. Friedrich, when he had the rare opportunity, asked about what had transpired in his absence. He knew that his next oldest brother August was not there and when he enquired as to his whereabouts they all said that Friedrich would have to talk to their father. Finally, one day Michel took Friedrich aside and informed him things had not been going well since he had left and that August had been sent to live in Canada. The reason for this was he had disgraced the family by getting the younger sister of his wife Ottilia pregnant. During the time Friedrich was away August had also fathered three children with his wife Ottilia; two sons and a daughter. The oldest boy was born a short time after Friedrich had gone to serve in the navy and he had been named Friedrich after his uncle. Both he and the second son had died of colic. August and Ottilia's third child was a girl and was now with her mother. Michel had sent both Ottilia and her daughter to live with Ottilia's widowed mother and of course, her pregnant sister. Ottilia was now waiting for her mother to raise money to send her to Canada to join her errant husband. Friedrich could not understand the reason why Michel felt that August's indiscretion was in some way the Kahler family's responsibility, and that it was their duty to send Ottilia to join her exiled husband.

Friedrich recalled the day Ottilia married August and how he would have liked to get to know her younger sister Martha, but she was only fourteen-years-old at the time. Why would August do such a thing? After all, Ottilia was a very nice and attractive woman so what was in August's mind to seduce the innocent younger sister of his wife? Michel went on to tell Friedrich that all the brothers had done well in their trades and professions much like Friedrich himself had done and that August seemed to have no more ambition than to while away his time with horses. After complaining about tribulations in the family Michel went on to say things were also not going well in all of Russia especially since the Bloody Sunday massacre in St. Petersburg on January 22nd, 1905. He said that Tsar Nicholas, Russia's supreme autocrat seemed to be losing his power and much animosity was growing across the country. The Russian peasants, especially the Mouzhiken, were causing problems wherever there were German colonies.

During the preceding century many German colonies had been established, ranging from settlements in the Volga River valley to those along the Dnieper River; German settlements had been established as far south as the Crimea, Odessa, Bessarabia, Moldavia and as far east as Kazakhstan. Friedrich could see that in the five years he was away much had transpired in both his family and among the settlers in the German communities that for the past century had called Russia their homeland. After becoming re-established with the family, Friedrich's main desire was to resume his connection with the Wendtland family: He especially wanted to see the father, August, who was Friedrich's blacksmithing mentor and as well, he wanted to see his boyhood friend Gustav Wendtland. Finally, one day in mid-February Friedrich was able to break away from family connections and went to visit the Wendtland household. The father said to him that he had always hoped Friedrich would soon be back home, since he was now getting too old to travel to all the different communities to continue his blacksmithing duties. None of August Wendtland's own sons had taken much interest in the blacksmith trade, so he asked if Friedrich would want to carry on the Wendtland blacksmithing tours of duty. Friedrich immediately said he would be glad to take on the task for he recalled how he enjoyed going to the various villages and how pleased the farmers were to get their machinery repaired and their horses re-shod. August Wendtland said he would go with Friedrich and re-introduce him to the work and the people in all the communities he had served after Friedrich had left for St. Petersburg in 1900. The following week August Wendtland called on Friedrich and said he was making a blacksmithing trip seventeen kilometres southwest of Nataliendorf to Adolin, and to all of the German villages between including Makowetz and Annette. Friedrich was pleased to go along, because he would be able to see old friends and relatives in Makowetz as well as those in the old mother colony of Annette. He also recalled the time he went with his oldest brother Eduard to fight the fire at Adolin where Eduard had met his future wife Henrietta.

Early the next morning, August Wendtland arrived and asked if Friedrich could come with his new buggy so that he could take along some of their equipment since he did not have enough room for it all in his wagon. This excursion brought back fond memories to Friedrich, as he got back to hammering out ploughshares, casting steel-rimmed wagon wheels and sharpening scythes and sickles.

The next day, on the way back from Adolin, Friedrich asked August why they were not stopping at the Russian villages along the way. August explained now that Tsar Nicholas II was steadfastly following the edict of russification that Tsar Alexander III had established to "purify" the nation through the mandatory elimination of ethnic minorities, more and more animosity was becoming evident. Germans were one of the more obvious minorities, since they were relatively affluent with nice farmsteads and thus were visible targets for ethnic cleansing. Friedrich immediately thought of his new brother-in-law Dmitri Bolislav—he had no quarrel with him being Russian and why should he for they had lived amicably in the same community all their lives. He also thought of the old Mouzhik who he would meet and spend time with when he was a boy, and the times they both revelled in the wonders of the Sluch River. Then there were his Russian shipmates who were his comrades-in-arms at Port Arthur and in the Battle of the Yellow Sea, where they all worked as a team and were closeted together in the flagship during the battle and also while they waited patiently for their release from internment at Tsintao. Friedrich found it difficult to comprehend this distinction based on race and culture. This too made him think of what had happened in his own family, for he found it hard to understand his father's decision to send his brother August to Canada and blaming the Kahler family for August's indiscretion.

On their way back from Adolin, they spent some time at Annette where Friedrich sought out the little homestead where his maternal grandparents, the Moller family had lived. He remembered riding one of the Zamel's horses over to visit them when he was about nine-years-old and his grandmother would always have oatmeal cookies waiting for him. His uncle, a younger son of the Moller grandparents, now owned the farm.

When they got back to Nataliendorf August Wendtland said he would let Friedrich take over the blacksmith work and would sell the anvils, forge, hammers and all the equipment to Friedrich, as well he would let him use his blacksmith shop as long as he wished. However, he assumed that Friedrich would eventually want to build his own shop nearer to Michel and Justina's larger farmstead.

After the summer of 1906, Friedrich continued travelling the established Wendtland routes and eventually extended them to villages even further away. One thing that helped him considerably was that his younger brothers showed a distinct interest in blacksmithing; they would help Friedrich at the forge and the anvil but really, their main interest was to listen to his stories as they travelled with him to the different villages. Friedrich's next youngest brother, Gustav no longer lived at Nataliendorf. He was married in 1903, and his wife Maria Bekker was from Dermanka, a village about thirty-five miles southwest of Nataliendorf. Maria was an only child so Gustav and Maria took over her parent's farm and only came to Nataliendorf on special occasions. Friedrich's younger brothers ranged from Michel Jr. nineteen-years-old, Emil about seventeen, Albert fifteen, Robert thirteen and Zamel eleven. They were constantly at Friedrich's elbow watching him perform magic with iron and as well listening to his stories about his naval adventures. By the time the summer of 1907 arrived, Friedrich with the help of his five brothers had built a new workshop on the Fischbuch farmstead and he had been able to pay August Wendtland for all of the blacksmithing equipment. On his travels through the countryside, one or even two of the brothers always accompanied Friedrich.

As time went on, they noticed the constantly increasing animosity toward them by any Russians they encountered on the roadways or in the Russian villages. The ethnic cleansing edict that Tsar Alexander III had established in the mid 1880's continued unabated. Tsar Nicholas II followed it religiously in his belief that through the hands of the Lord a true Russian identity must not be diluted by the encroachment of foreign migrants. Russification had now become the byword among the nomadic Mouzhiken who were now becoming increasingly aggressive.

Not only Michel and Justina's family, but also the whole Nataliendorf community were concerned about the unrest of the Russian populace following the massacre at St. Petersburg on Bloody Sunday, January 22nd, 1905. This coupled with the disastrous defeat of the Tsar's military in the Russo-Japanese war led the Russian people to see the weakness of the Tsar and the Romanov dynasty. It was now obvious, not only to his fawning bureaucrats, but also more importantly to the shiftless mass of peasants and Mouzhiken who were challenging the autocratic power of Tsar Nicholas. The loss of confidence in the Tsar's autocratic power began in the early 1890s, which was fuelled by a young lawyer, Vladimir Ulyanov, who later changed his name to Vladimir Lenin. Lenin's loathing of the Tsarist dynasty was triggered by the execution of his brother who with other revolutionaries had plotted the assassination of Tsar Alexander III. To avenge his brother's death Lenin began to propagate the socialist teachings of Karl Marx among the starving peasant workers. At about the same time another radical intellectual, Leon Trotsky, a brilliant Jewish student from Odessa also began trumpeting the socialist teachings of Karl Marx. These radical concepts, of course, were a direct contradiction of what the Tsar and his ministers had in mind for the working class. Consequently, it was not long before the Marxism of Lenin and subsequently that of Trotsky resulted in an escalating series of strikes among the destitute workers. Many were so impoverished that they would grasp at any straw to better their lives and working conditions, especially in the factories of the big cities.

To counter these insurrections the Tsar had both Lenin and Trotsky arrested and imprisoned in Siberia: Lenin in 1895 and Trotsky in 1900. They both subsequently escaped from their Siberian internment and were smuggled out of Russia. They met for the first time in London where they continued to foment Marxist concepts among radical British socialists, in an attempt to create not only a civil war in Russia but also a worldwide revolution. During their stay in London, Lenin's ideas shifted toward the radical socialist concepts of the recently emerging Bolsheviks, whereas Trotsky followed the more moderate Menshevik philosophy. This later led to a rift between these two doctrinaire revolutionaries who in 1905, both returned to Russia where their political philosophies diverged even more. Perhaps more importantly, both continued to create unending turmoil as the Tsarist regime continued to disintegrate. This then led to many new political factions to challenge the Tsar's autocracy. His frightened advisors suggested to the Tsar that he should institute some kind of parliament for the people to allow some representation from the masses. This parliament would be elected and have authority over the Tsar's appointed "cabinet." Nicholas vigorously objected to losing even a fraction of his power, for how could he tamper with a supreme autocratic dynasty that had ruled Russia for the last three hundred years. After all, was it not with God's blessing that he was to have supreme control over his subjects? Despite his angry opposition, he was forced to bow to the overwhelming demands of his ministers, the aristocracy and the striking and starving peasants who were bringing the Russian economy to a standstill. As a result, the first of four Dumas was formed in October of 1905. However, the institution was plagued by dissension from the time of it's inception with a multitude of political entities ranging from Bolsheviks, to Mensheviks, to moderate socialists, to Monarchists, to liberals and conservatives, all vying for control of the Duma.

# Chapter 11

## A Life Disrupted

In the late fall of 1907, as Friedrich and his brother Emil were returning from a long tour of blacksmithing at several German villages near Zhitomir some 30 miles to the east, they passed a Jewish village and saw that many of the houses were burning. Young boys and women were running with buckets of water in a vain attempt to put out the fires. Friedrich drove as quickly as he could and when they got to the village he and Emil ran to help the bucket brigade. Friedrich asked one of the women where all the men were. She replied that they had been taken away by a rampaging mob of Mouzhiken and that her husband and some of the other men who had refused to go were shot. Here now was a consequence of the continuation of Tsar Nicholas's ethnic cleansing of the Empire that was reaching ever closer to the villages near Novograd Volinskiy. Friedrich and young Emil helped the women carry the bodies of the three men that had been shot by the mob into one of the houses that had been saved. They told the women and children that they would hurry to the next village along their way back to Nataliendorf and tell them to send help. When Friedrich and Emil arrived home and told the family about the events of their trip Michel said it was time to get the family together and discuss what would be the best way for them to cope with this emerging turmoil. He knew it would not be long before the violence would affect not only those in the family at Nataliendorf, but also the family of Johann at Beresowka and Gustav at Dermanka.

The following Sunday, the family gathered at Michel and Justina's house. Michel asked them all to give an opinion as to what should be done. He suggested that the first opinion should come from the oldest son.  After a time Eduard rose and said that since he and Henrietta had three children: Robert, four-years-old, Olga three and little Ida just six months old, and that he and Henrietta had worked so hard to build their little farm that they would not leave their home even though he could see trouble was on the horizon.  However, he added that even though they knew they would be able to go to Canada since August had written and said that it was quite easy to get homestead land in Canada, they could not bring themselves to leave their established home.  August's wife Ottilia had just left for Canada with her little girl, so he knew that now they had a contact in his new world.  Nevertheless, it was his decision to stay in Russia.

The next brother to speak was Johann.  Here again was an elder brother who had three little children, but he said they had already decided to leave Russia.  Johann and Wilhelmina were married in 1899, and had a well-established farm at Josephine and against Michel's wishes, they had sold it with the intention of moving to Canada.   In the meantime, they temporarily rented a place at Beresowka a village about ten miles to the northeast of Nataliendorf.  It was here where their youngest daughter Elfrieda was born six months earlier.  Their other two children, Elsa who was now eight-years-old and Reinhold who was five, were born on the farm at Josephine.

The next oldest brother to let his preference be known was Friedrich.  He did not have a family so he would have been free to leave but he had other connections.  He felt an obligation to stay in the country that he fought for in the war with Japan, and he felt he should not leave the country of his fellow sailors for he could not forget the comradeship that had developed between them.  Furthermore, he had worked diligently to establish an even wider ranging blacksmithing business in just over a year than August Wendtland had done in over twenty years.  His decision, of course, was to stay and face whatever consequences arose.

The next brother to speak was Gustav, who did not hesitate to say that he and Maria wished to stay at Dermanka since their roots were well established in Russia and they would stay and face whatever happened.  Justina-Gustel and her Russian husband Dmitri Bolislav were now part of the Russian community so her wish was that the whole family would never leave Russia.

Michel Jr., who was nineteen-years-old and had no ties, as well as the younger siblings, all looked to their father to decide what would be best for them. Michel Sr., the last to give his assessment of what the family should do, said he was disappointed that Johann had decided to leave; here they had founded the farmsteads that he, his father and his grandfather had toiled for nearly a century to create productive fields and orchards from the swamp and forest of the Pilipovitshi estate. All of this would be lost if everyone in the family became frightened and ran away. Certainly, August had to leave for Canada because he had soiled the name of the whole family, but that did not make it right for any of the rest of the family to follow him. For a century the Russians had allowed the family to prosper and, therefore, he would like the family to carry on the Fischbuch tradition of hard work to make an honest living.

After the family meeting, Johann and Wilhelmina felt so guilty about their decision that they informed Michel they had decided to stay, even though they were still worried about what the future held for them. Without saying anything to the other families they knew if things got worse they could leave quickly and quietly, since they had money from the sale of their farm at Josephine and as well their children would be older, which would make it easier to travel.

Now that the decision had been made that everyone in the family was going to stay in Russia, at least for the next while, there was a period of relative calm among the family. However, toward the end of the summer outbursts of violence were becoming more common in the community. The younger brothers who still were enthralled by the fact that soldiers periodically passed through Novograd Volinskiy on their way to the Polish border, would slip away to see them parade through town. In the late summer of 1908, Albert who was now seventeen-years-old with Robert 15 and Zamel 13, rode their horses into Novograd Volinskiy to watch Russian troops transporting cannons to the Polish border. A group of Russian youths and several adult peasant men began to taunt the boys, calling them those Germans from Nataliendorf who came to Russia just to get free land.

The boys had always shown respect for the Russian people in the town, but the angry mob took their horses and told them they could walk home because the "rich" Germans in Nataliendorf had plenty of other horses that should rightly belong to the Russians anyway. As the boys walked home Zamel the youngest of the three asked what would they say to their parents after all, they had each worked so hard at their chores to earn enough to buy their cherished horses. When they got home, the boys suggested that the older brothers should go back with them and challenge the Russian thieves. However, Michel said this would only escalate the violence that had been becoming more and more common in the whole community. He said they would be better off to guard their homes and whenever they had to travel outside of Nataliendorf, they should go in a group.

Over the next few years, Friedrich shortened his blacksmithing trips to a few nearby villages and always gave wide berth to any Russian peasants on the roads. By the summer of 1910, he stopped going to any villages, for he had heard it was now common for Germans, Jews, Poles and even the Gypsies to be stopped on the roadways and robbed of their horses, their wagons or buggies, or whatever of value they had with them. Friedrich was concerned he might lose his horses and buggy, or his blacksmith tools. Late one night in the summer of 1913 Gustav, Friedrich's next youngest brother who had taken over the farm of his wife's family at Dermanka in 1903, came to Nataliendorf. Filled with despair he reported that a group of Russian peasants had stormed into his yard early the previous morning while they were still asleep, took all of the cattle out of his barn and set it on fire. The thatched roof burned quickly and he had to try to save the barn and stop the fire from spreading to other buildings. Therefore, he could not give chase to retrieve his cattle because he barely had time to rouse one of his neighbours to help him fight the fire. They carried water for several hours.and managed to stop the fire from spreading to their adjacent house or any of the other buildings. However, they did lose the barn. This rise in animosity was hard for the entire family to comprehend, for most Germans in the Russian Empire had been devout citizens but now as the Tsarist dynasty continued to disintegrate the local peasantry, which consisted mainly of itinerant ex-serfs, were becoming increasingly bolder.

Superimposed on this unrest were the spreading rumours that Germany was making threats of war against Russia, but the Tsar reassured everyone that even though Kaiser Wilhelm had declared war with Britain and France his good friend and cousin would not attack Russia. Nevertheless, the Tsar's tenuous hold on the Empire made many Russians uneasy. A war with Germany made Michel, Justina and their whole family concerned about their obvious German background and made them apprehensive about what the future held for them and their livelihood in Russia. On July 1, 1914, to the dismay of Nicholas, Kaiser Wilhelm's armies began marching toward Russia, which forced the Tsar to declare war on Germany. Surprisingly, even though the Tsar's popularity among the Russian people had fallen dramatically, the war aroused a fervent patriotism among the Russian aristocracy; it even gave the peasants a feeling of loyalty to the Empire. However, for the German-Russian population this was a traumatic shock, since they and their forefathers had been citizens of this country for over a century and their descendants were already suffering under the Tsar's proclamation of russification. With a war against their motherland, they would be treated as conspirators and spies for the German invaders.

The Duma immediately issued legislation that restricted the rights of Germans in all of Russia. There could be no assembly in German villages, the German language could not be taught or written and if it were heard spoken, the accused would be imprisoned. In the cities German shops, banks, factories and homes were looted and burned. No thought was given to the fact that many of the German-Russians had served in the military and the government, and for the past century had produced most of the countries agricultural needs. Then to add further to their injustice many German men were now being conscripted into the army to fight against their German ancestors. Sometime in the autumn of 1914 Eduard, Friedrich's oldest brother, was inducted into the army and sent to fight against the Turks in the Crimea. A short time later in the early part of 1915 two of his other brothers, Emil and Albert, as well as their younger sister's future husband, Emil Krampitz were inducted into the army and were sent to the Crimea. Only a few days were allowed for the brothers to prepare for their departure to the Black Sea city of Sevastopol. In the early summer of 1914, Emil Krampitz's sister, Lydia, had been selected by the community Matchmaker to become Emil Fischbuch's new wife. At the time, they hoped that living conditions would improve and had decided to wait until June of 1915 to get married. However, with Emil soon to depart and not knowing when or if he would return, they decided to get married in the short time they had left before he was to leave. Consequently, the wedding was quickly organized for the afternoon of the day before the three new soldiers had to report to the Army Commandant at Novograd Volinskiy.

After Emil, Albert and Emil Krampitz left the whole family was distraught, not only for the fact that three more of the family were taken away, but also because they had heard nothing of Eduard who had been sent to the Crimea three months earlier. His wife Henrietta and their three young children as well as the rest of the family waited patiently for news. They all wondered what would become of the four family men taken away to fight for Russia. There were now rumours that the German army was advancing rapidly into Poland and the Nataliendorf Germans feared it would not belong before they reached the Polish-Volhynian border, which was only a few miles to the west.

Friedrich did his best to calm everyone's concerns and helped his sister-in-law Henrietta with her livestock and chores but little could be done to curb the anxiety of the whole family. During this time, Friedrich lived at home with Michel, Justina and the remainder of the family. One day when he went to visit the Wendtland family, August told him he had taken all of his blacksmith tools and buried them in a carefully marked spot on his land so that regardless of what was stolen while he was away, he would at least have his blacksmith tools when he returned. Unknown to them both was that August Wendtland would never return, for he starved to death during the deportation that soon would be forced upon everyone in their community. Friedrich's main concern now, however, was that the July legislation of the Duma restricted every action and movement of anyone of German heritage. On July 5th, 1915, the Commander-in-Chief of the Russian Army, the Tsar's Uncle Nicholas Nicholaievich the uncle whom Empress Alexandra detested, accused the German Volhynians of carrying on espionage for Germany behind the Russian lines and he immediately issued a proclamation stating that all German residents of Volhynia were to be deported. It further stated that the July 5th decree of the Duma would be followed to the letter and every civil service worker with German heritage employed in Volhynia would be fired. It also stated that all titles of land owned by ethnic Germans would be rescinded immediately. On July 10th, 1915, the Final Proclamation was issued that German Volhynians were to be evacuated immediately. When the deportation order was delivered to Novograd Volinskiy, word was immediately sent to all the surrounding villages that when the Russian authorities arrived at randomly chosen German farmsteads the residents would only have a few hours to pack before being taken away. The Fischbuch families pondered what to prepare for their forced evacuation and what to do with their belongings and livestock. There was no time to sell anything and in any case, there was no one to buy their belongings. There was no indication of where their destination would be and once the deportation order was delivered the inhabitants, by national decree, would be forced to leave.

Friedrich had Emil's new wife Lydia, stay with her parents who assured him they would look after her until Emil returned. Just three days later, a contingent of Russian armed men or "strazhniks" arrived at the home of Johann and his family. Since the strazhniks had never owned property, they were ideal candidates for conscription into the Bolshevik fold. The strazhniks had been recruited into the Russian army and had been picked at random from the itinerant descendants of the serfs who had roamed the forested countryside ever since Tsar Alexander II granted their freedom in 1861. Johann was given eight hours to pack and have everyone ready to leave; when he asked where they were being taken, he was told to mind his own business and be ready at the appointed time. Johann hitched his two best horses to his wagon, rushed to the forest to cut and bent some willows to quickly to make a frame for a cloth covering over the wagon. He then let all of his livestock: horses, cattle, pigs, chickens and geese out of their pens in hopes that they could forage for themselves until he and his family were allowed to come home. Wilhelmina had baked bread and filled cans with lard hoping their travels would not be too long. With feed for the horses, a few blankets and extra clothing they hurriedly bundled their six children: Erhart 2, Meta 4, Arnold 6, Elfrieda 9, Reinhold 13 and Elsa 16 into the wagon and in no time they were on their way, but to where? At the home farmstead, Michel and Justina kept their remaining children: Robert 22, Zamel 20, Lydia 19, and Olga 14, close at hand.

As always Michel and Justina's home was the focal point for news, rumours and family connections. Robert had just returned from Dermanka and said that Gustav, Maria and their three children had been taken away the previous day. Their departure must have been sudden for Robert said an unfinished meal was still on the table. This news aroused even greater anxiety among them all. Michel had Robert and Zamel harness their two best horses and they let the livestock out into the pasture to make ready in case they were called upon to leave.

Two days later the next stop for the strazhniks was the home of Eduard's wife Henrietta. Here she was, all alone with her three children: Robert 12-years-old, Olga 10 and Ida 8. It had been assumed by the family that since her husband was away fighting in the Russian army she would be left alone. Their pleas with the leader of the strazhniks that the wife of their soldier brother would be allowed to stay and wait for her husband were ignored. He just laughed and told them to get her ready to go within the hour. Henrietta immediately sent her young son Robert to tell Friedrich, who was at the home farmstead with Michel and Justina, to come and help her get packed and ready to leave with the strazhniks. When Friedrich arrived, he could see how desperate their situation was and decided to go with them, since again they had no idea where or for how long they would be away. Friedrich told Michel to look after the house and livestock at Eduard and Henrietta's farmstead. They quickly took some clothes and food for the children and feed for the horses before they were forced to get on their way by the strazhniks.

As they left Nataliendorf, they were joined by several other wagonloads of deportees being herded along by contingents of strazhniks. Their captors forced the wagon train to travel in a general eastward direction, without letting them stop to eat or feed their horses. For several days, the strazhniks pushed their German captives along by whipping the horses pulling the wagons so they would go faster, but as the horses slowed from exhaustion and hunger the strazhniks, out of frustration and anger finally shot the horses and made the families proceed on foot taking along what few belongings they could carry.

Since the strazhniks now had no horse targets to whip, they stayed behind this slow moving human caravan lashing out at anyone who fell behind. As they were forced along the muddy roads, the first to fall behind were the young and the old. As Friedrich glanced over his shoulder, he saw a strazhnik's whip strike an old man who had fallen behind. The whiplash had hit the old man in the face. With blood streaming into his eyes the old man stopped and screamed for help but he was totally ignored and since he did not move a strazhnik struck him down with the butt of his rifle, and very casually walked past his body as it lay in the mud. Friedrich told Henrietta to stay at the front of the children and walk as fast as she could and that he would follow behind the children so that he could urge young Robert, Olga and little eight-year-old Ida to stay ahead of him. They struggled onward and as the children became tired and started to lag behind, Friedrich often felt the sting of the fine leather thongs of the whips as they struck his body. There was little pain but he soon felt the warmth of his blood trickling down his back. His thoughts went back to his youth and he wondered what had become of his beloved country and the Tsar, who he had fought for in the Battle of the Yellow Sea. Why was Tsar Nicholas now turning on the very people who were the lifeblood of his vast domain? Moreover, when would this nightmare come to an end.

Little did Friedrich realize that this was just the beginning of his and his family's long journey into hunger, misery, terror and sadism that would last the rest of his life. However, as history unfolded it not only lasted through his lifetime but also plagued the remnants of his family for the next seventy years. Friedrich would not find out until three years later that the day after he, Henrietta and the three children were forced to leave Nataliendorf, that most of the rest of the family: Michel Jr., his wife Emilia, Robert and Zamel would be taken away by the strazhniks. Michel and Justina with young Lydia and Olga would stay, but would suffer as much as the others under the rising tide of Bolshevik cruelties.

When the deportation order was decreed in July of 1915, a few of the colonist families in Volhynia hid themselves in the forest in the hope that they could await the arrival of the German armies. In this way some made their way to Austria and East Prussia. The Tsar's uncle, Commander-in-Chief Nicholas Nicholaievich, was pleased how meekly the German colonists submitted to the cruel deportation and he was smug in the fact that they had taken the precaution of previously arresting the pastors, kusters, felschers, mayors and other community leaders who may have organized resistance. In any case, resistance would probably not even have been thought of by the German colonists. After all, had they not made the forests of Volhynia bloom, as was the dream of Catherine in her famous manifesto. They had committed no treasonable acts against the state; in fact, they were overly conscientious in paying their taxes and debts. By years of great labour, they had converted the forest and swamp into productive farmland. They had taught the Russian peasants how to make and use the iron mould-board plough. They had taught the Russian language to their children. Their sons had fought in wars against Turkey and Japan and even now, they had sons fighting against their own ancestors for a Russia they had cherished and thought of as their own.

During this mass exile, thousands of colonists died under indescribable hardship and deprivation. In all cases, no one told them where they were going. No planning whatsoever went into the forced evacuation of these thousands of people. The authorities were more preoccupied with the requisitioning of locomotives and cattle cars from all over Russia to effect the deportation as quickly as possible. There was hardly a Volhynian family that half or more of its members had not died. The dead were buried along the way in the forest or on riverbanks where stops were made for water. Even bigger "cemeteries" were evident at some stopping places where Typhus was rampant. Sanitary conditions were non-existent, since the trains never stopped long enough to clean the excrement and human debris, including bodies, from the cattle cars. When the trains went through the Urals, central Asia and Asiatic Siberia the deportees were dumped off at random and if they survived they had to forage for themselves. The local people whether they were Russians, Mouzhiken, Kazakhstani's or Oriental Asiatics treated the German deportees with suspicion, since they were led to believe that these people were collaborating with the enemy and, therefore, were political criminals. Of the 120,000 Volhynians that were deported only about 60,000 returned. Meanwhile, during this time what was triggering these events in the nation's capital, St. Petersburg?

# Chapter 12

# Rasputin, Abdication, Execution

Right from the time that Friedrich arrived back at Nataliendorf in February of 1906, the Tsar was becoming more and more oblivious to the fact that he was losing control of his Empire. The disastrous conflict with Japan and the magnitude of Bloody Sunday in January of 1905 set the stage for unrest among not only the peasants but also the nobility, and even in some cases the Tsar's entourage of fawning relatives and bureaucrats. Among the general population, there soon arose a multitude of dissidents led by the adherents to Marxist socialism. This was an ideology that was gaining popularity under the guidance of Lenin and Trotsky, who trumpeted its virtues under the label of Bolshevism. This was followed by the more modest views of the Mensheviks, but simultaneously other factions arose: monarchists, reds, whites, left-wing liberals, right-wing conservatives and others all competing for a place in the Duma.

The Duma was to be the birth of a democratic system. However, three versions of it had failed since the first one was established in the spring of 1906. This had been a terrifying moment for the Tsar since it meant he would have to transfer a small portion of his power to the people. In fact, Nicholas burst into tears as he signed the constitution of the first Duma. At the opening of the first parliament, his wife Alexandra was overcome with grief for she felt that evil now surrounded the royal family and that God would never forgive the Tsar for giving away a portion of his God-given power. The Tsar's agony in granting a constitution for the Duma, which only slightly compromised his autocratic power, had only increased since he submitted to its creation in 1906. The first two assemblies were heavily socialist and collapsed within weeks of their inauguration.

However, in 1907 the newly appointed Prime Minister, Peter Stolypin reformed the electoral laws to allow the upper class to have more influence than the peasants.  Indeed, the country for a short time prospered under his leadership.  However, in September of 1911 Stolypin was assassinated at Kiev while attending an opera with the Tsar at the Kiev Opera House.  The Duma recovered but declined in effectiveness.  The Tsar became more convinced than ever that he had made an unforgivable mistake, and that God for the unholy act of allowing a parliamentary system to infiltrate his domain would punish him.

When the first Borodino-class battleship of the Russian Navy was launched in Toulon on August 18th, 1903, the Tsar christened it the Tsesarevich.  After having four daughters, he hoped this would be a good omen for the next child to be a son and heir to the throne.  Exactly a year later August 18, 1904, Alexandra gave birth to a son—Tsarevich Alexei.  In 1903 when the Tsesarevich was launched at Toulon, France Friedrich was proud to serve on Russia's first ironclad Borodino-class battleship. However, in the aftermath of the disastrous confrontations with the Japanese and the rise of Bolshevism at home, Friedrich wondered if his allegiances would ever again be tied to a Russia and a Tsar who now was sending him and his whole family into exile.

In the latter part of 1905, when Nicholas and Alexandra discovered that their son and heir to the throne had haemophilia, their royal physicians revealed to them that traditional medical treatment could not help him.  As time went on, they agonized over the painful sessions of their son's internal bleeding and decided to have him watched twenty-four hours a day.  A series of bodyguards, or in other words military nannies, were assigned to watch the Tsarevich to keep him from falling or hurting himself in any way. Empress Alexandra's constant state of fear about the health of the Tsarevich became an obsession, since their battery of royal physicians could only console them and give their afflicted son only slight relief for the pain.  With her strong belief in the Almighty, she became convinced that their only hope would be through divine intervention. Much praying and counselling by their priest of the Orthodox

Church ensued, but their son's health remained as precarious as ever. The Empress began casting about for any means of relief, or even a cure for the affliction of her son and heir. This made her vulnerable to anyone with mystical or spiritual connections. Montenegrin sisters guided her to various psychics and introduced the Empress and the Emperor to Rasputin. In fact, Rasputin was not connected with the Orthodox Church at all, he was not a priest or a monk and in reality, his ancestry was connected to the serfs who were freed by Tsar Alexander II in 1861. The serfs, who had been treated like cattle, were given no help in making their own way among the Russian peasantry and became known as Mouzhiken. Rasputin had roamed the Siberian forests near Tobolsk, which was a settlement east of the Ural Mountains. Incidentally, Tobolsk was a town that was near where the royal family would die in a hail of bullets. Rasputin grew up in the typical Mouzhik lifestyle that consisted of pilfering from established settlers and living off the land. Eventually, he discovered that he could influence people through a smattering of religious beliefs that he had acquired from various sources. He soon portrayed himself as an emissary of God and, indeed, often would portray himself as a reincarnation of Jesus Christ. As his clever antics improved, he influenced even more of the itinerant Mouzhiken around him and used his religious image to acquire everything from money, to food, to liquor, to fine clothes and of course, to amorous connections with any woman who took his fancy.

When the Montenegrin sisters introduced him to the Tsar and the Empress, the royal couple were quite impressed with his soothing demeanour and took him directly to see the ailing Tsarevich who at the time was suffering yet another session of agonizing internal bleeding. Rasputin had prepared for the occasion and when he was taken to Tsarskoe Selo he presented the whole family with gifts, and in his practiced religious eloquence soon had the four Grand Duchesses laughing and even Alexei smiling who momentarily had forgotten his painful leg. Rasputin leaned and touched the boy's leg and the bleeding stopped. From that time on, Alexandra was convinced that Rasputin had divine powers and called on him every time the Tsarevich had even the slightest bleeding problem. By 1913,

Rasputin was well entrenched with the royal family and, revelling in his exalted position became increasingly influential in his role as their royal religious and medical advisor.

In the early summer of 1914, the Tsar assured everyone that even though Germany was going to war with England and its allies, his close relationship with Germany's Kaiser Wilhelm would hold strong and there would be no conflict. After all, Nicholas insisted to everyone that the Kaiser was his cousin and close friend. Nevertheless, after the Serbian crisis in July of 1914, as Kaiser Wilhelm's armies were advancing, Russia was forced to declare war on Austria and Germany. The Tsar and the Empress, in their obsession to shelter the heir to the Tsarist throne continued to isolate themselves in their palatial residence at Tsarskoe Selo, and Nicholas had more or less let his appointed ministers run the everyday aspects of governing the country. The Tsar, in his retiring manner out of fear or concern over the Tsarevich seemed to be ignoring the problems facing his dynasty. They were many, ranging from the war that had just been declared against Germany, to the disastrous defeat in the Japanese conflict, to the slaughter of starving people on Bloody Sunday in January of 1905, to the destitute workers in all phases of industry who out of desperation were constantly striking in an attempt to supplement their meagre wages. In addition, and most important of all, he was ignoring the advice of his bureaucratic advisors, and even some of his Romanov relatives, to broaden the powers of the Duma. Instead, Nicholas and his family quietly continued to sequester themselves at their enchanting fairyland at Tsarskoe Selo with its ponds, waterfalls and paths covered with lilac bowers. Hardly a thought was given to any impending disaster. Alexandra, who had never really been a favourite among the aristocracy, or the complete Russian population for that matter, had always avoided public appearances and was becoming increasingly despised by the Russian aristocracy. Not just for her aloofness but also since war was declared with Germany she was regarded with suspicion because of her German ancestry. As she became more aware of the animosity toward her by the St. Petersburg elite and, indeed, most of the rest of the Russian people, she withdrew from any public appearances and closeted herself with her ailing son. This of course, resulted in her leaning heavily on the advice and admonitions of Rasputin. Even though Nicholas still believed in the mystical powers of the wayward Mouzhik, he tolerated his uncouth behaviour just for the sake of the Empress and of course, Alexei.

Rumours abounded that during The Empress's secretive meetings with Rasputin they were having an affair. This was not hard to imagine since he was having a field day among many women in St. Petersburg ranging from prostitutes, to peasant women, to the idle ladies of the aristocracy. It was not long before her intimate meetings wih, and lavish gifts to the Siberian "monk", raised eyebrows throughout the salons and clubs of St. Petersburg. In a short time, however, the war against Germany surprisingly kindled a spirit of allegiance among the Russian people and quickly spread throughout all of Russia. The fact that his subjects now saw him as the defender of the Russian Empire, Nicholas emerged from his sheltered existence at Tsarskoe Selo as the saviour of Russia.

He rose to the occasion by immediately ordering a general mobilization of the armed forces and had conferences arranged with his minister of defence and senior military personnel. As was the case with most of the Tsar's casually appointed ministers, his department of defence was bogged down in the usual bureaucratic maze under his Romanov uncle Grand Duke Nicholas Nicholaievich the Commander-in-Chief of all of the Russian Armed Forces. As the history of the Fischbuch family unfolded, it was none other than Commander-in-Chief Nicholaievich who declared that Nataliendorf and all other German villages in Volhynia to be forcibly deported to Siberia. When the call-to-arms against Germany was issued, the Tsar's generals were fully aware that the Russian Army was in no way ready for war. In reality, with political unrest rampant throughout the country, going to war loomed as yet another disaster. In the early days of the war, the country was flooded with optimism and the Tsar's political underlings felt that the war would be over by Christmas. Even the Empress was caught up in the frenzy of an early victory for Russia and, along with her two oldest daughters Grand Duchesses Olga and Tatiana, trained as nurses and nursing assistants.

However, Russian royalty, nobility and aristocracy who were quite aware that Alexandra had a brother and sister in the German royal hierarchy did not forget the Empress's German heritage. Indeed, anti-German sentiment by this time as well had permeated the citizens of all of Russia's allies. For example, Alexandra's British sister Victoria of Battenberg witnessed her husband's dismissal as First Lord of the Admiralty and his name was quietly changed to Mountbatten. The British royal family previously unconcerned about their German name of Saxe-Coburg, made it official that they were now to be referred to as the House of Windsor. In Russia feelings ran even stronger, Alexandra's subjects labelled her as a German collaborator and added resentment was voiced by the St. Petersburg aristocracy who were incensed by Alexandra's behaviour as the Empress of Russia. They made it be known at home and abroad that it was far beneath the dignity of a Russian Empress to serve as an ordinary nurse.

As far as the war against Germany was concerned, it was not long before Nicholas realized that things were going poorly on the battlefront. In the first year of the war, the Russian army had advanced well into East Prussia but a high price was paid since nearly one million Russian soldiers were killed. What followed in the spring of 1915 was even more devastating when the much better trained and equipped German war machine, that was now reinforced by troops from the French front, had by the late summer of 1915 driven the Russians back through Russian-held Polish territory and now threatened the Russian homeland itself. During this time, Alexandra had fallen more and more under the spell of the wily peasant, Rasputin. Alexandra detested the Tsar's uncle Nicholas Nicholaievich—the Supreme Commander of both Russia's army and navy. Her reason for this was that at every opportunity Uncle Nicholas made no secret of advising the Tsar in no uncertain terms to send Rasputin back to Siberia. Rasputin, fully aware of Uncle Nicholas's moves to have him banished, suggested to the Empress that Nicholaievich was responsible for the severe pounding the army was taking in Poland and that he should be replaced. Alexandra, with her dislike for the Commander-in-Chief eagerly urged Nicholas to dismiss his uncle and with his God-given power, he should personally take command of the armed forces. Always wanting to please the Empress, the Tsar agreed despite the strong advice of nearly everyone in his government including the Romanov relatives who realistically pointed out that Nicholas had no experience whatsoever in military matters. Nevertheless, in September of 1915, the Tsar left for the army's western headquarters that was located at Mogilev, at the headwaters of the Dnieper River in Belarus. With the Emperor away, Alexandra was now, by Russian law, the official leader of the country. This led to much concern in military circles, since with the dismissal of Nicholaievich they were fully aware of the influence that Rasputin had on the Empress. With a concoction of many incompetent ministers that had previously been randomly appointed by the Tsar, the government was already teetering on collapse. The Empress's unreasonable dismissals and appointments to governmental positions under the guidance of Rasputin continued to accelerate its demise. For a short while, the arrival of the Tsar at Mogilev boosted the morale of the troops, however, their lack of training coupled with his lack of leadership led to even further disarray and casualties among the ill-equipped soldiers.

By the summer of 1916, oblivious to Nicholas, the downfall of the Russia's autocracy was imminent. Russian soldiers were dying by the dozens from exhaustion, starvation, lack of ammunition and even firearms, but most of all the army was in disarray due to the disintegration of Russia's government. Along with the now pointless slaughter of soldiers in the war, the country was falling into economic chaos, which was most evident in St. Petersburg where turmoil was already bordering on revolution. Most of the members of the Duma recognized that political disaster was imminent, and among them talked openly that regardless of what they tried to do Russia was now being ruled by a deranged Mouzhik. They all wondered if the Tsar would ever come back to bring the obsessed Empress to her senses. By now, it was obvious to not only the Duma but also the nobility and the Romanov family that Rasputin would have to be removed. Yet, having been ruled for so long by an all-powerful autocrat the people in this turbulent atmosphere had no one to turn to, to rid themselves of this ruling peasant. The daughter of the Tsar's cousin Grand Duke Dmitri Pavlovich, whose husband was Prince Felix Yussupov, a homosexual who previously had intimate relations with Rasputin, joined together with a member of the Duma, an army doctor, and an army officer, had in concert for some time conspired to rid the Empire of Rasputin by somehow quietly killing him. However, on the night of December 29th 1916, after luring him to an intimate rendezvous with his previous lover, Prince Yussupov, they plied Rasputin with copious amounts of poisoned food and wine, but he remained unaffected. In desperation, they shot and stabbed him until he finally succumbed and dumped his body into the frozen Neva River. Unfortunately, his body was soon found and the news of his death quickly spread. When Alexandra was notified of his assassination, she was overcome with grief to the point of near collapse and in her sadness immediately ordered a private funeral for her holy advisor and healer. At his burial, she stated that as a martyr he would now look down and bless her and her ailing son from his rightful place, which now was—Heaven. Immediately following Rasputin's assassination the Empress called for Nicholas to return to St. Petersburg—an order to which he immediately responded. When he arrived at St. Petersburg, everyone thought that at last he would finally repair the damage that had been wrought on the government and the Empire by Rasputin's manipulation of the Empress.

However, despite the efforts of many of the royal family, including his mother Grand Duchess Elizabeth and his cousin Grand Duke Alexander Mikhailovich, as well as all of the members of the Duma, the Tsar would listen to no one but the Empress. She clearly stated that all of the talk about reforming the autocratic power of the Tsar with an elected Duma was ridiculous. Finally, a royal entourage of over a dozen members of the Romanov family demanded an audience with both Nicholas and Alexandra, they directly asked the Tsar to allow more power to be given to the Duma. Nicholas did not even respond, but ushered his relatives out of the room. The Empress demanded that Nicholas get rid of those in the family that were involved in the killing of Rasputin: Prince Felix Yussupov and Grand Duke Dmitri Pavlovich. As was her wish, he banished them to Siberia. In his obsession to cater to every wish of the Empress he seemed to become even more oblivious to the unrest among the people; the strikes, the riots and the crowds of people who desperately made heartbreaking demands for food. The requests of the royal family, the Duma and the aristocracy did not seem to stir the Tsar and it appeared as though he had compassion only for his wife and son—and for his role as supreme autocrat. By this time, the officers on the battlefront at Belarus were experiencing a wholesale collapse of the armed forces. Hundreds of soldiers were dying, not just from German attacks, but also most often from exhaustion and starvation. In desperation, the army staff at the front telegraphed the Tsar to return. Surprisingly, despite Alexandra's pleas for him to stay in St. Petersburg, on March 7th, 1917, he boarded the Imperial Train and returned to the battlefield. Only three days after his departure the unrest in St. Petersburg had escalated to the point where very few people went to work. Tens of thousands of people surged through the streets. The industrial core of the city was now at a standstill; a sign that the government of the Tsarist dynasty was out of control.

Several of the Grand Dukes of the Romanov family betrayed their Emperor and declared allegiance to the Duma. By now, the Imperial Guards who had been ordered to guard the Empress as well as the four Grand Duchesses and the Tsarevich, had abandoned their posts. The Empress kept sending telegrams to the Tsar at Mogilev but they were returned marked "address unknown". On March 15th, 1917, the General commanding the army at Mogilev, Nicholas Ruzsky requested an audience with Tsar Nicholas. The General had an armful of letters from nearly all of Russia's top Generals, several Admirals and some of the Romanov Grand Dukes, asking him to abdicate for the sake of the Russian Empire and to preserve the Romanov dynasty. Most of them stated that the unrest had gone too far and that a government under the Duma was the country's only salvation. Faced with this over-powering evidence Nicholas turned pale and said that if he had give up his throne it must be ceded to his son, Alexei. Deep down he must have known that his loss of power was because of his weakness in letting his wife dominate the kingdom. However, even his decision to relinquish power to his son was not to be, for his physicians told him that in his son's precarious physical health such a responsibility would be too much for the Tsarevich to bear. Nicholas was convinced by the other Romanov's to name his brother Michael as the Tsar-in-waiting.

Back at Tsarkoe Selo, the Empress refused to accept that her husband had abdicated and dismissed the news as viscous rumours. Even after she finally realized that his abdication was official, she smuggled letters to him telling him that he would eventually rise again to the throne of the Russian Empire. When the ex-Tsar finally arrived back at the Alexander Palace, he found that he was treated with disdain. Even his trusted former aides and servants treated him as if they no longer knew him. When he entered the royal quarters at the Alexander Palace and had to face Alexandra he could not speak, but broke into tears and asked for her forgiveness for failing to live up to his commitment to God to rule the Russian Empire.

The general consensus among the Russian people was that Alexandra was conspiring with her German relatives in the war effort to hasten the fall of the Russian Empire, and that the Tsar was doing nothing to stop her. From that time on, the ex-Tsar and his family were held captive at the Alexander Palace at Tsarskoe Selo with guards monitoring their movements twenty-four hours a day. As a result of the mounting cries that the Empress was a criminal and should be charged with betraying Russia the minister of justice, Alexander Kerensky, a leading member of the newly assembled government, was assigned to find evidence to show that the royal couple should be arrested for treason. Fortunately, Kerensky was a moderate among a wide range of political activists who had formed the provisional government that ranged from far left socialists or Bolsheviks to the moderate socialist Mensheviks to the right wing Whites. After interviewing Alexandra, Nicholas and members of the Tsar's bureaucratic hierarchy, Kerensky declared there was no direct evidence of treason but for their own safety, he privately set in motion a plan to have them quietly leave St. Petersburg. However, Vladimir Lenin who had been banished to Siberia in 1895 for his Marxist ideas that he had modified into Bolshevism, was now living in Switzerland. In early April of 1916, Lenin arrived in St. Petersburg

in a sealed train.  His return to St. Petersburg had been arranged
through the courtesy of none other than Nicholas's cousin -- Kaiser
Wilhelm of Germany.  The Kaiser was shrewdly aware of the
Bolshevik opposition to the war and calculated that if Lenin was
returned to Russia the Marxist father of Bolshevism would increase
the power of his party and pressure the Russian government to end
the war.  It was not long before the Kaiser's wish came true.  Lenin's
arrival in St. Petersburg was heralded with great enthusiasm by the
followers of the Bolshevik movement, and within the next six
months through the iron-fisted leadership of Lenin membership
nearly doubled to nearly half a million from its original three hundred
thousand.  This immediately set in motion calls for Nicholas and
Alexandra to be jailed in the Peter and Paul Fortress for treason.
Summary execution was threatened by the hard-liners that included
Lenin himself.  Behind the scenes, Kerensky worked quietly to have
the royal family find asylum somewhere among the Romanov royalty
in other countries of Europe such as Denmark, Greece, France or
England.  However, all requests for asylum were ignored.  Nicholas's
first choice of the country he would be most comfortable to live in
with his family was England.  A country where Nicholas's cousin was
king, King George V, but even here there was only silence from the
King of England on Kerensky's request for asylum—so much for
loyalty among the dukes, princes and kings of the Romanov family.

As the summer of 1917 unfolded, Nicholas and his family were
allowed to walk in restricted areas of the grounds of the Alexander
Palace at Tsarskoe Selo, which was constantly under the scrutiny by a
huge phalanx of guards who scrutinized them twenty-four hours a
day.  Even though he was closely watched, Nicholas continued to try
to monitor the actions of the Russian army, but his sources of news
were limited to asking an occasional cooperative guard or an
inquisitive bystander.  However, everything he heard was negative for
there had been nothing but massive defeats as the Russian army
continued to retreat.  Little did he know but by the early part of 1917,
nearly three million Russian soldiers had been killed or starved to
death.  For a short time, Kerensky became head of the provisional
government and during this time continued to seek a place of refuge

for the royal family. Nicholas in his idle moments, now aware that England had refused to grant the Imperial family asylum, often hoped that Kerensky would allow them to be sent to Livadia, their beloved summer palace in the Crimea. This was not to be, for Kerensky always aware that members of the emerging Bolshevik party would like nothing better than to have the royal family tortured or even executed, sought a place in Russia where there was as of yet limited unrest. The place he chose was Tobolsk, a small town in Siberia east of the Ural Mountains, which had a relatively large residence that had earlier been occupied by the local Governor. This he felt, would be sufficient for the family and a few of their servants and aides who were still loyal to the deposed Tsar and his family. The exiles were slated to leave at 1 a.m. on the morning of August 14, 1917, on a special train. Finally, at 6 a.m. after waiting all night they, with the limited amount of luggage they were allowed, were delivered quickly and unceremoniously to the escape-train. The windows of the carriages were curtained off and the train was disguised with a Red Cross emblem and carried a Japanese flag. Alexandra for some time had been packing things that were collected by the royal couple from the time that they were married. However, what was her first priority? She took as much dress finery as she could pack into the few trunks she was allowed to take. She had jewellery sewn into much of the Grand Duchesses clothing as well as her own. With great sadness and concern about what the future held for them in Siberia the royal family was on its way into exile.

Throughout the Empire, political chaos was now rampant and Kerensky not only feared for his position in the Provisional Government but also for his life, since Lenin's Bolsheviks were becoming more and more powerful. It had now come to the point that any opponents to the Bolshevik ideology were secretly banished to Siberia or quietly assassinated. Kerensky had a futile hope that the train would continue on to Vladivostok and in some way, the royal family might then be able to flee to Japan. The journey of the royal family to Tobolsk was long and with the heat of summer, the closed coaches were stifling. Periodically, the train would stop at small stations where the family was allowed to go for walks in the surrounding forest. As they reached the eastern slopes of the Urals, they passed through the city of Ekaterinburg that was the place where they would be taken to their final imprisonment and death. As they travelled slowly onward and as fate would have it, they passed Perovskia the town where Rasputin had lived. On August 18th, 1917, they arrived at Tyumen a port city at the confluence of three rivers one of which wended its way northward to the Romanov's relatively isolated destination, Tobolsk. Since there were no developed roads from Tyumen to Tobolsk, they had to be taken upriver by steamer. Several days later when they arrived at the dock at Tobolsk, they found that the mansion of the former governor was not ready for occupancy so they spent the better part of a week aboard their steamer before they went ashore.

When they were finally allowed to go ashore they were pleasantly surprised when many of the townspeople turned out to greet them. Most of them were people who had been deported to Siberia by previous Tsars and no animosity was evident. It was another case, however, with the soldiers who had been sent from St. Petersburg to guard the ex-Tsar and his family. The Commandant had them all photographed in front and by profile like common criminals. Nevertheless, life at Tobolsk was relatively comfortable. The Governor's mansion was adequate but not nearly equivalent to what the royal family was accustomed. Despite these shortcomings, the family made the best with what they had. The Grand Duchesses read, were tutored, would sew and do embroidery work. Nicholas and Alexei would work in the garden and as winter approached they would cut and split fire wood. However, boredom was always with them and much of their idle moments were spent wondering about their future. In this way, the weeks passed as their stay progressed into winter. During this time, they noticed that their guards became more and more oppressive. The family would regularly go out into the yard to exercise and get some fresh air or just to see what was going on around their prison, such as the changing of the guards or to be amused by the stares of curious onlookers. When a new contingent of soldiers was sent from St. Petersburg, they immediately built a high fence to block the family's view. At times when the four

Grand Duchesses were in the yard, the guards would make lewd gestures and shout crude comments at them.

As winter took hold, the Siberian isolation enveloped Tobolsk and communication was cut off from the rest of the country for weeks at a time. The rivers were now frozen and there was no regular mail delivery by steamship. The only mode of communication was by horse and sleigh. When news did arrive, it was sometimes three or more weeks out of date. In early December of 1917, the news finally arrived that Lenin and his lieutenants, Trotsky and Sverdlov, had engineered a coup d'etat by the Bolshevik party that overthrew the Kerensky provisional government. From that time on it was known as the Bolshevik October Revolution. Kerensky rallied sympathetic troops in an attempt to reinstate the provisional government but he was defeated and in fear for his life fled the country. Four years of revolutionary bickering continued until 1921, when at last Lenin's Communist ideology became firmly entrenched. Thus, the first Communist state in the world was established, unleashing a regime of terror that would last for three-quarters of a century.

The next news that arrived at Tobolsk was that wholesale looting and vandalism was taking place in St. Petersburg. The Winter Palace was totally ransacked and Tsarskoe Selo suffered the same fate. In a few days, the routine at the governor's mansion at Tobolsk changed dramatically. The guards were again replaced and Bolshevik-trained soldiers were sent from St. Petersburg. This occurred at about the same time that Lenin declared that the Russian capital would be moved to Moscow. The new Commandant at Tobolsk cut the food rations to the royal family and their servants to barely sustainable amounts. Several of those still loyal to the Romanov's were forced to leave.

In late March of 1918, the Bolshevik government signed a peace treaty with the Germans and had to relinquish over a third of Russian lands in Eastern Europe to Kaiser Wilhelm. By this time, Bolshevik zeal had spread throughout the country and major efforts were being made to rid the Empire of what remained of the royal family. Already Nicholas's brother Michael, the heir to the Tsarist throne had been murdered and most of the remaining Romanov's had fled the country. For external appearances abroad, the Bolsheviks announced that Nicholas would be tried in a Moscow court. However, the more radical Bolsheviks made no secret that the evidence against the Tsar was overwhelming and that he should be dispensed with immediately. As the controversy raged, preparations were being made to take them away, but to where? Furthermore, would they all be going together? In the early spring of 1918, steamer travel on the river from Tyumen was not yet possible and Nicholas, Alexandra and Marie were taken by horse-cart and sled to Tyumen, which was a tortuous journey that left them wet, numb and cold from fording streams and rivers and jarring along the rough and frozen ground. When they arrived, they were told that they were not going to Moscow as expected. Alexandra asked Vassili Yakovlev, the Soviet Commissar who had accompanied them from Tobolsk, if he would telegraph the family that was still imprisoned at Tobolosk, that they had arrived safely at Tyumen. Yakovlev went to the telegraph office and sent no message to Tobolsk but sent a long message to Moscow, undoubtedly, he had been told to contact Lenin and his two lieutenants, Trotsky and Sverdlov, in Moscow as to when he arrived at Tyumen with his captives. Apparenty, Lenin and Sverdlov overruled Trotsky and ordered Yakovlev to take them to Ekaterinberg—to their final destination.   On April 30th, 1918, the former Tsar, the former Tsarina and Grand Duchess Marie arrived at Ekaterinberg greeted by an angry mob of recently converted Bolsheviks who cursed, shouted obscenities and spit on the arriving Romanovs. They were taken to their new quarters, which were rooms in a large home that had conveniently been expropriated from a local engineer who owned it, which was a crime under the Bolshevik regime. Nicholas, Alexandra and Marie were greeted by their new Commandant Jacob Yurovsky. In fact, Yakovlev, their previous head jailer had been found to be too lenient with his prisoners and for this reason was accused of secretly associating with the right-wing White Army. For these trumped up suspicions he was found guilty of treason against the Bolshevik cause and was summarily executed.

In late May Alexei, Anastasia, Tatiana and Olga were allowed to join their parents and their sister Marie. By this time the river to Tobolsk was open and they travelled by steamer to Tyumen which made that part of the trip easier for the royal children. However, during their train travel to Ekaterinberg they were lodged in a coach with a group of Bolshevik supporters and soldiers. The soldiers called the girls Tsarist whores and cruelly raped the three Grand Duchesses in front of their ailing brother. Upon their arrival at Ekaterinberg, they were aghast how desperate the situation was for their mother, father and sister Marie. By this time their captors, revelling in the power they held over the ex-Tsar and his family, prided themselves in forcing whatever indignities came to mind upon the prisoners. In the house that was now their prison, their captors painted over all of the windows eliminating any view of their surroundings. All of the doors were taken out so the family had no privacy whatsoever, with guards watching their every move twenty-four hours a day. Each day they were served a bowl of gruel and the guards commonly would either spit or urinate into it before serving it to them. Whenever Nicholas would ask for even the most minor favour he was sworn at and reviled for having the temerity even to ask. Asking for a favour was an infringement of Bolshevik justice and when notified of Nicholas's misdemeanour Commandant Yurovsky threatened Nicholas that if this continued he would be sent to a slave labour camp to see what life was like for ordinary Russians.

The guns of an approaching White army could be heard in the early morning of July 16th, 1918, and since it was payday for the guards stationed at Ekaterinberg the drinking and carousing escalated. Undoubtedly, the guards were attempting to drown their fears and to bolster their bravado now that an enemy was approaching. Late that evening, when the Monarch and his family were preparing to go to bed, Commandant Yurovsky came into Nicholas and Alexandra's open living quarters and ordered them to get the family together and go to a vacant room on the lower level of the house. Thinking that they may be leaving the country, or at least were being taken to a more hospitable place, the Emperor agreed. Followed closely by his daughters and Alexandra, Nicholas had to carry Alexei down the three flights of stairs to the small unfurnished basement room. With no furniture in the room, they stood and waited. After waiting for a long time, they finally asked a guard for chairs for the Empress and for the ailing Alexei, since they were too ill to stand for long. They were surprised that their wishes were granted. In the meantime, Yurovsky had hastily commandeered a group of men from an array of drunken soldiers and guards that were carousing in the streets nearby. When the Commandant finally entered the "execution chamber" with about a dozen of his armed and drunken cohorts, he announced to the captives that the new government of Russia had ruled that they were to be executed for their betrayal of the Russian Empire. When the royal family saw the array of armament, the realization struck them that this was going to be the end. For a few moments, there was nothing but silence until finally Alexandra shrieked: "No, no, no" and the Grand Duchesses began to sob. Nicholas held Alexei close while the clicking of rifles and pistols being cocked was the only sound from the jostling crowd of men. One by one, the executioners began firing but with so many people in the little room many of the shots went astray. Since there was so much confusion some of the gunfire resulted in the assassins wounding each other.

Nicholas was the first to perish from the initial hail of bullets. In death, he still had his arms around his son. Remarkably, after the first volley Alexei was unhurt but still clung to his father and put his arms around his dead body. Alexandra was also riddled with bullets and died instantly, but the Grand Duchesses who had crouched down behind their parents were still alive and screaming for help. Even though bullets had struck them they seemed to be relatively unhurt, probably because much of the jewellery and coins that had been sewn into their clothing deflected the bullets. When some of the drunken executioners saw that the girls were still alive they began stabbing them with bayonets and smashing their heads with rifle butts. When it was all over some of the conscripted killers who, as they began sobering from their alcoholic state, were struck with the realization of what they had done and left in humiliation, disgust or fright. The Commandant had arranged to have trucks and wagons ready and with the few guards that remained had them carry the bodies to the waiting transport vehicles.

As the bodies were brought out it was later rumoured that at least two of the Grand Duchesses may still have been alive, but even so were thrown onto the waiting vehicles. In the dark of the early morning of July 17, 1918, the bodies of the former Emperor, his Empress, his four Grand Duchesses and his son Tsarevich Alexei, the future Tsar of the largest Empire in the world, were carted away like trash into the Siberian wilderness. No planning seems to have taken place as to where their bodies were to be hidden. It was later found that they were thrown down an old mining shaft in the forest near Ekaterinberg. One of the main concerns of the Bolshevik hierarchy was to keep the massacre of the Imperial Family secret, but the opposite occurred. By the next day, the whole city of Ekaterinberg had heard or were told of the gunfire and screams in the night. Furthermore, accounts circulated by the drunken assassins added even more tales about the events of the massacre.

It was not long before the general populace heard about the contents of the mineshaft and inquisitive voyeurs soon invaded the underground tomb. The Bolsheviks were now afraid that news of the botched execution of the royal family would spread like wildfire. Consequently, they quickly had the bodies moved further into the wilderness and buried in a shallow grave where they remained for the next seventy years during the silence of the Communist era. When Communism was dismantled and the Soviet Union dissolved in 1990, the Imperial Family's remains were exhumed and now rest in the Cathedral of Peter and Paul in St. Petersburg, and lie among the remains of all of the Russian Tsars and their families that had been buried there since the time of Peter the Great.

# Chapter 13

# The 1915 Deportation

After the Deportation Order came in July of 1915 and as Friedrich, Henrietta and the children were forced into exile by the strazhniks, they were now caught up in the crises that were evolving in Russia. There was the struggle to form a viable government in the Duma, Kerensky's establishment of the Provisional Government, the rise of Lenin's Bolshevism, and yet to come was the Tsar's abdication and finally the execution. There is little wonder that the tribulations of Friedrich, Henrietta and the rest of the families would only escalate.

As Friedrich, Henrietta and the children were being forced into exile the first few days were difficult but unknown to them their situation would only get worse. As the captives were forced along, the strazhniks seemed to take pleasure in their power to whip anyone who fell behind. Friedrich struggled to keep Henrietta and the children ahead of him and consequently the sting of the whip strands on his back became commonplace. As they plodded along day after day, he pondered about what the future held for them; surely this torture would some day end, but as each day passed there was no respite. At nightfall, they were allowed to stop and since the caravan was travelling along a river, they were able to get water and to eat the limited amount of food that they had been able to carry with them. On the eleventh day, they came to a large town and as always, they struggled to stay ahead of the ever-menacing strazhniks. About mid-day, they were allowed to stop along a railroad track and in the distance they saw a train. The strazhniks ordered them to wait as the train slowly steamed toward them. A few yards away Friedrich noticed an orchard with apples hanging from the trees. He took young Robert by the hand and since they were standing at the rear of the group, they quietly crept into the orchard. They quickly picked some apples and wrapped them in a shawl that Henrietta had quietly given them before they went into the orchard. They then casually slipped back to the end of the line of their group. The strazhniks and the deportees were engrossed in watching the approaching train and did not notice as Friedrich and Robert got back into line.

By this time, many of the exiles were near the point of exhaustion from the days of forced march. The wife of the old man who, when they were first forced to walk and had been struck down by one of the strazhniks and left to die, was now totally exhausted and in the past few days she had been helped along by fellow captives. When guards on the train saw her struggling to get into one of the cattle cars they pushed her aside and told the strazhniks to get rid of her. The strazhnik in charge grabbed her by her hair threw her down, and in one quick motion stabbed her with his bayonet. Some of the women in the group screamed in fear and terror, but the guards yelled at them to be quiet and said that if they were not able to get into the train the same would happen to them. The refugees rushed toward the train in the hope that they would not be singled out by the guards. Being at the end of the line Friedrich, Henrietta and the children barely got into the last open cattle car before the guards slid the doors shut. Once inside, they found there were only about ten other people with them. They were all so exhausted that no one noticed or even cared that there was nothing in their car to lie on, not even straw or hay. They either all sat against a wall or collapsed onto the floor. As the train passed slowly through the town, Friedrich stretched to look between the slats on the side of the cattle car and on the railway station he noticed the name "Poltava", which he knew was a small city about four hundred miles from Novograd Volinskiy. He surmised that their destination was to be Kharkov, but as he would soon find they would be going well beyond Kharkov.

Friedrich woke from a fitful sleep early the next morning to the clicking of steel on steel as the wheels of the train moved over the rails. Young Robert and Olga lay sleeping where they had dropped to the floor late the previous day. Henrietta was awake and sitting up holding sleeping eight-year-old Ida in her arms. When her mother moved Ida awoke and the first thing she said was that she was hungry. It was not long before Robert and Olga stirred and saw Friedrich standing over them asking if they were hungry. They all sat up and ate apples and some crusts of dry bread that Henrietta carefully divided for each of them. Their travelling companions at the other end of the cattle car looked at them eating their apples and since they appeared to have nothing to eat, Henrietta took the remaining apples to them. As the day wore on, everyone found they had to relieve themselves. The group decided they would use the far end of the cattle car as a toilet so they could stay as far away as possible from the smell. Late the next day, they were able to see that they were approaching a city. Friedrich assumed it would have to be Kharkov and felt that now that they were so far from Nataliendorf and Kiev that this must be their destination. However, the train did not even slow down and steamed on into the darkness. The next two days were agonizing for everyone; Henrietta's last bit of bread had been eaten and they had no water. The children were crying and every few moments would plead with Henrietta that they were thirsty.

Toward mid-day, the train slowed and everyone peered out through the slatted walls to see what might be in store for them. More and more houses appeared and everyone hoped that they were entering a town where the train would stop and they could somehow find some food and water. In a short time, they stopped at a railroad station where they saw that the name of the settlement was Woronesch and noticed there were many small tents and other makeshift shelters adjacent to the railroad station. As soon as the train stopped, the guards opened the doors to the cattle cars and ordered the prisoners to get out. When everyone had emerged from the train, the guards herded them to a large compound in the centre of the tent encampment next door. It turned out that the people housed in the tents were a group of other Volhynian refugees that had been here for some time.

Friedrich and Henrietta's group were taken to what appeared to be a soup kitchen in the centre of the compound. This was a relief to everyone for they could see people leaving the line-up carrying bread and bowls filled with what appeared to be soup. As Friedrich, Henrietta and the children waited patiently in the line they became even more hungry and thirsty now that food and drink was nearby. Suddenly, Friedrich heard his name being called. He turned to see who it could be, to his astonishment it was his brother Johann with his wife Wilhelmina. As they approached each other, neither of them could speak. Finally, Friedrich said that surely this ordeal would be over soon and that they both would be glad to get back to Nataliendorf where the rest of the families would be waiting for them. Both Johann and Wilhelmina looked tired and drawn. They said that by chance they had discovered Wilhelmina's parents who had been deported earlier and that they were all now staying together in a small tent. Johann said they were told that they would be taken to Samara, but had already been waiting for ten days and had no idea when they would be taken away. They said that they were allowed only one piece of bread and a bowl of watery soup each day, which was hardly enough to sustain them. Wilhelmina said that her mother was very ill and she hoped that it was not the dreaded Typhus. They were also concerned about the two youngest children, Meta and Erhart who were becoming very weak, so they hoped that they would be able to find less crowded conditions and some way to get more food when they got to Samara. Just then, a guard came up and demanded to know why Johann was talking to the new arrivals and ordered them to get back to their place in the compound. He then shoved his rifle butt into Johann's back and forced Wilhelmina violently along behind Johann. Friedrich and Henrietta had no time to say goodbye, or even wave because their own guard pushed them toward the bread line and told them to hurry and get their food for the train would soon be leaving.

Their concern about Johann and Wilhelmina was still on their minds as they hurried the children through the line-up. They were given a full loaf of bread and a small bucket of soup for the five of them. Their unrelenting guard quickly pushed them toward the train where they scrambled into the last cattle car just before the door was slammed shut. As they looked around they found that the car was filled to near capacity leaving standing room only. They made their way to a corner where Henrietta sat down and cradled little Ida on her lap, to feed her some of the thin barley soup while Friedrich, Olga and Robert quickly ate the remainder of the ration. Henrietta saved half of the bread and wrapped it carefully in her shawl. As she tucked it carefully behind her, she wondered what might be happening to Eduard and if he was getting enough food. When the children were born and they were all together back at Nataliendorf, no one ever went hungry so his was a new and devastating experience for her. Henrietta was often reminded of Eduard since the children at times would ask when they would see their father again. She desperately hoped that he would not be harmed in the war and tried to convince herself that Eduard would be back at Nataliendorf when they were allowed to return. One of the men nearby asked Friedrich where they were from and told him that they were from Zhitomir. The man said that when they were forced from their home, two of their children were away at school and when they pleaded with the strazhniks to wait for their children, they were forced to leave. He said that he and his wife were terribly worried about the children, and said that despite the ghastly deportation ordeal of the ethnic Germans, Friedrich and Henrietta were fortunate to have their children with them. He also told Friedrich that he had heard the guards talking at their stop at Woronesch that the train was going as far as Ufa, a city at the western foothills of the Ural Mountains and it was then to go back for more German exiles. The guards had also said that on their present route there would be no more stops until they got to Ufa.

The train travelled continuously for the next three days, and within the crowded interior of the cattle car in which they were enclosed the stench of feces and urine became overpowering. When the train finally stopped at a small railroad station, even the guards retched as they walked past the over-loaded cattle cars. Apparently, some of the Volhynians who had been waiting for days at Woronesch in desperation, had slipped unnoticed onto their train in the vague hope there would be better conditions at the train's destination—

wherever that would be. The extra human cargo in the cattle cars must have bothered the head strazhnik guard in charge to such an extent that the decision was made to rid the train of some of the smelly cargo. The doors were opened and more than half of the people were ordered to get out and fend for themselves in the surrounding countryside. No thought whatsoever was given as to where they were to go, or how they were to survive. Friedrich, Henrietta and the children had stayed in the cattle car when they heard the orders to get out and in a short time, those who had left the cars were gone. No one knew as to who was to go, families were separated, some were old and weak from hunger and some were children who were alone and crying for their parents. All were begging for food and water but the guards forced them off into the forest.

Several of the guards were then ordered to swab out the cattle cars with mops and buckets of water. As a guard came by, Friedrich asked him if he could clean out the excrement in their cattle car. The guard was glad to hand him a big bucket of water, a mop and a shovel. Friedrich immediately poured some of the water into the pail that they had been given at Woronesch to carry their soup, so that they for a while would have a bit of water to drink and to be able to wash. With Henrietta's help, they quickly did their best to scrape and scrub the smelly deposits out of the cattle car. Just before the door was rolled shut, the guard reached in for the cleaning utensils, but Friedrich held out only the mop and shovel and kept the large pail so that they would be able to use it to relieve themselves. As they looked around, they found that they had only about a dozen travelling companions. For the next four days they travelled much as before, but now had room to move around and were able to avoid some of the smell of the passengers relieving themselves by using the big bucket. When they arrived at Ufa, everyone was anxious to find out what would happen to them now that they were at the end of the train route. As before, the guards opened the doors and ordered everyone out, but again they were only interested in getting rid of their prisoners. When the deportees were released, they wandered listlessly in various directions. They now were all weak, hungry, thirsty and cold. As night came Friedrich, Henrietta and the children along with several other people walked as far as they could toward the centre of town hoping that somehow they would find some food and shelter. They approached some people on the street and asked them where they could find some help but the men in the group said that they had known for some time that the ethnic Germans were being sent to Russia's interior for collaborating with the German invaders, and there was no way they would find refuge among the native people.

Friedrich's destitute group finally found shelter in an old barn near the outskirts of Ufa, and at last got a bit of respite by sleeping on the straw that was scattered in one corner of the barn. The next day the men and a few of the women went into the main part of the city to try to seek some work to get some money to buy food. They were greeted with nothing but suspicion since the city had been inundated with ethnic German exiles, not only from Volhynia but also from the Crimea, the Volga, Belarus and Odessa. As a last resort, several of the women in the group went out and begged for food near one of the markets. One of them came back with several loaves of mouldy bread that they divided among their companions in the barn.

After a few days, some of the group drifted off on their own to try to find some means of survival. Friedrich said to Henrietta that perhaps they should go into the forested countryside where they might somehow put together a dwelling of sorts out of trees and branches, and gather roots and berries to quell their hunger. Friedrich also thought that he might find work at some isolated farmstead away from places where people were not so aware of the ethnic German refugees. Two days later, they decided that despite the fact they would be leaving their fellow exiles, they left taking with them a few vegetables that Friedrich and Robert had stolen from a nearby garden the night before. Since Friedrich and Henrietta, and especially the children, were weak from hunger, they did not travel far the first day. Then after several days of wending their way toward the mountains and deeper into the forest, they found wild berries that they ate with great relish and found plenty of fresh water as they followed a stream that would have emanated from the Ural mountains far to the east. Friedrich, Henrietta and the children found a spot protected by a grove of trees with overhanging branches beside the stream.

Friedrich left Henrietta and the children resting under this cover and scouted the surrounding area. About four miles further along the stream, he discovered a farmstead. For a time he stood and watched, wondering if it would be safe to approach and ask if he could do some work for them. As he thought of their desperate need for food and shelter, he finally decided there was no other choice but to approach the Russian farmer who he saw was working in the yard. As Friedrich cautiously approached, the farmer was startled to see him and it was obvious that he rarely saw any travellers. When Friedrich greeted him in polite Russian the first thing the farmer said was, "Are you a German refugee from the west? Are you from the Crimea, the Volga, or Volhynia?" Friedrich's heart sank for he did not think that it was so well known in the back woods of Siberia that the hated ethnic Germans had been exiled to central Russia and beyond. However, the farmer smiled at Friedrich and said that he did not believe that the so-called German criminal "land owners" from the west, who had always been known across Russia as "those good German farmers", could not all be bad people and asked what he could do for him. Friedrich immediately replied that he would like to work, work at anything in exchange for some food or a bit of money for the children and their mother. The farmer explained he had a lot of work to do but he did not have much money. However, if Friedrich was willing to work for vegetables or other food he could really use the help, since his son had been conscripted into the army. Friedrich said that he would come to work the next morning, but he asked the farmer if he could spare some food to take back even if it was only enough for his children. The farmer went to his root cellar and returned with two old tin buckets filled with potatoes and turnips. When Friedrich got back to their camping spot by the stream, the children and Henrietta were delighted to see that they finally had some food. The children each took some potatoes and turnips and ate them raw. Henrietta started a fire and made some soup and they all ate until they were satisfied.

Early the next morning, Friedrich set off for his first day of work and arrived just as the farmer and his wife were getting up. Friedrich sat on the front step and waited for them to have their breakfast. The farmer came out and asked Friedrich to come in to eat with them. He said that surely he would need nourishment because he had a lot of work for him to do. Friedrich did not argue and went in to a meal of sausages and eggs with fresh bread—more food than he had in the last month. He told them that he could not thank them enough, but he would have to stay out of sight if anyone came because he would not want to be recognized as a German exile. The farmer agreed that Friedrich would be well advised to keep his family hidden in the forest. He said that twice already bands of Bolsheviks had come by and each time they took whatever they wanted, including food that the farmer and his wife had put away for the winter. The second time, the passing Bolseviks took his best team of horses and a wagon. The farmer said that he knew now that he too was labelled as a kulak. The Bolsheviks were becoming so strong that the whole country now seemed to be at their mercy. The farmer said that if this new political group deposed the Tsarist regime that not only the hapless Germans, but every Russian who owned land, would be a criminal. During the next few weeks, as winter was approaching, Friedrich worked diligently for the farmer cutting hay with a scythe, milking cows and repairing fences. Now that the farmer knew that Friedrich was a blacksmith, he had him repair some of the farm tools. As the cold weather was setting in, Friedrich and Henrietta knew that they needed a better shelter than the woven branches and logs that they had hastily put together earlier. With a shovel that the farmer had given him, Friedrich cut blocks of sod to build a "home" by the stream. Day after day, he piled the blocks on each other to make walls until they had a relatively comfortable place to survive the coming winter.

As each day grew colder, Friedrich brought as many vegetables home that the farmer would allow him to have. From his trips back from the farm, he had acquired a good supply of potatoes, beets, carrots, cabbages and beans. Friedrich and Robert earlier had dug a makeshift root cellar to store this cache of food. Friedrich had made various utensils for the farmer and made a knife for Henrietta to use to shred the cabbage that they packed it into a large crock to make sauerkraut to add to their winter food supply. By late October, snow already was permanently on the ground and Friedrich was concerned that if anyone passed through the area they might see his tracks in the snow that he made going back and forth to the farm that led to their sod hideaway. Therefore, he was always careful to walk under the trees where there was little snow so tracks would not be obvious. As they struggled to survive the cold of winter during their first year of exile, from December 1915 to March of 1916, Friedrich continued to work at the Russian farm with no visitations by any looting Bolsheviks.

One day in the latter part of May 1916, on his way to work Friedrich noticed a haze of smoke coming from the farm site. As he approached the farm he saw that both the house and the attached barn were burning. Immediately fearing that a Bolshevik raid had taken place; as Friedrich got closer, he became more and more concerned that the Bolsheviks had raided the farm. Friedrich and the farmer had previously talked about the future of Russia and that the German settlers in western Russia would not be the only ones to be singled out as criminals; the Bolsheviks would soon take the properties of all independent Russian farmers.

As Friedrich got to the house, he could see that both house and barn had already burned nearly to the ground and there appeared to be no sign of life. He was sure that the Bolsheviks were responsible so he stopped and waited to see if the perpetrators were still in the vicinity. After a time no movement was obvious anywhere around the farm, so he carefully edged his way toward the burning farmhouse. As he crept closer the first thing he saw was the bloody body of the farmer's wife in the doorway with one arm outstretched toward her husband whose lifeless body lay partly into the house. In the farmer's hand was a kerosene lantern. Before he was shot, he obviously had set fire to his cherished house to avoid letting the Bolsheviks confiscate his home. As Friedrich carefully made his way into the farmyard, he noted that the invaders had taken whatever they could carry with them and that much of the livestock was gone. All of the horses were taken, but the calves that were too young to be herded along had been shot; no live animals were left. Friedrich found a spade and dug makeshift graves for the farmer and his wife at the edge of the well-manicured flower garden. He put a large rock at the head of each grave to mark the property where they had worked so hard for their livelihood.

From that time on, whenever Friedrich would go to the farm, he would often stand by the graves, knowing that this would also be their own fate if the Bolsheviks discovered their hideaway. Fortunately, the road through the forest that went by the farm went off in a direction away from where they had built their sod house by the stream. In case marauders would again appear, Friedrich made a point of obscuring the small trail that had been worn through the forest where he had gone back and forth to the farm. From that time on, Friedrich and the children would periodically go to the farm to salvage anything that they could use to survive. Henrietta had saved the seeds from their winter supply of vegetables and had planted a garden. As summer appraoced Henrietta and the girls carefully tended their prized potatoes, beets and carrots.

However, it had been a long time since they had tasted bread so one day Henrietta told Friedrich she had quickly sewn some money into one of her skirts before they were forced out of their home at Nataliendorf. She asked if he and Robert could go to Ufa and get some flour so that she could bake a bit of bread. Their main concern was that Friedrich and Robert might be recognized as German deportees. It was a long way to Ufa, which meant that they would have to walk for several days. Nevertheless, Friedrich decided that since he could speak well in Russian, without much of a German accent, he felt that he could easily pass as a Russian peasant. Furthermore, he was anxious to find out what was happening in the war and if the animosity against the German evacuees was still ongoing. He warned Henrietta and the girls to watch carefully, and if they ever heard horses approaching not to wait to take any belongings but quickly run into the forest and hide.

The next day Friedrich and Robert packed some food, dressed in their typically Russian clothes, and were on their way to see what was transpiring in Ufa. It took them three days to get to the city, and when they got there Friedrich was astounded at how many German exiles were roaming the streets. It was obvious that they were destitute to the point of desperation. He saw many of the women begging on the streets and was glad that they had their refuge in the forest. Friedrich made a point of avoiding the Germans but spoke to some of them when he could see there were no Russians nearby. He found that not only the German villagers near the Polish border were sent to Siberia, but also those as far south as the Crimea had been exiled. He soon saw that the Bolsheviks had taken over the city and were revelling in their newly found power. He heard that the war was going badly and the Russian armies had retreated into Russian territory. However, the most disconcerting news of all was that Lenin had arrived back in St. Petersburg and now was the leader of the Bolshevik faction. It was obvious to Friedrich that control of the Empire was slipping away from the Tsar and it would only a matter of time before Lenin and his brutal Bolshevik party would have control of the country. Friedrich had to enquire at many different places before he finally found an underground market where he could buy flour, sugar and tea—all at inflated prices. Nevertheless, he had enough coins to get as much flour as he felt that he and young Robert could carry on the long way back to their sod house, but he knew that Henrietta would be happy finally to have some flour. It had been a long time since they had bread, especially freshly baked bread.

When they arrived back at their secluded sod house, Henrietta was anxiously awaiting their arrival for she had to tell them what had occurred in their absence. She said that shortly after Friedrich and Robert had left and when they were in the forest searching for roots and berries, they heard horses approaching and men talking so they quickly hid in some bushes. As the cavalcade passed nearby they heard the men say that when they had gone by the farm it was obvious that someone had been there and had buried the kulak farmer and his wife, after they in their role as "authorities" had seized the possessions that rightfully belonged to the state. They went on to say that someone else must be living nearby and that when they passed this way again they should check the area more thoroughly. This close encounter was an indication of what the future might hold for them; Friedrich felt they were fortunate they had not yet been discovered. After all, they had been hiding here for nearly a year and he feared that it was only a matter of time before they would be found. The rest of the summer passed relatively uneventfully and they began to prepare for the next winter, harvesting their vegetables and picking roots and berries. However, in late November of 1916, Robert and the girls had wandered well into the forest through the freshly fallen snow. Early the next morning they woke to the sound of men shouting and heard the pounding of horse's hooves.

The wandering Bolsheviks had finally found them. Friedrich knew there was no way that they could escape, so he told the children and Henrietta not to resist and go along with anything the marauders wanted. Three men came storming into the sod house and when they saw there was little of value to take, they said that it was obvious that these were escaped German traitors and spies. "Should we waste bullets to kill them, or should we take them to Ufa and use these traitors to work for the Bolshevik cause?" Friedrich was told to get them all out and start walking and they were being taken to Ufa to work to compensate for their spying for the German enemy. As they left their sod house, Henrietta quickly picked up their jackets that were by the door and they were on their way into the freezing cold. For the next three days, their captors forced them to walk through snow that sometimes was up to their waists. When they faltered, the Bolsheviks would ride their horses against them. After the second day, Friedrich had to alternate carrying young nine-year-old Ida and eleven-year-old Olga. By the time they arrived at the outskirts of Ufa all five of them were stumbling along near total exhaustion.

During their march, they had no food or water. It was only when their captors stopped to feed their horses that they were able to eat handfuls of snow. As their captors stopped to rest and were arguing as to which Bolshevik encampment they should deposit their captives Henrietta, Friedrich and the children fell into the snow and lay there hoping to rest for a few moments. Suddenly, gunfire erupted from the nearby forest and the Bolshevik leader fell from his horse with blood spurting from a wound in his neck  The others, not knowing where the shots were coming from, leaped onto their horses and headed toward the cover of the forest where they were met by another hail of bullets.  The captor in the lead fell from his horse during the first volley and the remaining four fled into the forest.  When this new wave of attackers emerged from the forest, they spotted Friedrich, Henrietta and the children.  One of them rode up to where the family was huddled in the snow and asked if they were part of the Bolshevik group.  Friedrich explained that they had been deported from near the Polish border and now had to wait for their exile to end so they could go back to their home.  The man said that he was a soldier in the White army and that as long as Kerensky was head of the Provisional Government the White army was the official armed force of Russia.  He then told Friedrich to go where he wished, but to stay away from the Bolsheviks.  With that, he turned and rode away with the rest of his armed men.  Friedrich and Henrietta looked at each other and did not know what to make of their situation.  Here they were no longer prisoners but were cold, weak and hungry.

## Chapter 14

## Bolshevik Internment at Ufa

Since Friedrich, Henrietta and the children needed shelter and food, the only thing they could do was to get to Ufa as soon as they could in the faint hope that they could get some help; night was falling and it was bitterly cold. As they struggled their way toward the city, a sawmill was the first set of buildings they encountered. No one was in sight so they made their way to an open structure, which contained piles of sawdust and shavings. Exhausted as they were, they dug their way into the shavings until they were completely covered and they all immediately fell fast asleep. Early the next morning the noise of the workers in the sawmill woke them and they cautiously crept out of their bedding place and carefully stayed out of sight of the workers until they were well on their way from the sawmill. When they entered the city, they encountered people on the streets, but found no stores or markets. Finally, Friedrich spoke to a man, and told him that they had had nothing to eat for the past week and asked where they could find a place to get food. The man said there was a market about a mile away but by this time of the day there would be very little food left.

They walked on in a desperate hope that they could find something to eat, even if they had to beg for it. When they got to the market most of the stalls were closed. Young Robert spotted some wilted cabbage leaves on the ground in one of the empty stalls and all five of the family hurried into the stall and ate them as soon as they found them, even the ones that had been trampled into the mud. As they slowly wandered on into the city a kindly appearing Russian man came up to them and said, "You must be German exiles from the west". He told them he knew of a place where they could find work and have food and shelter. With this, he started to walk away and motioned them to follow. Friedrich thought about their situation for a moment and even though he was afraid of what they might be getting into. He truly hoped this was another sympathetic Russian like their farmer friends were. However, Friedrich realized that even though the farmer and his wife were Russians, there was no quarter given and the Bolsheviks just for the dire sin of owning property murdered them.    The man led them to a building where they saw a row of tables and a back room that appeared to be a kitchen; he told them to sit down and he would get them something to eat. In a short time, he came back with a pot of watery cabbage soup and some dry black bread. Henrietta first dished up soup for the children and then measured out the rest for herself and Friedrich. There was just enough to take the edge from their hunger. They were soon to find that the "kind" man was the Bolshevik Commandant of a communal farm that consisted of several smaller farms that had been owned by a group of Mouzhiken who had seen fit to rise above their itinerant existence. This now was the Bolshevik headquarters in Ufa.

Within the next few days, they became aware of their fate; all of the Germans detained at the Bolshevik compound were assigned to a contingent of workers. Friedrich was put to work in the fields, and even though it was still winter they had to haul manure onto the fields to fertilize the soil for summer planting. Henrietta and the girls were kept in the camp to clean the Bolshevik living quarters and work in the kitchen. Robert was assigned work in the cattle barns, milking and feeding cows. Henrietta and the children were not allowed to stay with Friedrich but were assigned to separate barracks. The German men were housed in an old barn far removed from the women and children. Undoubtedly, this was done to discourage anyone from trying to escape, since fathers would be less likely to leave without their wives and children. After his twelve hour shift, and as he sat at the tables where they ate their limited amount of food, Friedrich would occasionally get a glimpse of Henrietta or the children at the evening meal, but there was little opportunity to communicate, since a guard was posted at the end of each table.

When they were finished their meal the men were herded like cattle back to the barn where they had to sleep on a cold plank floor. However, some of the workers that arrived early were able climb into the few straw-filled mangers. This became the continuous routine for Friedrich—work twelve hours a day for seven days a week, sleep on a hard wooden floor and suffering constant hunger; the food ration consisted of mouldy black bread and watery soup once a day. His only respite was that after they found out that he was a blacksmith they allowed him to shoe their horses. For Henrietta and the children their routine was no better—washing clothes, making food for the Bolshevik elite and catering to their every wish. After all, they were German spies and had to be constantly kept busy so they would not be able to escape or send messages to the enemy.

It was now late in January of 1917, and every day Friedrich tried to think of some plan to escape from their internment. One day Friedrich heard the camp guards talking about the turmoil in St. Petersburg and that the Tsar was still at the battlefront, supposedly in command of the Russian army. They laughed at the fact that he had failed miserably to halt the wholesale retreat of the Russian army. They also said that the Tsarina's lover, Rasputin had been murdered in St. Petersburg and that even though Kerensky was still head of the Provisional Government it was only a matter of time before Lenin would overthrow Kerensky's shaky hold on power. They said now that Lenin was back in the country he had already invigorated the Bolshevik cause. After hearing this, Friedrich wondered if they would ever get away from their sentences as Bolshevik slaves. He resolved that in some way he must try to escape and get them all back to Nataliendorf; however, how would he be able to get Henrietta and the children away? Henrietta, isolated from any contact with Friedrich, despaired every day about being held hostage. She agonized about the fate of her husband; was Eduard still in the Crimea and was he fortunate enough to survive as the Russian army was collapsing? Now that the Russian armies were in full retreat, perhaps he got away and was back in Nataliendorf. If that were the case, he would be desperate to know what had happened to his family.

As the incarceration of Friedrich, his separation from Henrietta and the children unfolded at the Bolshevik encampment, Friedrich constantly thought about how he could improvise an escape. However, it would take Friedrich nearly another year before an opportunity to get away would present itself.

Early in the morning on the 18th of March 1917, there was great rejoicing throughout the Bolshevik camp. Friedrich was later to learn that the Tsar had abdicated. For the next few days, the whole encampment was alive with shouts of, "We should kill the Tsar before Kerensky allows him to escape from the country!" Through the summer and fall of 1917, life for Friedrich, Henrietta, the children and their co-workers became an agonizing ritual as they were forced to work from early morning until the dark of night. Then in December, they heard news that was even more distressing. Kerensky's Provisional Government had been overthrown by Lenin's far left Bolshevik regime that Lenin had renamed the Communist Party. Lenin immediately decreed that all land owned by individuals, including the estates of the aristocracy, nobility, or anyone else, be confiscated and divided among the landless peasants by rural peasant committees. Adding more turmoil to the unrest in the country there was widespread mutiny in the army against the officers -- the army was now in total disarray. Mass desertions followed and the deserters were joined by roving bands of Mouzhiken and peasants who looted and destroyed property as they moved from community to community. Further discontent and even rebellion arose among the nobility, the dispossessed landowners, the heads of industry, the Russian intelligentsia, and even the clergy. Nevertheless, Lenin did not heed the masses and launched a deliberate campaign of terror that resulted in the arrest, imprisonment, and execution of thousands of "dissidents" with no regard to their guilt or innocence. The looting, rape and murder escalated as the various political factions were bickering among themselves until Lenin's Bolsheviks finally got the upper hand. This now marked the beginning of Lenin's October Revolution.

By January of 1918, Friedrich had become more and more doubtful about ever being able to escape and even if they were able to get out of the camp how could they ever get back to Nataliendorf. He often thought about what had become of the rest of the family after he, Henrietta, Johann, Gustav and their families were so quickly arrested and deported. He hoped against hope that none of the others were forced into a similar hell that they were experiencing since they had been taken away from their comfortable life in Nataliendorf. By February of 1918, Friedrich as often as possible had been carefully listening to every conversation that he was able to listen to among his Bolshevik captors, and found that all was not going well with Lenin's "Communist" takeover of the fragile Kerensky Provisional Government. The quarrelling among the political factions, the uprising of the soldiers, peasants and rebellious former landowners had now left the Ufa Bolshevik encampment in disarray. Many of the members had left to subdue looting peasants or to commandeer more properties. Adding to their duties, the new government ordered their Bolshevik underlings to arrest or kill any landowner not submitting to the escalating expropriations. By the time Kerensky's Provisional Government fell, the Russian army was no longer a functional body. Starvation and desertion in the army had already been rampant for some time, but now even officers had abandoned the battlefront.

On March 3rd, 1918, the Bolshevik/Communist government was forced to end the war. What followed was total surrender to Germany's Kaiser Wilhelm who demanded nearly half of Russia's European territories. Lenin wasted no time negotiating and a peace treaty was hurriedly signed at Brest-Litovsk. Now that the war with Germany was over and the Bolshevik followers were engrossed with the problems of evicting landowners and trying to control other rebellious factions, little attention was being paid to the German exiles. With so many Bolsheviks gone from the Ufa encampment relatively few were available to guard the German deportees. When Friedrich learned that Russia had surrendered to Kaiser Wilhelm, he noted that there were fewer and fewer guards monitoring their movements. When they were marched over for their evening meal there were now only token guards at the tables. Friedrich felt that the time had come to make a move to escape. One day in early April after the evening meal, Friedrich saw no guard in sight so he quickly went to the kitchen door and asked one of the German women to tell Henrietta to wait by the kitchen door after the meal the next day. When he finished his meal the following day he was relieved to see that the only guard at the other end of the dining area was already gone by the time the meal was finished. This left him plenty of time to speak with Henrietta. He quickly told her to get the girls and Robert together and wait for him just after dark the next day on the forest side of the kitchen area. She said that she would try her best to contact Robert but he was now housed in a separate barrack. She said that the two girls were clearing the garden of weeds to get it ready for planting so it would be easy to get them ready. However, she did not know how to get word to Robert, but said that she would volunteer to take the noon ration of food to the cattle-barn workers and probably could alert Robert. She told Friedrich that she would try desperately to get them all together. That night Friedrich went over his escape plan, a plan that he had gone over many times in the past year and had often wondered if they would ever be able to flee the Bolshevik encampment.

He had devised a route through the forest to get to the railroad at the point where they had arrived at Ufa nearly two years previously. The next day he waited patiently for darkness to fall and when it arrived he filled two cans with water and carried them along with his few other belongings: his overcoat, as well as a pair of shoes that he had stolen from in front of a doorway to the Bolshevik guard house. When he got to the backside of the kitchen /dining area, he breathed a sigh of relief to see Henrietta waiting with all three children. They were overjoyed to see him, the girls were crying and Henrietta was trying to keep them from talking too loudly, but they were so happy to see Friedrich that they wanted to tell him about all of the hard work they had been doing; washing and cleaning the Bolshevik barracks. Robert, who was now fifteen-years-old, told Friedrich that in addition to his cattle duties that he was forced to haul wood from the forest after milking cows. The firewood that he brought from the forest was used to heat the Bolshevik buildings. He said that wherever they were in the forest the wolves would often threaten them, especially when darkness came. Henrietta had brought a sack of vegetables and bread for each of them to carry. Friedrich was thankful that Henrietta was able to bring along bread and potatoes, for now they had food and water to last them for several days. They wasted no time in leaving and immediately followed the route that Friedrich had been planning for the past year. All night long, they wended their way through the forest and shortly after sunrise, they got to the place where they had left the train on their arrival at Ufa. They found a grove of evergreen trees near the railroad where they lay down under the boughs for a much-needed rest. They all soon fell asleep, but they had only slept for a short time when young Robert woke to the sound of a train whistle. He quickly got up and ran toward the railroad track where he saw a train slowly approaching from the east. By the time he got back to their sleeping shelter the others were wide-awake. Friedrich was happy to see that the train was pulling empty coal cars.

As the train approached, they hid in the trees until the locomotive had gone by and then ran alongside the train as the empty coal cars went by. Robert got onto the train first and with his help, Friedrich got the girls and Henrietta into one of the slow-moving coal cars. Since it was only the middle of April the nights were still quite cold and for the next four days, they huddled in a corner of the coal car. Henrietta had brought along a blanket but it was hardly enough to keep them all warm. Early one morning Friedrich saw that they were entering a large settlement and hoped that they would stop so that they could get away from the grimy coal dust, but the train just kept steaming on. As they passed the station, he noted that they were passing through Samara, a city about 300 miles from Ufa. Finally, on the morning of the eighth day, they again were entering a city and Friedrich recognized it as Woronesch, the place where they had encountered Johann and his family on their way to Ufa. During their eight-day train ride, gusts of wind had covered them all with coal dust until they could hardly recognize each other. It reminded Friedrich of his career as a stoker, and how he and the other stokers on the Tsesarevich would be covered with coal dust for days on end. As the train slowed, Friedrich had them all make ready to get off, wherever the train would stop. They were now out of food and had only a bit of water, so they all were eager to get off. The train finally stopped at a station where the locomotive began to take on water and coal. As they climbed down the side of the car, they did not notice that two trainmen were coming toward them from the train station. There was no time to run or get away and in their fear, they remained frozen. As the first man approached he said, "You dirty, black people must be German traitors returning from Siberia, why not stay on the train and continue on your way home?" Then to Friedrich's relief the men just turned and walked away. In a moment, the train began moving again, but they were too tired, hungry and dirty to want to get back into a dust laden coal car. Their hunger pangs brought them back to reality and they immediately thought of finding some food and water.

There were no houses to approach to beg for food and there were no shops anywhere in sight. However, since they had no money buying food was out of the question. It was still only the latter part of April, so there were no gardens to raid for vegetables. Their only alternative was to gather the short but tender grass blades that were sprouting along the side of the road. They were careful to pull up the roots as well so they could get the full nourishment from the whole plant. In a low spot at the side of the road, they found a pond, and even though the water was muddy, they drank it and filled their pails to take water with them. They then took off their outer clothes and even though it was late afternoon and getting cold they tried to shake as much of the coal dust out of their clothes as possible. Young Robert could not resist the temptation to take his clothes off and leaped into the pond. He did not stay long and came out shivering, and quickly pulled on his clothes. Henrietta, Friedrich and the girls were more cautious and knelt beside the pond to wash their faces and arms, at least to rid themselves of some of the coal dust. After eating a portion of their newly found "salad", they huddled together under Henrietta's blanket and waited patiently for another train. About midnight they woke to the whistle of an oncoming locomotive. Friedrich hoped that it would stop because in the dark they would have a hard time climbing aboard a moving train.

Fortunately, it slowly came to a stop to load coal and water like their previous train. Friedrich was relieved to see several cattle cars near the back of the train and as they hurried along the side of the tracks, they spotted an empty car and quickly climbed aboard. They then waited patiently long into the night while the locomotive finished loading. To keep warm they sat close together under their only blanket. Just as daylight was breaking, the train slowly started to move and they all breathed a sigh of relief that they were finally on their way. For the next two days, the train rumbled along as they listened to the click of the wheels on the track. Their meagre diet of grass and grass roots had only briefly satisfied their hunger and again they were hoping that the train would soon stop.

As they watched the passing countryside, several houses appeared and soon there was more and more evidence that they were approaching a settlement. Friedrich said that he hoped that this would be the city of Kharkov, the place where they had ended their forced march by the strazhniks. However, the train did not stop. Hour after hour, the train steamed on and as their hunger pangs got worse, there seemed to be no end to their travel. The second day another town appeared and they all stood at the doorway waiting for the train to stop but it kept moving on. When they had passed the town, Friedrich assumed that it was Poltava and said to Henrietta that probably there would be no more stops until they got to Kiev. He said that it was still a long way away and would take at least another two days to get there. This meant only one thing; they would have to suffer even more hunger and thirst. On the afternoon of the next day Olga and little Ida kept begging for water and could hardly cry anymore since their tongues were dry and swollen. Finally, the train began to slow and at last came to a halt at a water tower—they had arrived in Kiev.

Robert and Friedrich climbed out of the cattle car and walked toward the tower; the trainmen saw them coming carrying their empty pails and immediately knew that these two wasted souls had been housed on the train during the long trip from Woronesch. One of them laughed and said, "These must be German refugees who are finally getting back to where they came from; hopefully they will keep on going—right back to their homeland!" With that he turned a water hose on them until they were both soaked to the skin. However, in the process they both were able to fill their pails as the water was sprayed over them. They said nothing but turned and made their way back to Henrietta and the girls, who by this time had climbed out of the cattle car and were walking toward them. Henrietta allowed them to drink only enough water to take away some of their thirst so that they would not become ill. Robert immediately began asking about food and said that he had seen a small farmstead a short way beyond the locomotive. In no time, they were knocking on the farmhouse door and an old woman appeared. When they asked her for some food she said, "I have hardly any food for myself but I have some sour milk and some potato peelings that I was going to feed to my pigs. You can have some of it, but leave some for the pigs." With that, the old woman pointed to a wooden barrel in the corner. Without hesitation, young Robert went over and filled one of their pails with the fermenting food that the old woman had offered. As they left the farmhouse, Robert was the first to dip his tin cup into the unappetizing slurry, Henrietta and the girls hesitated but when they saw how Robert was relishing every mouthful they all filled their cups and ate until the bucket was empty.

They were still over 50 miles from Nataliendorf and since there was no rail connection west of Kiev, they would have to walk the distance. Their only hope would be to get rides from other travellers on the road. They walked to the western outskirts of Kiev and when night arrived, they found a bit of shelter in a grove of birch trees. They all stretched out together under Henrietta's blanket and quickly fell into an exhausted sleep. They rose early the next morning and began walking along the road to Zhitomir, the German settlement that was about halfway to Novograd Volinskiy, and home. They walked for over four hours and encountered only two men on horseback who were riding in their direction. As they continued to walk along their pace became slower and slower. Finally, a horse-drawn wagon appeared behind them and they all stopped to watch it coming toward them with great hopes that they would now be able to get a ride. As the horses drew alongside of them, Friedrich asked the driver in Russian if they could ride along with him. To all of their surprise the man replied in German and said that he knew that they must be German refugees coming back from their Siberian exile and needed help. He said that he himself had just returned from exile in late 1917 to his farm located on the other side of Zhitomir. He then told them all to get into the back of the wagon and to move his supplies to the front, so they would have enough room to sit in comfort. They all crawled into the back of the wagon and arranged their few belongings around them. Robert snuggled up against a bag of flour and immediately fell asleep. Henrietta took exhausted little Ida and held her close until she too fell fast asleep. Now that they were getting closer to Nataliendorf and home, she dearly hoped that Ida's father would be waiting for them.

Several hours later when they arrived at the man's farm his wife and two children were standing in the yard waving at the oncoming wagon. They were happy to see their father back with them again, for he had been gone for nearly a week. Since it was already early May the mother was eager to get busy and clean up their overgrown fields and garden to start planting grain and vegetables. When they got to the farmhouse, Friedrich noticed some of the windows had boards over them and that there were a few new panes in the smaller windows. The farmer said they could hardly recognize their home when they got back. The barn and granaries had been burned, and the house had been used as a refuge for raiding transients. The farmer's wife said that they all should come in to eat with them and spend the night, since they all looked tired and hungry. After a hearty meal of borscht and crusty freshly baked bread the farmer's wife took them to their only bedroom, and had them lie down on her thick straw-filled mattresses. In no time, they were all fast asleep.

The next morning they found that the farmer's family had slept on makeshift beds in the kitchen—what a difference from the treatment they had had at the Ufa Bolshevik encampment. Waiting for them on the table was a breakfast of fried eggs and crusty bread. The farmer's wife then took out a long ring of sausage that her husband had brought from Kiev. She cut most of it off, took the last loaf of her bread, put it all in one of Henrietta's pails and said, "You will need this and more for your long trip to Novograd Volinskiy, but it is all I have to give you." Henrietta hugged her and thanked her for doing so much for them. She could not hold back the tears and in a choked voice, she said they would remember the kindness of her family for the rest of their lives. Friedrich then said that they must be on their way for he too was fighting back tears. They all walked along briskly, now that they were well fed and rested and by noon they had covered quite some distance. They had just stopped to rest for a while when they saw a group of men on horses coming toward them from the west. As they approached, they could hear one of them say, "Here comes some more of those German refugees, but I doubt that they will find much left of their treasured farms." As they passed one of them shouted at Friedrich: "German traitors have no right to use the roads of the Proletariat, so get out of our way!"

After the Bolshevik cavalcade was gone, they again started on their way to Novograd Volinskiy. Friedrich quietly wondered what would greet them when they got home to Nataliendorf, but said nothing to Henrietta and the children since he could see that they were upset by the comments of the Bolsheviks. In the late afternoon, they spotted an old barn and Henrietta said that she was very tired and that they should stop here to get a bit of shelter. It had started to rain and as well, they needed to rest and have some of the food that the farmer's wife had sent along with them. In the morning, they rose to bright sunshine, which lifted their spirits knowing that now they were nearly home. No sooner were they on the road when an old creaking cart, drawn by oxen and driven by an old man stopped beside them. He shouted to them in Russian to get on the cart if they wanted a ride and asked them how far they were going. Friedrich said that they were on their way to Novograd Volinskiy. This made the old man aware that they were going to one of the many nearby German villages. For the rest of the day they slowly creaked along the rough and rutted road and whenever Friedrich spoke to the elderly Russian man he rarely would answer, probably because he felt compassion for this destitute family, but also felt guilty for helping German deportees. By nightfall, they slowly made their way into Novograd Volinskiy, Friedrich could see that nothing much had changed, except that the streets were littered with trash and little was being done to keep the buildings neat and clean.

When the old man stopped to let them off, Friedrich told everyone to thank their benefactor for the ride, but all the old man did was crack his whip over the oxen and left without a word.

# Chapter 15

# Bittersweet Family Reunion: The Birth of Communism

As it was now late in the evening Friedrich, Henrietta and the children were tired and hungry, but now that they were so close to home, they set out with new energy to walk the last two miles to Nataliendorf.  When they got to the road going into Michel and Justina's farmstead it was very dark, but they were relieved to see a light in one of the windows.  When they knocked at the door Michel had been sitting reading and Justina who had gone to bed awoke to hear talking and crying and came out from the bedroom.  Everyone was trying to talk at once and Henrietta kept asking about Eduard, surely he would be back from the war and was he at their farm?  Finally, Justina said that all of the talk about family could wait until morning for now they must have something to eat and get some rest.  She said that they did not have much food but she would get them something.  Michel said that he would go and get some beds ready, since there was too much to talk about and they should eat and rest for the night; everything else could wait until morning.  After having some borscht and small crusts of bread, they all went to bed wondering what they would hear the next morning of the trials of the rest of the family during their absence.

Even though she was deathly tired, Henrietta could not sleep; deep in her mind she felt something was wrong or why did Michel or Justina not say anything about Eduard?  She was still awake when the early morning light filtered through the window so she got up hoping that Michel or Justina would soon be awake.

When she got to the kitchen Michel was already up and had started a fire in the cook stove and Justina was busy making porridge. Henrietta immediately asked them to tell her anything they had heard about Eduard, for surely he should have been back from the war by now. Michel hesitated, and finally said that late in the evening one day in July of 1916, about a year after the deportation order was issued, that Emil Krampitz, the young neighbour man who would soon marry Eduard's younger sister, Lydia, arrived at their house with a fellow soldier who also was from Nataliendorf. With them was Eduard and he was very ill, very weak and unable to talk. Albert, Emil Krampitz, Emil Fischbuch and the young man from Nataliendorf had been conscripted in late 1914 and had been sent to fight the Turks in the Crimea. Some time later Emil Fischbuch was sent to Poland and Emil Krampitz and his Nataliendorf friend were assigned to the same regiment as Eduard. Michel said to Henrietta that he anxiously asked Emil Krampitz to tell him what had happened to Eduard. Emil Krampitz then told Michel that their Russian Commander had given Eduard a ration of nine bullets for the day and told him to select two volunteers to stay with him, for he was taking the rest of the regiment back to their headquarters at Sevastopol. The Turkish army was forcing them back through the small town where the Russian advance had been stalled for some time. He told Eduard to use his two volunteers to delay any Turks that appeared until nightfall and when darkness came, for them to slip away and find their way to Sevastopol. After the regiment had left, the two Nataliendorf companions volunteered to stay with Eduard. However, Eduard told them there was no point in all three of them staying since between them they had only nine bullets and that once they were out of ammunition they would all three be taken prisoner by the Turks -- that is if they were still alive. So he told his two volunteers to give him their ammunition, and for them to go to the southern edge of the town and hide in the deep ditch full of rushes that they had all seen when their troops had entered the town earlier. He said that if he were able to stall the Turks until nightfall he would join them there.

Several hours after Emil Krampitz and his friend left, Eduard spotted several Turkish soldiers coming toward him. From his cover behind one of the town's buildings Eduard shot once to let them know that the Russian army was still there. He then saw about a dozen Turks cautiously crawling up the embankment toward him and he thought that if he was able to hit one or two of them with the eight bullets he had left, soldiers at the rear might retreat. After carefully shooting his eight rounds, he hit several of the advancing soldiers. However, Eduard saw that the remaining Turks kept moving forward, so rather than waiting to be discovered, Eduard stood in full view holding his hands high waving a white handkerchief in surrender. However, the Turks paid no attention to his signal and began shooting. A bullet hit Eduard in the chest and when he looked down blood was running down the front of his uniform. He then must have passed out, and as he lay unconscious the approaching Turks saw all the blood and must have assumed that he was dead. They continued on their way looking for more Russian soldiers in the village.

Emil Krampitz and the other soldier waited until well after dark and when Eduard did not arrive, they decided to risk going back to see what had happened. When they found Eduard, they too thought he was dead but could hear a faint gurgling so they knew he must still be alive. They carried him as best they could, made their way to Sevastopol and arrived there late the next morning. Emil Krampitz then told Michel and Justina about the difficult time they had to get Eduard back to Nataliendorf. Michel told Henrietta that Emil Krampitz then said that he must go to his home and see what had happened to his parents and if any of his family was back from their exile.

Another reason that Emil Krampitz wanted to get back to Nataliendorf was that he had to see Eduard's sister, Emil Krampitz's future wife, Lydia, for they had talked about setting a wedding date before he was sent to the Crimea. Even before he left for the Crimea Emil Krampitz had talked with Lydia about leaving Russia. As the next ten years unfolded, he and Lydia made elaborate plans. Somehow, they would find a way to leave this oppressive land and flee to Canada.

Michel told Henrietta that they had been terribly shocked when Emil Krampitz and his fellow soldier had arrived back to Nataliendorf with Eduard, and found that he was barely conscious and coughing up blood when he was carried into the house. Whenever he could speak, he kept asking about where Henrietta and the children had been deported. During the first night Justina, fifteen-year-old Olga and Lydia, Eduard's younger sisters took turns through the night to sit a few moments with Eduard. At the time, they had been forced to cook food and serve a contingent of passing Bolsheviks. All that night, Justina sat with Eduard and toward morning he took Justina's hand and in a whisper said that several weeks earlier as his regiment was passing by a field there was a dead Russian soldier lying by the roadside. When he looked closer, he saw that it was his brother Albert and it appeared that his body had been there for some time. All he was able to do was to quickly dig a shallow grave and bury his brother. Eduard could say no more as blood was welling up in his mouth; he passed out as Justina tried to clear the blood away with a wet cloth. In a few moments he stopped breathing.

The next day they buried Eduard in the Nataliendorf graveyard. Michel and Justina had no way of doing very much for Eduard in the short time that he was with them. They were in a crisis themselves since the beginning of the unrest in 1915, since they had been forced to accommodate transient Bolsheviks, raiding mobs of Mouzhiken and wayward peasants. All of whom, now in their newfound hatred of landowners had taken anything that they could use or sell and would force these helpless people to feed and accommodate them.

Whenever they found nothing on the premises to their liking, they would set fire to the buildings. All of Michel's outbuildings had been burned, including the neighbouring community Bethaus or prayer hall, Nataliendorf's place of worship. They had left Michel and Justina's main house and attached barn intact, and knowing that it was occupied, they used it for a place to rest themselves and their horses, and took great pleasure in forcing the family to act as servants. After all, they were nothing more than despised kulaks.

When Friedrich and the children emerged from their beds that morning Henrietta was too distraught to say anything, so Michel took Friedrich, Robert, Olga and little Ida to another room and told them about their father, Eduard, and the sad news about what had happened to their Uncle Albert. Later that day, after everyone had time to absorb what they had heard about Eduard and Albert, Michel said that Friedrich and Henrietta were the last of the family to get back from the deportation ordeal. They then went to see what was left of Eduard and Henrietta's farmstead and when they got back he would tell them the circumstances of the return of the other families.

Upon their return, Michel told them that Johann and Wilhelmina were the first to get back nearly six months earlier and it was a very distressing account of their deportation. Friedrich told Michel that by chance they had met Johann and Wilhelmina at Woronesch but did not have much time to speak with them, because they had been forced back onto the cattle train to continue to their eventual exile at Ufa. Michel told Friedrich that when Johann and his family arrived at Woronesch they by chance discovered Wilhelmina's parents and that in the horrible conditions that they all were living in, both of the younger children and Wilhelmina's mother were very ill.

Johann, his family and the in-laws were kept there for over a year and that their two youngest children, little Erhart and Meta and Wilhelmina's mother had died. They did not know whether it was from Typhus that they had contracted earlier, or if it was from starvation. During their time in exile, they had to make do with only a little tent to house all of them, but to get enough food was their main dilemma. With only a crust of bread and a small bowl of watery soup for each of them every day, it was not long before they all became weak -- they probably remained alive by a sheer will to live. For a time, they traded their few belongings for food but soon they had no belongings left and could add nothing to the little food they had for the sick children and their grandmother.

When they finally got back to their farmstead at Marianin, they found that all of their farm implements and tools had been stolen and most of their carefully built barns and granaries had been burned to the ground. Undoubtedly, this was done by roving bands of newly converted Bolsheviks as they passed their farmstead. The vandals had given no thought to who owned these well kept premises and they took whatever they wanted—after all this was now state owned property so who cared. The devastation was traumatic for Johann and his family, but the damage was done and no one would ever know who the culprits were. Was it the dreaded Bolsheviks, the ever-present Mouzhiken or the Gypsies -- possibly, some of it was taken by their Russian neighbours. Johann and Wilhelmina often thought that if only they had not been influenced by Michel's advice and left for Canada when they had the opportunity to leave. With the trauma they since had gone through regardless of the influence of Michel and the rest of the family, they decided to get out of Russia at the first opportunity.

The next family to return was that of Gustav, his wife Maria and their three children: Lilli who was now about thirteen-years-old, Bernhard ten, and Reinhold seven. When they arrived back at their farmstead at Dermanka, they found all of their buildings relatively intact, but they had been left in shambles by passing bands of vandals who had taken all of the belongings that they had so hurriedly left behind. When the strazhniks had forced them to leave their farmstead they were taken only as far as Poltava. Here they found an old abandoned farmhouse where they lived quietly, passing themselves off as poor Russian squatters and survived by trapping rabbits and growing vegetables during the two summers that they were in exile.

Michel Jr. and his wife Emilia were the next ones of the family to return from exile. Their farmstead was near Michel and Justina's home and had been ravaged as much as the others, but since their return they had kept to themselves and apparently found it too traumatic to speak about their exile. Michel said that perhaps it was too painful for them to talk of their deportation, since their only son Herman who was only a baby when they left had died during their exile.

Emil had arrived back at Nataliendorf sometime in the fall of 1917, and was now with his wife Lydia at the farm of her parents. The buildings that Emil had started to build in 1914, on his new farmstead had been ransacked and torn apart, leaving no shelter for anyone to live there. After they were hurriedly married in 1915, and shortly after Emil was sent to the Crimea, Lydia and her parents were deported to Siberia. They had a long and exhausting trip in open cattle cars. When they stopped by a stream somewhere in the Ural Mountains to dump the excrement from the train and to have a short time to use the stream water to drink and wash themselves, both of her parents along with several other older deportees were late in getting back aboard. With no hesitation, the Bolsheviks shot her parents for the only reason that they were too slow getting into the cattle cars. Lydia had returned sometime in August of 1917, in the company of another family who were from the nearby village of Annette.

Shortly after Emil, Albert and Emil Krampitz arrived at Sevastopol in the Crimea, Emil was promoted from a private to a non-commissioned officer and in the summer of 1917, he was sent to Poland to fight against the Germans, since they were now rapidly advancing across Poland toward Ukraine. Emil's promotion in itself was surprising, since Nicholas Nicholaievich the Commander-in-Chief of the Russian Army had labelled Volhynian Germans as spies and traitors to the Russian Empire in July of 1915. What was even more unusual was that Emil was then sent to fight against the very Germans for whom he had been accused of spying for. When Emil arrived in Poland, the collapse of the Tsarist dynasty was imminent. The Tsar had abdicated and now was incarcerated with his family in Siberia. The country was in a state of chaos and all along the battlefront the Russian armies were in total disarray; ammunition and even guns were at a premium, which made the Russian soldiers relatively helpless targets for the well-equipped and well-trained German soldiers. Whenever an opportunity presented itself, it was quite common for disheartened Russian soldiers to drift off into the Polish countryside hoping to find relief from the German guns. One day after exhausting his limit of bullets, Emil hid in a small grove of trees feigning that he was dead and hoped to remain unseen by a passing contingent of German soldiers. However, one of the German soldiers saw him move and shot at him to make certain he was dead. As blood spurted from his leg, he did not move and the German soldier assumed that he was dead and kept on his way. By the time they were out of sight, Emil had lost a considerable amount of blood and with the last of his strength, he bound his leg with his shoelaces to stem the bleeding. He then must have passed out for when he came to, it was dark. He knew there would be no help for him from his fellow soldiers, since they were in full retreat and would be miles away by now. Even if they had been nearby, they would not have been much help, since all the while he was in Poland there had been no medic and no medical supplies available for his contingent.

As darkness fell, he saw a light in the distance and started to crawl toward it hoping that he could get there before it was put out for the night. Finally, after a long struggle of dragging himself through a ploughed field he used the last of his strength to pound on the door of the lighted house. A grey-haired man cautiously opened the door and when he looked down and saw a bloody and dirty man lying on his doorstep, he quickly called for his wife to come and help him. They carried Emil into the house, and the Polish farmer and his wife washed him, carefully dressed his wound and brought him a bowl of soup. Emil tried to thank them for their kindness in the few words of Polish that he knew to somehow let both of them know how grateful he was for taking him in. He then told them that he was a German from Novograd Volinskiy. The Polish farmer replied in German and said that he would help anyone who was from Volhynia, since the Germans who had fled Germany to settle in Volhynia were good neighbours to the farmers in Poland and that he was glad to help. To Emil's relief, for the next three weeks the farmer and his wife carefully fed and looked after him. Although, they were as nervous as he was, for all three of them were always afraid that the passing German army might search their farm and discover that they were harbouring a Russian soldier. As soon as he was able to walk with relative ease, Emil knew that he could no longer impose on the people who had risked opening their home to a Russian soldier; they had put themselves in great danger from the advancing German army. Therefore, early one morning he bade farewell to his benefactors and told the farmer and his wife that he would always be grateful to them for saving his life and nursing him back to health.

During the next month, Emil made his way to Nataliendorf by walking at night, hiding and sleeping during the day. As he neared Novograd Volinskiy, he climbed onto an open rail car and finally arrived home sometime in the fall of 1917. In the meantime, his wife Lydia who after she and Emil were married for only a few days before he was sent to the Crimea in 1915, had been staying with Michel and Justina. Lydia, with the help of Robert and Zamel had worked hard to repair and rejuvenate their home that was only partly built when Emil was conscripted and sent to the Crimea. It had been ravaged by the various passing vandals much like those that had been left vacant by the other relatives. There was great rejoicing when Emil arrived home, and he immediately wanted to get his new wife into the home that he had started to build earlier.

All of the family had now been accounted for. Sadly, however, because of the deportation, seven members of the family perished, having been shot or starved to death because of the rising tide of Bolshevism. Two of Michel and Justina's sons were killed in the Tsar's ill-conceived war; son August had been banished to Canada in 1906. Their young son Herman had died of unknown causes sometime prior to 1910. This now left ten of Michel and Justina's children still at Nataliendorf, but as they prepared to rebuild their farms, their villages and their lives, they had no idea that even more suffering and bloodshed was yet to come.

During the summer of 1918 Friedrich, with the help of Henrietta and the children worked at finishing Eduard's house and tried to get the fields back in order. Life was very difficult not just for the returned exiles of Nataliendorf, but also for anyone regardless of their ethnic background. Any Russian who had owned property was now also "officially" labelled as a kulak. When Lenin overthrew Kerensky's Provisional Government he immediately issued a proclamation that all property now belonged to the state and that any dwelling and property, including household items, farm equipment and grain must be confiscated. It soon became obvious that the continued pillaging by Lenin's Bolsheviks could not continue without disastrous results. By 1920, over half of Russia's arable land was no longer under cultivation with the obvious result that grain shortages quickly arose. The colonist's great social institution, the community granary that so often had tided the farmers through droughts, hail and locusts in other times was gone. Even seed grain had been confiscated along with any other farm produce that was spotted by the raiders. Inevitably, a famine struck, swiftly and harshly and began soon after Friedrich and the rest of the families got back to Nataliendorf. It spread like wildfire across the whole nation and by 1922, it was not only the German colonists who were targeted, but any other citizen of the Empire who had means of survival was designated as a kulak. By the Soviets own figures at least six million people starved to death from 1918 to 1924. In desperation, Lenin proclaimed his New Economic Policy, which allowed people to retain ownership of previously held land. However, this flew directly in the face of Bolshevik socialist policy and irritated many of Lenin's colleagues.

From December 1917 onward, after Lenin had overthrown the moderate Provisional Government under the leadership of Alexander Kerensky, Lenin's Bolshevik political police that he had officially named his "Cheka police" as well as any faction that felt hard done by during the Tsarist regime. This included itinerant peasants, criminals that Lenin had released to join the Revolution, Mouzhiken and even the omnipresent foot-loose Gypsy's, who all now were free to pillage the vulnerable German or other colonist's farmsteads. The multitude of German colonies in the western part of Volhynia were especially vulnerable. This, of course included the villages in the general Novograd Volinskiy area where so many of Friedrich's relatives had laboured since the early 1800's to drain the swamps and cut down the massive trees to expose the fertile land to establish their productive farmsteads. The raiding bands were most interested in settlements where they were able to see activity on abandoned farms that had previously been ransacked and where the returned "owners" were now trying to re-establish their livelihood. Therefore, the decimated German colonists who had just returned penniless and hungry from exile, like those of Michel and Justina's family were obvious targets. The returned exiles now were desperately trying to acquire seed to grow grain and vegetables and were slowly striving to obtain livestock and tools to provide themselves with some means of survival.

Even though the Bolsheviks had become more powerful after Lenin overthrew Kerensky's Provisional Government there were still fierce and powerful opponents. The White Russians were becoming aggressive in the area east of the Urals, there were the dissident Reds who had split from the Bolsheviks, there were the restless Mensheviks and there were moderate socialists. Furthermore, dissension was becoming evident among Lenin's own lieutenants in the Politburo. All was not well among its members; this included such influential Bolsheviks as Zinoviev, Trotsky, Kamenev, Bukhoven, Rykov, Tomsky and—the General Secretary, Stalin. Lenin detected a growing animosity between Trotsky and Stalin and spent considerable time refereeing between the two. While the Bolsheviks were struggling to increase their power, Lenin sensed the ruthlessness of Stalin. By 1921, Lenin became more and more concerned about the increasing influence of Stalin in the party, and secretly was laying plans to have him demoted or removed entirely from the Politburo. However, fate intervened when in March of 1923, Lenin was smitten with a stroke that left him almost totally incapacitated to the point where he could not even speak. He desperately wanted to have Stalin replaced as General Secretary or better yet have him banished from the party. However, his health continued to fail and he died in January of 1924, unable to voice his wish to purge Stalin from the Bolshevik hierarchy.

Lenin's widow Krupskaya, confided to various people that prior to his stroke Lenin was going to have Stalin removed as General Secretary. Rumour had it that Stalin had become aware of what Lenin's intentions were and was somehow instrumental in his death. Lenin's death triggered a power struggle among all of the members of the Politburo that lasted for the next five years. At first power was held by a triumvirate consisting of Stalin, Kamenev, and Zinoviev. However, Stalin still in his position as General Secretary cleverly manipulated the members against each other. His first priority, of course, was to destroy Trotsky who he fervently disliked. Most of the party elite were aware of the animosity between Trotsky and Stalin. Stalin, initially to give the appearance of promoting unity in the party refused to take any action against Trotsky. Then, to create as little dissension in the party as possible he quietly dismissed Trotsky as Commissar of War. By 1926, Zinoviev and Kamenev realized Stalin's subtle ambitions to head the party and joined forces with Trotsky in an attempt to undermine Stalin. However, Stalin immediately retaliated and in his position as General Secretary without hesitation expelled Trotsky from the Politburo despite the fact that he risked offending many party members who had risen in the party alongside the flamboyant and eloquent Trotsky. Then in early 1927, emboldened by his success he had Trotsky banished from the party and deported, firstly to Siberia and later as Trotsky, now constantly fearing for his life, was forced to flee his Russian homeland entirely. For years, Trotsky moved from one country to another and was able to avoid Stalin's assassins. However, in 1940 after Trotsky secretly found asylum in Mexico the ever-persistent Stalin assassins found him and had him duly executed.

Between 1925 and 1928, Stalin made short work of any other of his rivals. Following Trotsky's banishment he deliberately and efficiently by any means at his disposal including deportation, prison or execution decimated most of his rivals. He eliminated not only the two remaining members of the triumvirate, Zinoviev and Kamenev, but also most of the remaining members of the Politburo including Bukharin, Rykov and Tomsky as well as anyone in the party who in his paranoid state either posed a threat to his leadership or in some minor way fell out of his favour. As his confidence grew, so did his ambition and in his fear of anyone who even vaguely challenged his authority, they were deported, imprisoned or put to death. He was now Supreme autocrat of the Communist Party and had complete control of the Russian Empire. Ironically, this was now very similar to the Tsarist autocrats who had controlled the Russian Empire for the past two centuries. History was repeating itself. For the next twenty-five years, his purges continued and became even more aggressive and ruthless right until the day he died in March of 1953.

Stalin was born in 1879 somewhere near Tiflis in Georgia, which lies between the Black and Caspian Seas. Both his mother and father were illiterate serfs and roamed the Russian backwoods. His drunken father periodically found work as an itinerant cobbler; he was a violent man and beat his wife and his young son. The mother in her misery was devoutly religious and had named her son Josef after the husband of Mary the mother of Jesus. Friedrich was also born in 1879 at Nataliendorf some 1500 kilometres to the west of Tiflis. As both of their lives unfolded during this turbulent period in Russian history, life would eventually become a tragedy for both of them as well as for their Russian homeland. Whenever Stalin's father came home between drunken binges, he would abuse young Josef and the mother mercilessly to the point where they both dreaded to see him come home.

Fortunately, the father died from injuries during a drunken brawl when Josef was eleven-years-old. His mother got work as a servant for a priest, and when Josef was thirteen-years-old she enrolled him in a seminary where she hoped he would graduate as a priest. He stayed at the seminary only long enough to learn to read and write and when he was nineteen-years-old he left. By this time, the abuse he had endured from his father had affected his personality and as well, he developed an inferiority complex about his stature for he was less than five feet four inches tall. Therefore, to enhance his image among his peers he changed his name from Josef Djugashvili to Josef Stalin (Man of Steel). His psychological instability manifested itself in other ways as well. He became very sensitive about authority and developed animosity toward any superior who gave him orders to perform even the most menial task. He acquired a narcissistic obsession with himself, which gave him a basic anxiety of being isolated in a hostile world. He had no feelings of compassion for anyone only for himself. His teachers at the seminary labelled him as a socialist heretic and no doubt were relieved to see him leave.

Stalin immediately joined a revolutionary force and worked at organizing strikes at railroads and factories; this resulted in him being arrested and exiled to Siberia. The fact that he was criminally charged and forced into exile only increased Stalin's hatred of authority. He immediately plotted an escape and soon manipulated his way out of captivity. In 1916, Stalin went to St. Petersburg where he worked diligently at organizing strikes and demonstrations; it was not long before Lenin and Trotsky noticed his efforts. The rise of Bolshevism was now under way and any radical was being recruited to spread the Marxist philosophy among the Russian workers to promote enough revolutionary zeal to overthrow the dreaded Romanov dynasty ruled by the weak and timid Tsar Nicholas II. Once associated with Lenin and Trotsky, Stalin rose rapidly through the Bolshevik hierarchy and he quickly became General Secretary of the Politburo, the centre of power of the Soviet Union, which laid out all Politburo policies and was the centre of power of the Soviet Union.

# Chapter 16

# Agony in Nataliendorf during the Rise of Lenin, then Stalin

One day in early 1918, Friedrich and Robert went to Novograd Volinskiy to see if they could find something to do to earn money, or to barter some of their threadbare belongings for tools to work their land. When they got there, lines of people were waiting not only for work but also for handouts. In frustration, Friedrich decided that he would go back to the farmstead rather than waste his time competing with so many people. Robert said he would stay and search the alleys to see if he could find anything that they could trade or use at home. When evening came and Robert still had not come home, Friedrich went to look for him and as he reached the outskirts of Novograd Volinskiy, he found Robert lying semi-concious beside the road. He was incoherent with one eye swollen shut and had a massive bruise extending from his eye to his ear. As Friedrich was helping him up, Robert said he had spent the whole day going through garbage in the back alleys to find potato peelings with eye sprouts so that they would be able to plant them in their garden. As he started on his way home, a band of Russian youths tried to take his collection of sprouts from him, and when he resisted they knocked him down and kicked him until he was unconscious. One blow struck the side of his head and from that time on, and for the rest of his life, he was completely deaf in that ear.

A few days later Johann, Wilhelmina and their four children had walked to Annette to see if they could get vegetable seeds from friends and relatives that lived there. On their way back, and as they came around a turn in the road they saw two men standing by a freshly dug hole in the adjacent forest; surrounding the two men was a group of Bolsheviks all holding firearms. As Johann and his family hesitantly walked past the ominous assortment of men little attention was paid to Johann and his family. Johann said nothing as they passed and he hurried everyone along as fast as he could to get them past this armed confrontation. When they got further down the road they heard several shots and feared the worst for the two men but what could they do—the rule of law no longer existed. They hurried home as fast as they could and shuddered to think what would happen to them if the Bolsheviks appeared at their farm. About an hour after they got home a man came running toward their house with blood oozing from a wound in his shoulder. When he got to the house, he explained that he had been shot by the Bolsheviks and was unconcious when he fell into the makeshift grave. Luckily, the Bolsheviks had only partly filled the hole with dirt. Johann quickly tore off the man's shirt and Wilhelmina washed the wound. She found an old shirt and tore it into strips to bind the injury. She then said that he should lie down and rest and she would get him something to eat, but he said he was worried that the Bolsheviks could come at any time and Johann's family would be their next target just for taking him in. He thanked them for their help and added that the Bolsheviks had killed his wife and son, so all that was left for him was to hide somewhere in the forest. He said no more and left. They never saw the man again.

From the time that Friedrich, Henrietta and her children were forced into exile when the deportation order came in 1915, and until the time that they arrived back at Nataliendorf, Friedrich had spent much of the past two and a half years with Henrietta and the children. After Robert's encounter at Novograd Volinskiy and the execution that Johann and his family had witnessed on their way back from Annette, Friedrich was concerned about leaving Henrietta and her children alone at their farmstead. Since they had been together during their exile in Siberia Henrietta and the children had become very close to Friedrich. With Lenin's proclamation that the Bolsheviks had the power to confiscate whatever they wished, it had become a daunting task for them to get re-established in what was left of Henrietta and Eduard's home, as it was for any of the German colonists who survived the deportation. Faced with the uncertainty of Henrietta and the children living alone, Friedrich decided that he would ask Henrietta to marry him and that it would be much better to be together as a family. They were married sometime in December of 1918. It was a quiet performance and took place in Novograd Volinskiy with only Michel, Justina and the three children present.

Unfortunately, they had to forego the traditional two-day reception and celebrations that commonly followed a German wedding, since everyone in the family was destitute and constantly were afraid to leave their homes. They had to be continuously on guard to protect their few prized possessions and livestock that they had been able to gather since they got back from exile. As the power of the Bolsheviks and Lenin's Cheka forces increased from 1917 to 1924, so did the harassment of the people who had spent a lifetime working to own land, many of whom clung to their homes and buildings as the Bolsheviks concentrated on confiscating all of the grain and produce that the farmers accumulated. The situation deteriorated to the point where there was not only confiscation of produce, but also the helpless colonists were vulnerable to other atrocities as well. Looting continued as usual but as the Bolsheviks became more aggressive their actions soon escalated to rape, torture and sometimes murder, especially in areas where the roving Bolsheviks had easy access to farms and businesses that were near well-travelled roads and those adjacent to larger settlements. One documented example of the Bolshevik devastation was the case of the village of Friedenstahl, which was located about forty miles from Nataliendorf. German colonists had established the settlement sometime in the early 1800's. In late July of 1919 the villagers, despite the fact that they had little access to seed grains and equipment, were happy that a better than average crop was about to be harvested. When the harvest was completed, the Bolsheviks hearing of this prosperity came to confiscate the grain. For three days, the villagers kept them at bay with pitchforks, clubs and a few firearms. However, the Bolsheviks had no problem getting reinforcements and soon overran the village. A mad rampage of murder, rape and robbery followed. The villagers were pursued and shot in their homes, in the fields or anywhere they attempted to hide. Those that desperately covered themselves with hay or straw were bayoneted to death regardless of their age or sex. Since the church was the largest building in the community it was used as the centre for a great drunken orgy. It was the focal point where they gathered the women and children. They then entertained themselves by raping the women and children while the husbands, brothers and sons lay dying in the streets and fields. After the Bolsheviks had satisfied their lust and their thirst, they took the little remaining food, clothing, grain and tools that were left in the village. Not even a chicken was spared. When news of this rampage became known in Nataliendorf the Fischbuch families tried to arm themselves the best they could. Friedrich kept their pitchforks and scythes at hand and he and Robert made clubs from the birch trees that surrounded their farmstead and kept them near at hand. However, their tools were of little defence against any Bolsheviks with firearms.

Friedrich decided that they somehow must get a rifle or pistol so they could at least delay a Bolshevik raid, in the hope that they would have some chance of saving some of their produce that they had struggled so hard to grow. Whenever they had the time, Friedrich and young Robert went to Novograd Volinskiy and took grain and vegetables with them in hopes of bartering them for some type of firearm. They loaded their treasured produce in the rickety buggy that they had been able to resurrect from various pieces of machinery that the looters had not taken during the deportation, to see if they could trade their goods for a rifle or a pistol. They had previously met a Mouzhik in town who was carrying a rifle, but he refused to take any of their produce in trade. The third time they went to Novograd Volinskiy they saw that a group of Bolsheviks had left their horses standing in the street and were on the banks of the Sluch River carousing and drinking. Friedrich stopped before he got to the bridge to make sure that the Bolsheviks, occupied as they were in their revelry, would not see or hear them when they went over the bridge. He was about to turn around and go home when Robert noticed that one of the horses had a rifle lashed across the back of its saddle. Without saying a word to Friedrich, he looked around and seeing that there was no one in sight jumped out of the cart, ran to where the horse was tethered and quickly untied the rifle. As he was about to leave he spied a box of ammunition in the saddlebag, took it as well and ran back to the cart. Friedrich, by this time had turned the cart around and had their old horse headed toward home. Friedrich scolded Robert for taking such a chance, but because of Robert's youthful bravado, they now had some armament to give them at least a semblance of defence if they would have to face a Bolshevik raid.

Friedrich and Robert had earlier dug a root cellar-like storage pit some distance into the forest to hide a few sacks of their grain, potatoes, beets and carrots that they had harvested at the end of the summer of 1919. The remainder was stored in the only granary that had not been burned by the roving bands of vandals while they were away during the deportation. As the weeks went by, they heard of more atrocities on the farms of neighbouring villages. In the autumn of 1919, Johann's eighteen year-old son Reinhold came by, and told Friedrich that his older sister Elsa was to be married in early February, and Johann would like them to come to Novograd Volinskiy to stand for Elsa at the ceremony, since that was the only time that a Lutheran minister would be in the area. The other relatives wanted to come, but were loath to leave their farmsteads for fear of being raided by the Bolsheviks while they were gone and losing what little food or belongings they had. The wedding ceremony was quickly performed because the minister had to leave for Zhitomir to perform two more weddings the next day. For him caution was necessary in his travels, since Lenin had already implemented his cruel suppression of the churches. All pastors of any denomination were being arrested, as were any community leaders such as felschers and kusters who along with pastors were taken and either imprisoned or sent to slave labour camps.

Emil, who lived at the northern part of Nataliendorf, had already lost his grain to the Bolsheviks but, fortunately, like Friedrich he had buried some of his produce in the forest. At Dermanka, the

Bolsheviks appeared late one night and took all of Gustav's grain, vegetables and some of his livestock. It was mid-winter and not only Gustav, but also all of his neighbouring colonists were critically short of food. Gustav tried to seek some relief from his neighbours, but they had very little to lend or give him for they were hungry and destitute themselves. In desperation he had his oldest son Bernhard, who was only thirteen-years-old, walk the nearly twenty-five miles to Nataliendorf to see if the relatives there would be able to help. Like most of the German colonists they had little to give, but joined together and each family gave whatever they could spare, loaded it on Friedrich's cart and Robert, with his young cousin Bernhard, took it to Gustav's family at Dermanka. As winter progressed, Gustav and his family had less and less food to sustain them as they waited patiently for spring and the growing season to begin. Their food supply had dwindled to the point that they were starving. Their oldest daughter, fifteen-year-old Lilli, in her run down condition, contracted the dreaded Typhus -- Lilli died a short time later.

By the end of 1921, the economic record of the new Communist regime was disastrous. Famine and pestilence struck southern Russia on an unprecedented scale, since agriculture had been completely disrupted throughout the breadbasket of southern Russia. The war, the Revolution, the absence of law and order, the confiscation of the prime farmland of the German colonists and as well as the grain that they had produced from their prrzed farm land led to nearly an eighty percent drop in production. The rural communities had been in a crisis since the 1915 deportation. Fortunately, the harvest, even though it was small, had been good in 1919 and 1920. Still the colonists were left with little or no grain since no sooner than it was harvested it was immediately confiscated by the Cheka. Lenin was pleased with his policy to export over half of the grain that he had forcibly taken from the farmers to finance the newly born Communist regime. However, in 1921 disaster struck in the form of a severe drought that resulted in a near complete crop failure. Lenin, now aware of the sudden drop in the quantity of grain collected and in his obsession to forge ahead with his Marxist Solution, increased his army of "grain collectors" -- the ever-feared Cheka. In 1922, as could be expected, because of the drought he found there was no grain to confiscate and his exports fell dramatically. Too late, he realized that the farmers needed seed to replant and their granaries were empty. They did not even have enough to hide for their own personal survival. The starvation and disease became so grave that foreign countries had become aware of the famine after it became known abroad that thousands of Russian farmers and artisans had died. The American Relief Administration set up stations in various parts of the country, especially in southern Russia. By July of 1920, the organization was feeding nearly ten million people daily in Russia's agricultural heartland alone. The collapse of the farming communities had such an effect on the economy that Lenin was forced to modify his Marxist solution.

Lenin, now faced with the common sense factor of survival, finally realised the fact that farmers needed incentives to produce food. To quell dissent at home and abroad Lenin, as he searched for a solution, decided that despite opposition from his followers that requisitioning farm produce without compensation could not continue. Therefore, to provide some incentives to produce food he instituted his "New Economic Policy," which allowed the farmers to retain title to their land. When the farmers, and in particular the Fischbuch families, along with all of the German colonists, heard of this radical reversal of Communist policy they breathed a sigh of relief and immediately set to work to restore their shattered farms. With this departure from the iron-fisted Communist doctrine, the families at Nataliendorf had hopes that the rule of terror was ending. By 1922, Lenin had eclipsed most of those vying for leadership, and had risen through oratorical ability and sheer ruthlessness as the unchallenged dictator of the Communist party. Unfortunately for him, an event that would have dramatic implications for the Communist Party occurred in 1923, when Lenin had a stroke that left him paralyzed and unable to speak. He died on January 21st, 1924, at the age of fifty-four. This left the leadership role open and all of the elite members of the Politburo especially Trotsky, Zinoviev and Bukharin, as well as the other members of the Politburo. As could be expected, they all rose again to vie for the now vacant role of the all-powerful supreme dictator of the Communist party. However, during the next four years Stalin, who had remained relatively unnoticed, systematically and meticulously eliminated all of his competitors, and by 1928 was in full control of the Communist Party. By this time, he had the OGPU, Stalin's new and more powerful version of Lenin's Cheka, serving at his command. Under Stalin's direction they now had the power to confiscate any property in the Soviet Union and to administer a prison term or death sentence to anyone who obstructed them. From 1924 to the latter part of 1927, Friedrich and the rest of his brothers, buoyed by the "graciousness" of Lenin's New Economic Policy, were relieved that they again had control of their land and worked diligently to get it back into production. Little did they realize, however, that Stalin as Lenin's successor was systematically taking full control and would make their country into an even more oppressive regime than had earlier been envisioned by Lenin.

Despite the tribulations that their family had suffered since 1915, Michel and Justina who now were in their seventy's, were still adamant that the family must stay together, but there was much discontent among their nine remaining siblings. After having lost his two youngest children to starvation during their deportation in 1915, Johann looked back with much regret to the time when Michel and Justina had called the family meeting in 1907 to decide whether they should stay in Russia. He had reluctantly given in to Michel's wishes and had foregone the opportunity to leave Russia and go to Canada. He and Wilhelmina recalled with great sadness that they could have left when they had enough money and their family was still intact. Despite the fact that in 1923 Lenin's New Economic Policy had given them new hope, Johann and Wilhelmina were suspicious of the subtle return of dictatorial socialist confiscation under Stalin's leadership -- they again resolved to leave. They would have to work hard and somehow amass enough money to bribe authorities for passports and to pay for their train and ship travel to Canada. Another problem for them was that their oldest daughter Elsa was now married, and would she and her husband be willing to leave as well? The remaining six brothers: Friedrich, Gustav, Michel Jr., Emil,

Robert and Zamel all felt that they should leave but they had just started to acquire seed grain, cattle, horses and livestock and would have to give up what they had struggled so hard to acquire. Then there was the problem of being noticed by the rising power of the new and more viscous OGPU political police. The final step would be the most difficult; how would they be able to bribe their way through the new bureaucracy to get the proper documentation to leave?

Michel and Justina's oldest daughter Justina-Gustel had not been close to the family after she married Dmitri Bolislav and had become part of the Russian community. They had moved to Kiev in about 1907, not long after they were married. However, during the deportation of all the German colonists in Nataliendorf in 1915, Michel, Justina and the others had lost contact with her and in 1925, they heard that she had died of unknown causes in about 1920 when she was just thirty-eight-years-old.

By 1927, Friedrich's two youngest sisters, Lydia and Olga, were now married. Lydia had married Emil Krampitz who had been in the Russian army with Eduard and Albert in the Crimea and was now the only survivor of the three that had gone through that military ordeal. Emil Krampitz and Lydia were married in February of 1919 and Emil vowed that he would get them out of Russia by any means possible. After his return from the Russian army in the Crimea, he got work as a labourer on the railroad and noted that many of his co-workers needed clothing. At night, with his wife Lydia's help he practiced his tailoring skills and became quite adept at sewing men's clothing. However, not many people had enough money to pay for his efforts, but when he caste about for clients that could afford his clothing he found that the Jewish communities, relative to the German colonists, were the most affluent of the ethnic minorities in southern Russia. He became aware of a large Jewish settlement at Zhitomir and would often make the long trek to that city to sell his wares. As he became familiar with them, he found that for a price they had an underground method of getting travel documents. By the end of 1927, he had accumulated enough money from his tailoring to pay the inflated amount for passports for himself and his family and as well, he had saved enough money to get the Jewish underground to obtain the train and ship tickets he needed to get his Krampitz family to Canada. Emil Krampitz's sister Lydia had married Emil Fischbuch in 1915, just before both Emils were conscripted to go to the Crimea.

Going back to 1921, when the families were still struggling to make a living, and were slowly recovering from the Bolshevik revolutionaries, they had hopes that their lives would soon be back to normal. It followed that the Matchmaker was set to work to find a suitable mate for Olga, Friedrich's youngest sister. A prospective husband was found in nearby Warwarowka. His name was Ewald Degen and Olga and her father Michel were requested to go there to meet him and the family. Michel could see that his youngest daughter, twenty-year-old Olga, was rather apprehensive so he told her that if she did not want to go through with the marriage he would understand and take her away, but she would have to let him know if she did not like the Matchmaker's choice. As they were going through the forest by horse and buggy to Warwarowka, Olga spotted some yellow flowers and told Michel to stop and she would pick a bouquet of them, and if she did not like Ewald, she would throw the flowers down. Unfortunately, by the time that they arrived at the Degen's home, the scent of the flowers had given Olga an allergic reaction and she began sneezing. When she met Ewald and his family, she could stand her flowers no longer and put them down. Michel immediately took note and stated firmly that they were leaving. Olga quickly drew her father aside and told him that she really liked Ewald and she had thrown the flowers down because they had made her sick. The wedding took place in June of 1921, as was the custom. It was soon found that Ewald had already laid plans to leave Russia because of his families devastating tribulations during the deportation, and he had been working at several jobs to get enough money to leave. When he found that Emil Krampitz had connections to get passports and visas he soon convinced Olga that they must leave despite what her father wished.

During this time, Friedrich and his other five brothers and their families had put all of their efforts into restoring their farms, but by 1927, they too were completely disenchanted with Stalin's rising

Communist atrocities.    Earlier they had agonized over Lenin's Marxist view that all religion was evil.    However, Stalin had now moved even further and had decreed in no uncertain terms to abolish religion completely.    He followed this by confiscating all church properties.    His next move was to arrest, jail or send to Siberia any identifiable ministers and church advocates.    This made everyone in the family concerned about Michel, since he had been the lay minister (Kuster) at the Bethaus (Prayer-hall) in Nataliendorf.    However, this did not faze Michel for he still felt strongly about his Russian homeland and continued to rationalize the ominous rise of Stalin.

In 1921, when Lenin's New Economic Policy came into effect Friedrich and Henrietta were convinced that a new economic order would soon be restored and concentrated their efforts on building up their farmstead.    They and the three children worked at any job in and around the neighbourhood doing much work for even a few roubles, or they would barter any spare items that they had for livestock and seed grain for their oat, barley and wheat fields.    Friedrich and Robert scouted everywhere they could for any old iron implements so that Friedrich could make tools and farm equipment to upgrade their newly titled properties.    As they concentrated on restoring their home and fields, they paid little attention to the political infighting among the contenders vying for the leadership of the Communist Party after Lenin's death.    However, the creeping influence of Stalin's brutality would soon come to haunt them.

In the spring of 1924, Friedrich and Henrietta's oldest daughter Olga, who now was nineteen-years-old, was working along the roadway between nearby Makowetz and Annette herding cattle and helping to milk the cows.    She worked with a young man named August who was one of the sons of the Krause family who lived at the northern limits of Annette.    One day they announced to each family that they wanted to be married and that there was no need for the services of a Matchmaker.    Henrietta frowned on the proposal but agreed to give them her blessing.    They were married in the autumn of 1924 and for the time being lived with his parents.

Henrietta and Friedrich's youngest daughter Ida who was only sixteen-years-old was married the following summer to the son of a neighbour family named Missal. They had known this family before the deportation order came in 1915. The Missal's also had felt that everything was going to be better under the Stalin regime and had worked diligently to rejuvenate their farm. With this renewed optimism of their future in the new Russia, young Robert Missal was fired with ambition and worked hard to obtain a farm of his own. Shortly after they were married in 1925 Robert and Ida with their hard-earned savings bought a well-kept farm in the mother colony of Annette. They soon rebuilt the old log home and with Friedrich's help, Robert Missal had good machinery to cultivate his twenty-hectare plot of land. However, in their enthusiasm to build their farmstead they paid little attention to the dark political clouds that were emerging under Stalin's increasing command of the Communist Party.

In September of 1927, Friedrich and Henrietta were informed by the local Matchmaker that the Krause family from Annette had called her to find a husband for their daughter Ottilia. The Matchmaker had selected Robert, Friedrich and Henrietta's twenty-five-year-old son as an ideal mate for Ottilia. This came as a pleasant surprise to Friedrich and Henrietta, since Ottilia was a cousin to their son-in-law August Krause, Olga's husband. The Krause family was one of the first families to settle in the mother colony of Annette and were located just across the road from the farmstead of one of the other early settlers—the ancestors of Robert's grandmother Justina (Moller) Fischbuch. Even though the two families had limited resources, the

wedding was an affair that attracted all of the relatives as well as many friends of both families. It was a welcome break from the uncertainty they all faced during the emerging Communist confiscations.

Robert and Ottilia moved into the old farmstead of Ottilia's parents, however, no one knew if anyone would have homes, for there was always the threat of a visit by Stalin's powerful OGPU police patrols. Ottilia had been a close friend with Elfrieda, Johann and

Robert & Ottilia (Krause) Fischbuch
Abt. 1927

Wilhelmina's daughter who was now in Canada and Ottilia would periodically write letters to Elfrieda, but she had yet to get an answer; mail was already being censored or even confiscated by Stalin's new regime. As living conditions deteriorated the newly-weds were faced with added responsibilities; in 1929 Waldemar, their first of three sons was born. A second son Gerhard was born in 1930 and a third son Willi was born in 1933.

By 1928, Stalin had quietly eliminated his chief rivals, which included Trotsky, Zinoviev and Kamenev as well as others, some of whom were only remotely a threat. His rise in power was becoming more and more obvious and it was apparent in that his OGPU political police were becoming more aggressive. Most of the families heard of properties in neighbouring communities that had been confiscated, regardless if the residents had the new titles to their land that had been issued when Lenin proclaimed his New Economic Policy. On November 7, 1927, during the celebration of the October Revolution Stalin announced his plan to move Russia directly into an "Ideal Communist Society." Firstly, his aim was to accelerate heavy industrial production that lagged far behind that of Europe and other industrialized countries during the Tsarist regimes. It now was at a virtual standstill due to the strikes and walkouts that had occurred since the October Revolution. To accomplish an increase in industrial productivity he ruled that manpower would be recruited from the deposed landowners (kulaks) and their sons. This, of course would also include those that had gained land titles under Lenin's New Economic Policy. Secondly, agricultural production was to be accelerated by combining the confiscated properties to create large communal farms. Each of these communal farms would be known as a "kolkhoz." Thirdly, he proclaimed that on January 1, 1929, Russian borders would be sealed and anyone apprehended leaving the Soviet Union would immediately face the death penalty.

This was devastating news for all of the Fischbuch families; the exceptions were the three families who had anticipated and prepared for this Stalinist disaster -- Johann and Wilhelmina, Lydia and Emil Krampitz and Olga and Ewald Degen. The others, including Friedrich and Henrietta were now at a loss as to what to do. There now was no way to get travel documents. They feared that their land would soon be confiscated. Their personal property was worth nothing since there was no one to sell to and all of them had only a pittance of cash left to bribe officials or the Jewish community for travel documents. By October of 1928, all three of the departing families had divested themselves of their farm equipment and livestock. Most of it went to other members of the Fischbuch families and some to friends. Although, really what was it worth to anyone now that Stalin's political police force the OGPU would soon confiscate all land and belongings? Friedrich, Henrietta with the rest of the Fischbuch families met at Michel and Justina's home for a final gathering to say farewell to the three departing families, who would be leaving Nataliendorf—never to return. Michel had finally come to the realization that his siblings would no longer be together in the village in which he had so much pride; he had always felt that Russia would be the homeland for his family forever. Michel and Justina were now eighty-years-old, their health was rapidly failing and they depended on the family to come and help them through their daily lives.

Taken 1928 just before the 3 families left for Canada
Beate/Zamel   Elsa/Robert "Lydia/Emil Krampitz" "Ewald/Olga Degen"
Emilia/Michel jr.   Justina Michel  "Johann/Wilhelmina"
Emil/Lydia

Michel and Justina looked back with great sadness to the dreams they had for their healthy and robust family of fourteen. Little Herman had died so young, August had been sent away, Eduard and Albert had died serving the Tsar in a senseless war, and Justina-Gustel had died without her family even knowing where she was buried. Now three more of their children were leaving along with their families. In an attempt to ease the pain of departure, Michel looked away and said, "Goodbye my

children, but never mind, we will all be together again -- in Heaven."
Johann, Wilhelmina, their two sons, Reinhold twenty-six, Arnold
nineteen and their daughter Elfrieda twenty-two, were the first to say
goodbye to the remaining relatives. Their oldest daughter Elsa and
her husband Julius Riev had been so certain that Lenin's New
Economic Policy would be their salvation that they, along with most
of the others in the family, had renewed hope and put their efforts
into rebuilding their homes and farms. Following Lenin's death they,
like so many had misjudged the ruthless and methodical rise of Stalin.
Furthermore, Johann and Wilhelmina did not know that Elsa and
Julius would soon perish in one of Stalin's slave labour camps. They
had already lost their two youngest siblings during the deportation of
1915, so this would come as yet another blow to them some five
years later when news of their daughter's demise was smuggled out to
them some time after they arrived in Canada.

The next ones to say goodbye were Lydia and Emil Krampitz and
their family, which now consisted of two daughters, Alma eight-
years-old and Meita two-years-old. Their only son Albin died in 1923
when he was only one-year-old, probably of starvation. They too
were now anxious to get on their way for they all knew that Friedrich
and Robert were anxiously waiting and ready with a team of their
best horses and a covered wagon to take them all to the railroad
station at Minsk, in the province of Belarus.

The last ones in line to say goodbye were Olga and Ewald Degen
with their son Arvid who was five-years-old and their little daughter
Lilly who was two-years-old. By this time, the tears were flowing
freely and Friedrich made a point of quickly ushering the three
families out to the waiting wagon. He left them just enough time to
wave goodbye to all of those left behind. Friedrich breathed a sigh of
relief to get them on their way to a new life—to whatever awaited
them in their new country. The wagon ride to the railway station at
Minsk took them a full two days and everyone was cold, hungry and
tired when they arrived. However, this was nothing compared to
what they were to endure on their train trip to Riga in Latvia the port
on the Gulf of Riga that opened into the Baltic Sea—and to freedom.
The coaches of the train were packed to the point where there was

standing room only; crowded with people who had the foresight to get travel documentation and train fare to the Latvian port. Their five-day train excursion was a long and arduous affair especially for the children; in fact, it was not much different from their deportation ordeal in 1915. When they arrived at Riga the trainload of fleeing refugees, were separated into groups with each group having to wait for an outbound ship. In the meantime, they were given accommodation in barracks of sorts where they had to share their space with others.

Fortunately, being that there were fourteen members in the three families they were able to stay together in one of the allotted rooms. They were relieved that they did not have to share their accommodation with strangers. Day after day, they waited and anxiously watched while the occasional group was sent down to the dock to board a ship to take them away from the repression they had faced under the Bolshevik-Leninist-Stalinist regimes. After six weeks of casting about Riga for food and anything to keep them warm Lydia Krampitz's little girl Meita became very ill, probably from the dreaded Typhus, but no one really knew what her illness was since there was no doctor to consult. A few days later she died. Since it was mid-winter, the men in the family dug a shallow grave for her in a nearby cemetery. Finally, one day in early February all three of the Fischbuch connected families were sent to the dock and boarded a ship bound for Liverpool, England. When they arrived at Liverpool, each family was assigned to a different ship for the arduous trip across the Atlantic. On the 28th of February 1929, the Krampitz family arrived in Canada at St. John, New Brunswick. Johann and his family arrived at Quebec City in early March and Olga and Ewald Degen landed at the same Canadian port a week later. They all then faced the long train voyage across the vast stretches of Canada to a barren and cold winter in the province of Saskatchewan.

Meanwhile, what was happening back at Nataliendorf?

# Chapter 17

## Nataliendorf, 1930

As the Russian winter set in at Nataliendorf after the three families had left for Canada the remaining six brothers, their offspring and Michel and Justina fearfully waited to see what was in store for them under Stalin's increasingly oppressive Communist regime. Stalin's announcement on November 5th, 1927, that he was going to recruit kulaks to serve in the heavy industry of central Russia and to collectivize the agricultural sector, was now becoming more and more obvious. Within the next few years the youth of the Communist party became fervently enthusiastic to enforce the Marxist philosophy that had been so eloquently presented to them by Lenin and Trotsky, which now was further being imposed on the populace by Stalin's terror and propaganda machine. It soon followed that armies of labourers were initially recruited from the ranks of the hated kulaks, all of whom were unskilled in industries such as mining, metal working and manufacturing. Later, however, as more workers were needed the itinerant Mouzhiken as well as anyone that had shown even the slightest opposition to Stalin were pressed into service; all were loaded into cattle cars and sent to distant factories and mines.

Simultaneously, on the agricultural front the communal farms, or kolkhozes, were randomly located on the lands expropriated from the German colonists, as well as on any other lands that had been privately owned, regardless if the land had been owned by native Russians or colonists of any other ethnic group. As the kulaks were forced from their properties, the buildings were either burned or moved to the kolkhoz compound. However, many of the buildings collapsed in the process of moving them. This resulted in only a small portion being of any value to the kolkhoz, which led to severe overcrowded conditions for the kolkhoz slave labourers.

Late one night a group of Stalin's OGPU secret police arrived at Michel and Justina's home and ordered them to leave immediately. They were informed that the buildings, livestock and farm equipment were going to be moved to a communal farm two miles south of the village of Annette. Michel and Justina were taken away without even being able to contact anyone in the rest of the family. They now were over eighty-years-old and were forced to walk nearly six miles to the communal farm. When they arrived there, they were taken to live in an old barn that had just been moved onto the compound. Here they had to make their beds in cattle stalls that had only bits of straw on which they laid the one small blanket that they had brought with them.

Several days later, when the rest of the family finally found that their parents had been taken away Emil, Zamel and Friedrich scouted in all directions from Nataliendorf until they finally heard from someone at Annette that several people had been taken to the kolkhoz south of the village the previous night. When they arrived at the kolkhoz, they found Michel and Justina in the old barn where they were very distraught and ill. From then on, every day some of the family would quietly go to the kolkhoz to do what they could for their parents. However, after a time they saw that Michel and Justina were despondent and weak and by this time appeared to be suffering from pneumonia. The only place they had to lie down was on the hard wooden floor of their straw covered planks in the old barn. Lydia had Emil and Friedrich take some blankets and some sacks of straw for a mattress to them, but their health continued to fail. Several days later when Zamel went to visit his parents, he found that Michel had died during the night. Justina told Zamel now that Michel was gone nothing mattered to her any more and she wished that she too would die. Zamel stayed with her through the night, but by morning, she too had passed away. Being taken from their treasured farmstead that they had worked so hard to build they undoubtedly succumbed not only from their age, exposure and hunger, but from broken hearts, since their early dreams for their family's future were now in tatters. Friedrich with his son Robert and his brothers Emil, Michel Jr. and Zamel dug graves for their parents in the Annette cemetery. Here they laid their parents to their final resting place in their Russian homeland -- the country in which they and their ancestors had taken so much pride in building productive farmsteads to nurture the future generations of their family.

Right from the time of the October Revolution in 1917, Friedrich and his brothers were concerned when it became known that new prison camps were emerging to house the ever-increasing numbers of kulaks and enemies-of-the-state who had dared to challenge Lenin during his rise to power. Now that Michel and Justina had been forced from their home and died in the process, it became obvious that with the rise of Communism the lives of certain Russian citizens were expendable commodities, just like cattle or any other livestock. Even the optimists among the Fischbuch families now feared for their future. After all, they were all kulaks so what would emerge for them under Stalin's evolving regime?    As Bolshevism that had evolved into Communism spread across the nation, Stalin's penal institutions were becoming more numerous and everyone was becoming familiar with the term "Gulag." The history of Russian Gulags goes back as far as the seventeenth century when the Tsars had kept forced-labour brigades of criminals in isolated camps in the Siberian wilderness, well away from the searching eyes of the common people.    However, since the Revolution these institutions were now showplaces for everyone to see that Stalin would not tolerate those opposed to the Communist dream. Therefore, the Gulags progressed from isolated and hidden Siberian enclaves to ones conveniently built in populated communities all over Russia. Beginning in the early months of the Revolution many aristocrats, religious leaders, merchants, kulaks or for that manner anyone that could be defined as an "unreliable element" of the state were sent away to be "rehabilitated."

During the five years of Lenin's leadership, from 1917 to when he died in 1924, an additional eighty-four penal camps were added to the ones that had evolved in Siberia during the Tsarist dynasties.

However, after 1929 the camps took on an even more insidious purpose after Stalin brought in his measures to use forced labour to speed Soviet industrialization. Now that Stalin had eliminated many of his powerful enemies: Lenin, Trotsky, Zinoviev, Bukharin and others the Soviet penal system had become too slow and cumbersome for him to carry out his recruitment goals, as well as his increasing need to quell any resistance to the Communist cause. He needed quick and decisive action. Therefore, to expedite the process he gave his secret police the OGPU, the additional power to take control of the Russian penal system. Consequently, the influence of the Russian justice system was reduced to deal only with minor offences. This streamlined the process to the point where "enemies of the state" could be arrested, convicted and sent to prison by a single declaration of any OGPU officer whose only qualifications were that he had voiced his allegiance to Stalin and the Communist Party. From 1929 to 1939, mass arrests were instituted to bolster the need for fodder for Stalin's goal to build a Communist industrial giant. Consequently, ever-increasing numbers of Gulags were soon established in all of Russia's provinces. By the mid 1930's they were a common sight throughout the nation from the Polish border to Russia's Pacific Coast. They became common sights from the White Sea in the Arctic to the temperate shores of the Black Sea to the south.

The speed and ruthlessness in which Michel and Justina had been taken away and the callous way that an indoctrinated Russian Communist family was even brought to live in their home, until it was to be moved or demolished, was very distressing for all the rest of the families. Many times Friedrich and Henrietta would discuss their situation far into the night, but what could they do. It was now well into the summer of 1929 and leaving the country was out of the question, for many reasons. Firstly, no longer were passports or visas available. Secondly, there were newly recruited guards at every border crossing and anyone apprehended was eagerly taken as fodder for the Gulags. And thirdly, their properties and belongings were now rapidly being confiscated and no one had enough money to finance an escape. All that could be done was to wait for the secret police to appear at their doorsteps. Friedrich and Henrietta agonized throughout the next year as the food from their garden and the meat from their few pigs and chickens began to dwindle. They had no money and often their hunger was only surpassed by their anxiety for what the future held for their three children and nine grandchildren. They were particularly worried about their youngest daughter Ida and her husband Robert Missal and their three children: Wanda who was seven-years-old, Arvid four, and Friedbert two. Ida and Robert had worked hard to establish a nice home and since it was near the roadway to Novograd Volinskiy, their property was an obvious target for expropriation by the OGPU. Any destitute neighbour or Stalinist sympathizer passing by could easily inform the local political police and the Missal family would be gone. Their other daughter, Olga and her husband August Krause lived on a farm on the east side of Nataliendorf, which was near the Sluch River where Friedrich in his younger days would take his brother's horses to drink and bathe, and where he and his boyhood friend Gustav Wendtland would cut willow shoots for August Wendtland to make baskets. Olga and August Krause had three children—Waldemar who was four-years-old, Mehta two, and Paul one. Olga and August kept to themselves and had little to do with the other family members except when they needed help themselves. August Krause would commonly ask Friedrich or any of the other relatives for money to supplement his alcoholic cravings. However, he rarely had success with the relatives and, therefore, spent most of his time sponging vodka from any transient Mouzhik or wayward peasant.

As time went on Friedrich and Henrietta's son Robert and his wife Ottilia, who were having more doubts about Stalin's Communist regime, had devised a plan to slip across the Polish border some dark night, but were afraid that it would be too risky with their two little sons, Waldemar and baby Gerhard who was only one year old. Even though they were desperate to leave Russia, they decided to stay. Later his plan to escape was further complicated by the fact that early in 1933 another son, Willi was born.

Friedrich was having less and less contact with his five brothers and their families, since each of them were preoccupied with looking after their own children and grandchildren, as well as avoiding Stalin's political police.

Since Friedrich's old friend, Gustav Wendtland, lived nearby Friedrich and Henrietta would occasionally go to visit him and his family. A month previously Gustav Wendtland's son had gone to Novograd Volinskiy with some vegetables to see if he could barter them for other food -- he never returned. When Gustav went to look for him the next day a shopkeeper told him that three members of the OGPU had forced him into a window-less Black Maria and drove off in the direction of Zhitomir. The Wendtlands never heard from their son again. Ever since Stalin had sealed the borders in 1928, everyone lived in fear of being arrested when they heard the Black Maria drive by in the dead of night, for they knew that one of their neighbours was being taken to some far-off slave labour camp. From that time on, none of the families dared go to Novograd Volinskiy to barter some of their few belongings for food, especially for flour since they all hungered for bread. However, their hunger was now overshadowed by the fear of encountering the dreaded OGPU and their Black Maria. One day in the early summer of 1931, while Ida and Robert Missal were planting their garden with seed that they had hoarded over the winter, a group of horsemen rode into their yard wearing the banner of the OGPU. The horsemen announced that the entire Missal property now belonged to the state and it was needed for the new kolkhoz just south of Annette; the place where Michel and Justina spent the last days of their lives.

The Missal property would eventually be incorporated into the communal farm as the kolkhoz was expanded. They were told that their house and buildings would become part of the kolkhoz but they would be allowed to live there until further notice. Meanwhile, all of their tools, farm equipment, livestock and furniture was to be taken to the kolkhoz in the next two days. Stalin's police then mounted their horses and rode off leaving Ida and Robert wondering how they would be able to carry on, and how they could now feed and clothe their three little children. The next morning the OGPU arrived and took everything that Ida and Robert had worked so hard to get together in the last four years. They were now left with only the barren house to live in and even then, it was only for the next little while.  When the other members of the family heard of Ida and Robert's dilemma they rallied with whatever little food and furniture they could muster.  For the rest of the summer Ida and her family made do with what they could, especially with the bit of garden produce that they had, but when fall came, they had little food to carry them through the winter.  Friedrich and Henrietta canvassed the other families to see what they all could spare for Ida and the children but it was never very much.  Whenever Henrietta would appear at Ida's house with a bit of food Ida would say that they had plenty and not to bother, since they needed the food for themselves and the other relatives.  After the hard winter of 1931–1932, Ida was very thin and weak, mainly because she was giving most of the little food they had to Robert and the children and was eating less and less herself.  By July of 1932, she was giving most of the food to the children even though her husband urged her to eat more and leave less for him.  Ida eventually became so ill she could no longer function.  Ida died sometime late in July of 1932.  Ida was only twenty-five-years-old and she tried desperately to save her three young children from starvation; they were only nine, six and four-years-old.  After Ida died their father, Robert Missal spent most of his time searching for food for the children and struggled to make life bearable for himself and the children.

Friedrich and Henrietta did what they could for Robert and the children, but here again, they had very little food for themselves so could do little more than sympathize with Robert Missal's dilemma. Late one evening in December of 1932, Robert had just put the children to bed when there was a loud knocking and before he could get to the door three men burst into the house -- it was the OGPU. They immediately demanded that he get his clothes on and leave with them.  He said, "But what about my children, I can't leave them alone?"  They retorted and said, "Damn the children!  Let's get going before we have to hobble you and drag you out."  Robert quickly ran to the bedroom and told the children to get dressed and go to their grandparent's house.  It was a long way for them to find their way in the dark of night but he had no other choice.  He kissed them all and said not to worry, for Friedrich and Henrietta would look after them, and that he would be back as soon as he proved to the OGPU that he was not a kulak. Sadly, however, this was the last time the children would see their father. For the next ten years neither Friedrich, Henrietta nor any of the families would know what happened to Robert Missal. When Friedrich questioned others who had their loved ones sent away, they had heard only rumours about where anyone was sent. Friedrich finally found out from a man that he knew from his blacksmith days that a man named Robert Missal and other detainees were taken to a prison in Zhitomir. He said that they were held there for nearly a month and survived on a little amount of bread and water the local people were able to bring them. Then, one day they were all taken in chains to a waiting train and forced into an open cattle car that was already filled to capacity with other unfortunate prisoners.

Nearly a decade later Friedrich and Henrietta heard that Robert had been sentenced to ten years at hard labour and was sent as a slave labourer to work at the Belomor Canal. This was Stalin's grand scheme to build a shipping canal all the way from the White Sea high in the Russian Arctic through Lake Ladoga to the Baltic Sea. Since Stalin's new Communist regime had no heavy equipment for such a major project he, nevertheless, had his unlimited supply of slave labourers. To mobilize enough manpower he sent his trusted OGPU out to conscript as many bodies as they could find, regardless if they were kulaks or anyone even remotely opposed to Communism. By this time the Gulag population had become a major source of manpower for Stalin's other projects. Many more men and women were needed for the high Arctic and were recruited from the multitude of slave-labour camps across the country. The Gulags had blossomed into a wide array of institutions. They included: "Trudarmee" or traditional slave-labour camps, punishment camps, criminal and political camps, women's camps—a favourite among the guards who utilized these particular institutions to satisfy their sexual desires, and children's camps, where youngsters were taken and forced to work in the deep and narrow shafts of the coal mines that were too small for adult miners.

At this time, the Belomor Canal was the largest undertaking in the Soviet Union and since so many labourers were needed, no record of how many people were sent to work there was ever revealed by the Soviets. However, a crude estimate made after Stalin's death in 1953 was that at least 170,000 men, women and children were sent to the White Sea most of who perished from freezing to death, being worked to death, starving to death or a combination of all three. Heavy equipment was too expensive to buy abroad because Stalin's need to save money was paramount. He reasoned that the cheapest and most available and convenient method to build the canal was to use the vast quantity of manpower in the Gulags—many of which were populated by the colonist kulaks of southern Russia.

All the slave labourers were provided to work with during the twenty-one-month construction period were picks, axes, hammers, chisels, handsaws, wooden shovels and wheelbarrows. With these crude instruments, they were required manually to carve a twelve-foot deep trench through frozen tundra, bedrock, and swamp. This also included building five dams and nineteen locks that stretched 141 miles along the route from the islands of the White Sea to the northern shores of the Baltic Sea. . Upon its so-called completion in 1934, his Communist compatriots as well as many observers in other countries heralded Stalin as a hero. To ensure that all of Russia and the world would be made aware of Stalin out-performing Tsar Alexander's feat of bringing ships from the White Sea over land to capture the island of Noteburg from the Swedes, Stalin had thirty-six Soviet writers compose a treatise expounding the virtues of Stalin's socialist slave labour accomplishments. It was titled "Stalin's Belomor Canal" and was published everywhere by the international media. The media in Russia regularly praised the virtues of Stalin's Belomor Canal with such eloquent phrases such as was published by Isvestiya in Archangelsk, which read:

"The harsh environment, the work regime, the fight against the forces of nature will be a good school for all of Russia's criminal elements."

As Friedrich and Henrietta would later find, other members of their family would also be sent to slave labour in the High Arctic.

When Ida and Robert's children arrived at Friedrich and Henrietta's door late on the night when their father was taken away their grandparents were appalled by the callous way that Robert was taken away and such little children were left to fend for themselves. They comforted them as best they could but Friedbert the youngest boy who was only three-years-old, was hard to console since it was not long since he had lost his mother and now that his father was gone as well, it was difficult for him to understand. Henrietta told him not to worry and that as long as his father was away he could always be with them. As the days went by Friedrich finally got the word that Robert Missal had been imprisoned at Zhitomir and was sent away by cattle train. To ease the children's fears he told them that it would not be too long before they would hear from their father but deep in his heart, he knew that it probably would be years before the children would see their father again. The only comfort that Robert Missal would ever have had during his arctic ordeal is that he would have always known that his children were in the care of their grandparents.

Less than a year later in the autumn of 1932, the OGPU again appeared in the dark of night, this time at the home of Olga and August Krause. When they arrived, they demanded that the whole family get ready to leave within the hour. Olga quickly gathered clothes and as many belongings that they could carry before they were all forced into the Black Maria. Since August and Olga Krause had little to do with the rest of the family no one heard of their departure for several days. As Friedrich and Henrietta would much later learn they were all taken to the railroad station at Karkhov and shipped on a cattle train to work in a kolkhoz near the village of Taintscha in northern Kazakhstan. After they left Friedrich and Henrietta heard nothing of their whereabouts. However, unknown to them Olga and August Krause and their family in 1938, six years after their incarceration at the Taintscha kolkhoz, were sent to the northern Urals to a Gulag housing workers that did not fill their kolkhoz quotas. They were interned there until 1946, when they were sent back to their "home" kolkhoz at Taintscha. Ironically, this is where Friedrich would later spend the last days of his life.

As time went on, Friedrich and Henrietta survived from one day to the next hoping to be able to provide enough food for themselves and Ida's three children: Wanda, Arvid and Friedbert. In the early spring of 1933, they looked forward to planting a garden with the little amount of seed that they had. They had saved every eye from the potato peelings that they ate during the winter. Potatoes had become a staple food for them since their deportation in 1915. Friedrich spent much time with Arvid and sometimes-young five-year-old Friedbert down at the Sluch River fishing, much as Friedrich had done when he went fishing with the old Mouzhik when he was a boy. These fishing expeditions helped provide them with food until mid-summer when they were able to harvest some of the vegetables.

In May of 1934, the Black Maria again arrived late in the evening at another family farmstead. This time it was at the home of Emil and Lydia Fischbuch and their seven children. Emil was shown documents that labelled him not only as a Tsarist army officer, but also as a kulak. They showed him an itemized document that listed his belongings. This document was unearthed at the Zhitomir State Archives by Donald N. Miller in 2003 and reads as follows:

"Comrade Kaz, head of the village council and Comrades Kowalski and Bizhkiviski members of the local collective visited Emil Michael Fischbuch's 14-hectare farm at the village of Nataliendorf on March 6, 1931. and itemized his property as follows:"

"House, made of wood, covered with straw, two sheds made of planks, a stone fruit and vegetable cellar, a threshing machine shed, a small mill, scales, an iron-wheeled cart, a drill, an iron plough, three cows, two heifers, a 1½ year old horse, a seven-month-old colt, eight pigs, five piglets, five geese, four ducks, 15 hens, a sheep with a lamb, 15 puds of wheat, six puds of rye, 8 puds of barley, 10 puds of oats, about 100 puds of hay, 100 puds of potatoes, a glass buffet, a bureau, a wardrobe and a table."

This proved without a doubt that Emil Fischbuch was a kulak. Therefore, the leader of the new and now powerful NKVD group promptly convicted Emil as an enemy of the state and on the spot sentenced him to ten years at hard labour to be served at a Gulag near the Siberian city of Tomsk.  Much to the despair of his wife and children he was quickly taken to the waiting Black Maria.  His wife Lydia never saw her husband again; and his seven children never saw their father again.

**Emil Fischbuch's Family 1938**
**Reinhold, Richard**
**Ergard, Lydia, Margarita, Antonina**

For the next year, Lydia tried to make ends meet with the help of the two older children, Reinhold and Antonina.  Reinhold was sixteen-years-old, Antonina fourteen, Richard eleven, Ergard eight, Gerhard six,

Margarita four, and little Erwin was one-year-old.  In the early spring of 1935, a caravan of Stalin's military police again arrived at Lydia's farm.  This time they confiscated the few household items that Lydia had collected from relatives and friends to survive: one pig, a few chickens, and two pails of potatoes.  They then forced Lydia and the children into a wagon and announced that they were being taken to Woroschilograd, a kolkhoz that was located some 500 miles to the southeast of Novograd Volinskiy near the city of Dniepropetrovsk.  There was no time to send messages to the remaining Fischbuch families.  All that the relatives subsequently knew was that Emil, Lydia and their children were gone.

By the next year, in the summer of 1935, Friedrich's family and their son Robert's family were able to produce enough food to keep them fairly well fed.  In total, the two families had been able to find enough food, clothing and firewood for them to survive, but already they were beginning to dread the approaching winter.  Both families often thought of the sad way Ida had died and the cruel way her husband Robert was arrested and forced to leave his children; this grim reminder was always with them.  Furthermore, these memories were coupled with the painful recollection of the departure of the other daughter Olga along with her alcoholic husband and children. All of these traumatic incidents were never far from their minds. They agonized about who would be next to be taken away. Then, one day in the autumn of 1935, as they had all had dreaded for years the NKVD arrived at Friedrich and Henrietta's home. Stalin's newly named police force was now the largest bureaucratic movement in Russia and to this end, it had been re-named the NKVD because of its ever-increasing importance to the Soviet economy. The population of Gulags at this time had risen to over one million inmates and many more were to come. The mania for arrests and executions spread quickly through the Communist Party hierarchy, since no Communist would dare challenge any direct order that was given by Stalin. Consequently, this then established a class of loyal leaders who left no stone unturned to arrest anyone even for the most mundane reason. By 1935, Stalin was approaching the zenith of his dream to show the world how a Communist society could flourish by using the labour of "criminals". To hasten the growth of his slave labour force he had the NKVD establish quotas for all the districts of Russia. In Volhynia, which included the area from Zhitomir to Novograd Volinskiy the NKVD was given permission to arrest an additional 30,000 "criminals", regardless of whether they were kulaks, Mouzhiken or any other trumped up "anti-Soviet" element.

When the NKVD arrived at the doorstep of Friedrich and Henrietta much as with the relatives that had been arrested earlier, they, along with the three children, were ordered out of the house. The NKVD leader said that they were there to prepare the house for removal to a nearby kolkhoz. Friedrich and Henrietta quickly gathered the children together, took a few belongings and while the police were concentrating on examining the house they quietly slipped unnoticed from the yard and went to Robert and Ottilia's house. Friedrich and Henrietta had devised this plan with Robert previously, so if and very likely when the NKVD would come to either of their places they would try to quietly leave and go to the other's home -- any attempt to avoid being taken away in the Black Maria. A few days later Friedrich and Robert went to see if their house had in fact been moved away and found there were only a few boards left where the house had been standing. In some respects, Stalin's political police were very efficient. They had burned the barn and other outbuildings however, for some reason they had left one granary standing. Friedrich told Robert that perhaps he, Henrietta and the children should come back and stay in the old granary. Therefore, if the NKVD came to Robert's house they all would not be taken away together. It was becoming more and more obvious that the buildings on Robert's farmstead were relatively intact and the premises were being lived in, since most of the homes in Nataliendorf had already been either moved away or burned. For the next year Friedrich, Henrietta and the children lived in the sparse accommodation of the granary. The winter of 1935–1936, was long and harsh for them all, especially for Ida's children who were now twelve, nine and seven-years-old. In early May of 1936, Friedrich and young Friedbert had just come back from fishing at the Sluch River when to their dismay they saw the Black Maria stopped at the door of their granary home. Since Friedrich and Friedbert were not home, there was no opportunity for Henrietta to get away, for she had to wait for them to get back from the river. When Friedrich came into the house, the police told him to get into the Black Maria and that he was not allowed to take anything with him because all of the household items belonged to the state.

Friedrich desperately wanted to get his naval documents and the Cross of St. George that he had treasured for the last thirty years. Not because it was presented to him by the Tsar, but for the memories he had of serving with his naval companions: Admirals Makarov, Rozhdestvensky, and Witgeft, Captains Grigorovich and Kozlowski and his friend and co-stoker Lubomir Radomsky. As well, there were all of the other stokers with whom he had sweated and toiled with in the bunkers during the Battle of the Yellow Sea. The NKVD leader did not allow Friedrich and Friedbert to go back into their granary home, but rather they were forced into the dreaded van where Henrietta, Wanda and Arvid were already waiting for them. Since Henrietta knew that Friedrich would want to keep the mementos of his naval career she unobtrusively had taken the two items that she could find; the medallion that he got for his service in the Russian Navy and the Cross of St. George that had been presented to Friedrich by the Tsar. While waiting in the Black Maria they were able to peek through the curtained window and watched the NKVD police bring out their few belongings and put them into a waiting wagon. The police then piled straw and some firewood against the granary and set it on fire. This is the last distressing memory that Friedrich and Henrietta would have of their once beloved Nataliendorf.

# Chapter 18

# From Nataliendorf to Jasnaja Poljana

The first stop for Friedrich, Henrietta and the children was Zhitomir where they were all kept in a prison cell for two days. They were then taken to the railroad station at Kiev where they were put on a cattle train, which had now become Stalin's standard mode of transportation for his slave labour army. Friedrich, Henrietta and the children then suffered through a twenty-eight day cattle-car ordeal that was similar to what they went through during their deportation in 1915, only this time they had three young children that suffered along with them. When their cattle train finally arrived at the small settlement of Qiyali south of Petropavlovsk, they emerged to a completely new world. As they were soon to find, they were nearly 3,000 miles from Nataliendorf and on the broad, barren steppe of the far northeastern part of Kazkhstan, an environment completely alien to their forested and fertile farmsteads far to the west.

They were forced to march several miles to their assigned kolkhoz near the village of Jasnaja Poljana. When they arrived, they were herded into a large building where many other people were housed, there were no rooms or even stalls and everywhere there were families huddled together in little groups. The next day the Commandant came early in the morning and assigned the new people to different tasks. Friedrich was selected to clean manure from the livestock barns, which housed the horses, cattle and camels. Henrietta was sent to work in the communal kitchen. The children were mentioned only briefly at the end of the session when the Commandant said that when any of the younger detainees reached the age of seventeen they would be sent away to work in the Trudarmee. Nothing more was said about their care, so obviously they would be left by themselves among other strange children that they knew nothing about. This was devastating for any family that had young children, since babies and younger children would have no one to look after them, since both parents would be assigned specific tasks on the kolkhoz.

They were told that when any children reached the age of sixteen or seventeen they would be assigned work at Jasnaja Poljana, or would be sent to any other kolkhoz that needed workers. However, if they did not behave they would be sent to a Gulag. Henrietta delegated her granddaughter, Ida's thirteen-year-old Wanda, to look after her two younger brothers and watch over their few personal belongings. Several weeks later, some of the inhabitants of their "Kazakhstani home" were transferred to another dwelling that had just been moved onto the kolkhoz. This now left more room for those that remained. Friedrich, Henrietta and the children quickly sought a more private place in one corner of the building where they put up a barrier of sorts with some boards that Friedbert and Arvid had found in the yard. Each day Henrietta brought the allotted ration of food for the family from the kolkhoz kitchen; it consisted of nothing more than a bowl of watery soup and a slice of dry black bread for each person who was a worker. This meant that Friedrich and Henrietta each got full rations of a large bowl of soup and a thick slice of bread. The children on the other hand were allowed only half that amount since they were not workers. Often times the children would waken during the night and cry because they were hungry, especially young eight-year-old Friedbert.

By the beginning of October, it was obvious the winter of 1936–1937 was approaching. The nights were getting too cold for them to sleep on the hard dirt floor, especially since they only had the two blankets that Henrietta had been able to smuggle out of the house before the NKVD took them away. As the weather became colder, they made mattresses out of potato sacks filled with straw that the boys had carefully gathered from a nearby field. By the end of November, some of the older inmates had become seriously ill, forcing the Commandant to allow them to bring in some metal barrels and metal pipes to make crude stoves. The men then cut holes in the side of the building for the stovepipes to guide the smoke outside. Since there were few trees on the plains of Kazakhstan the only fuel that was available was straw and dried cow and camel dung. Rarely did they have small amounts of coal that an inmate would have stolen from the kolkhoz. This, however, was short-lived when one of the workers was caught taking a small sack of coal and was sent away to serve a sentence at hard labour in one of the Criminal Gulags.

The following winter was long and difficult for Friedrich, Henrietta and the children. However, when spring arrived at least the children were able to be outside during the day and away from the closely packed inmates in their communal "home." As May passed into June, during the little time he had away from work, Friedrich dug a garden plot well away from the compound. Here they planted vegetables and potatoes with seeds that Henrietta had been able to smuggle out of the communal kitchen. They then had Wanda and the boys weed the garden and monitor it, so nothing would be stolen by fellow inmates. They now had extra food to supplement their sparse allotted rations. In this manner, they survived the summer and the winter of 1937-1938.

One day in mid-July of 1938, as Wanda was coming back from their garden she heard one guard say that a new group of inmates was arriving the next day. The next morning, Wanda and the boys left their duties at the garden to watch as the new people were brought into the compound. Again, the new arrivals would have had a long and arduous journey in one of Stalin's cattle trains. As she and the boys watched the haggard and frightened souls being marched toward their barrack, they noticed that most of the people were in family groups, but there was one woman alone with an armload of belongings. She struggled along holding the hand of a young boy about six-years-old. Following were two other boys who were being forced along by one of the escorting guards. As the long column of people approached, Wanda recognized the mother as her aunt Ottilia and the young boys as her cousins, Waldemar, Gerhard and six-year-old Willi. Wanda ran up to them and saw her aunt's eyes light up when she recognized a relative so far away from home. Wanda told her that her mother and Friedrich would be so surprised at last to see someone from the family, and to find out what was happening back at Nataliendorf. She then told her aunt that they should come with her and they could stay in their boarded off corner of the barrack.

When they got to their private little corner, Wanda asked about their father, her uncle Robert, and if he was coming later. Ottilia said she would wait and tell them all what had occurred in the past two years, when Friedrich and Henrietta got back from work. When Friedrich and Henrietta got home, they were astounded that someone from home was now with them; their daughter-in-law and their three grandsons. The first question Friedrich asked was, "Where is Robert, and will he come later?" Ottilia began to cry and said that Robert was no longer with them. She then told them that the NKVD and the Black Maria arrived at their house late on the night of September 19, 1937. Stalin's all-powerful military police demanded that he get into the van immediately or there would be dire consequences. As Ottilia and the children watched from the doorway, they heard Robert say, "I must go back into the house and say goodbye to my wife and children. Where and why are you taking me?" When he pulled away and left to go back into the house, one of the police drew his revolver, held it to Robert's head and pulled the trigger.. With blood flowing from his wound and as he fell his family saw him reach toward the house; two of Stalin's police took him by the legs and arms and threw him into a waiting truck. Robert's wife Ottilia and their three sons stood in the doorway of their home and in horror had witnessed the execution of her husband and the children's father. This is the last memory that Ottilia had of Robert, and the last memory the three boys had of their father.

As time went on, Ottilia and the boys struggled to survive and wondered how they would fare through the coming winter. There were still a few remnants of other Fischbuch families that had not yet been arrested and taken away. The ones who were nearby helped Ottilia through the winter with food and wood, but they too had their own problems. By 1938, all five of Friedrich's brothers who had remained in Russia had been arrested and sent away -- to Gulags, to Archangelsk in the Russian arctic, to Perm in the Ural Mountains, and to the Muslim states of Kirgistan, and Kazakhstan. Like Ottilia, some wives and children were still living in whatever accommodation they could find on their dispossessed farmsteads. In their common dilemma, they helped one another as best they could to get through the winter of 1937–1938.

With the influx of the new inmates into the Jasnaja Poljana kolkhoz, the accommodation in their bedroom building again became cramped, as bad as it was when Friedrich and Henrietta had first arrived. As the population of the kolkhoz communities increased in numbers and size, the problem of educating the children arose; therefore, in 1938 the Supreme Soviet decreed that at least four years of schooling was to be provided for children below the age of sixteen. The families in all of the kolkhoz compounds heralded this with considerable enthusiasm. There were a total of six children under the age of sixteen in Friedrich's family group, consequently, Friedrich, Henrietta and Ottilia were thankful that at least this small concession was being provided for the children.

Friedrich thought about what he had seen two of the other inmate family heads had done the previous year. They had worked late at night building sod houses for their families in various places outside the compound. As time passed, the men had smuggled materials from the kolkhoz to make furniture of sorts, wooden boxes for chairs and barrels, which they made into stoves. Now that Friedrich's family group had increased to nine he decided to build their own sod-house accommodation. This became an exhausting task, for after each twelve-hour shift during all seven working days of the week, Friedrich with the help of the children, cut blocks of sod. They had to cut a lot for they had to make a relatively large dwelling to house the nine members of the family. By the fall of 1938, their sod house was complete; the boys had found two big rocks on which they put the big suitcase that they had brought to carry their belongings when they left home and used it to serve as a table. They also had found four blocks of wood that served as chairs. The boards that they had used to isolate their corner in the big barn-like barrack they used as a base for their beds, on which they put sacks of straw for mattresses. Now as their second winter approached they were better prepared than they were for the previous winter, even though the family had increased by four. During the winter, they not only were able to supplement their food rations that were issued so sparingly by the kolkhoz, they had been able to save some vegetables and potatoes from their precious garden for the coming winter. The five boys: Arvid, Friedbert, Waldemar, Gerhard and young Willi had dug a small root cellar to store these priceless food items. The winter of 1938–1939 was similar to the previous year, however, this time they were better prepared. The sod house was relatively warm since the boys worked diligently to make sure they had a plentiful supply of straw to burn. During the coldest nights, one of the boys would stay up to keep adding straw to the fire. In addition, they were able to increase their food rations with vegetables from their root cellar.

Sometime in the February of 1940, Henrietta heard from other workers in the communal kitchen that a large addition was being made to the Jasnaja Poljana kolkhoz adjacent to, and immediately to the south, of the one they were working on. This new kolkhoz was to house German colonist kulaks who were being brought from east of the Dnieper River, and were inmates in kolkhozes in the Woroschilograd and Donetz areas. However, Henrietta did not know that when Emil was taken away in 1934, that he had been taken to a Gulag at Tomsk, which was only about a hundred and fifty miles from their internment at Jasnaja Poljana. Ottilia had said that in 1935 Lydia, Emil Fischbuch's wife and their seven children, had been taken away, but was not aware that they had been sent to work at a kolkhoz at Woroschilograd.

When Lydia and her seven children arrived at the Woroschilograd kolkhoz, they had no living accommodation, but with the help of the older children, they tacked together a building of sorts with logs and scraps of lumber and subsisted by eating grass. They eventually grew some vegetables while all the time Lydia had to work in the fields of the kolkhoz. As they struggled to survive with their limited amount of food and sparse accomocation, in 1936 little Erwin died probably of starvation and/or pneumonia.

One day in 1937, Lydia was given a letter from Emil by an inmate who had just been sent to Woroschilograd from Tomsk. In the letter Emil said that he was assigned to feed and live with the pigs, and he was allowed only the food the pigs did not eat. The letter was not finished. One of his fellow inmates had written on the bottom of the letter that Emil had died -- his name was signed "Krause."

A short time later, the Commandant arrived at Lydia Fischbuch's accomodation and announced that her oldest son Reinhold, who was now eighteen-years-old, was to be sent to Archangelsk to work on a railroad being built to the White Sea where the Belomor Canal opened into the frozen Arctic Ocean. The next day guards appeared and Reinhold was taken away. His mother never saw him again.

# Chapter 19

## The Chelyabinsk Gulag: Family Tragedies

In the early summer of 1939, rumours of another war with Germany were circulating through the Jasnaja Poljana kolkhoz hierarchy. The inmates, most of whom were German colonists from Volhynia, Bessarabia, the Crimea and other German colonies in western Russia, overheard many of these conversations. It soon became obvious that the ethnic German colonists were now being looked at with even more suspicion. Even though the colonists had no contact with Germany and had been productive citizens of Russia for over a century, they were perceived as spies and traitors. In Friedrich's case, it was even worse since some of the inmates had heard about his service in the Tsar's navy and this fact was soon passed on to the kolkhoz Commandant. In early June, Friedrich was called to report to the NKVD representative of the kolkhoz. When he entered the Commandant's office, he was informed that he had been found guilty of stealing barrels and boxes that were kolkhoz property and, therefore, he would have to serve a sentence of five years at hard labour.

He was not allowed to go back to the little sod house to say goodbye to Henrietta and the rest of the family, but was forced into a waiting Black Maria along with two other prisoners who were already in the van. As Friedrich found later, they also were German colonists from somewhere in the Crimea. The three of them were taken to a railroad station at Petropavlovsk and put into the usual NKVD transport method—an overcrowded cattle train. As he found later, their destination was Chelyabinsk, a Siberian city on the eastern slopes of the Ural Mountains. From there they were taken about 30 miles through a forested area to the Gulag, a desolate and foreboding structure surrounded by a high barbed-wire fence. Here the slave labour force had been brought to work at a logging operation cutting and hauling logs to a nearby river. Ironically, the Tsar and his family had been taken to their imprisonment from nearby Tyumen to Tobolsk in August of 1917, on the same river. As Friedrich was soon to find, the Gulag had very specific behaviour and work rules.

What evolved in the first five years following the October Revolution is that the Gulags served mainly as death camps. However, it was not long after Lenin's death that Stalin realized the potential of slave-labour camps and the Gulags became a potential economic engine for the new Russia. However, it took until 1937, for him to gain total command of the Communist party and during this time, he methodically created more and more detention centres to amass his army of slave labourers. He wanted to show the world that Communism would transform Russia into an industrial and agricultural giant. To accomplish this, Gulags were to be his source of power to rejuvenate the Russian economy and show the world the virtues of a Communist society. To this end, he transformed the role of the Gulag from the hidden detention camps of the Tsarist era to a source of human muscle for the economy. The NKVD administrators in charge of the Gulags continued to be steeped in the brutal methods of operating the camps in the same manner as in Tsarist times. They were very unconcerned with preserving human life or respecting human dignity. Consequently, the daily life for the inmates of the new era of Gulags, detention centres and kolkhozes that arose after the October Revolution had changed very little, the only exception being that most inmates were innocent colonist farmers that were incarcerated with criminals, political dissidents, disenfranchised Russian nobility, Mouzhiken and Gypsies.

As Friedrich was brought into their place of accommodation, he saw that it was not much different to that at Jasnja Poljana. It was a barrack, but was constructed of logs with only a dirt floor and boughs of fir and cedar trees to serve as mattresses for the inmates. As daylight dawned on his first day at the Gulag Friedrich and the other inmates were ordered into an outer courtyard. Every second man was given an axe and a long crosscut saw with a handle at each end. This meant the worker next to him was his partner for the day to fell and chop the branches from the trees.

They then were arranged in lines of four men abreast with armed guards one each side. The guards informed them that if anyone was seen stepping out of line it would be a sign that they were trying to escape and they would be shot without warning. One team of oxen pulling a metal sled and driven by two labourers, who must have had special rights to have this easy task, followed the entire entourage. By mid-morning Friedrich was already tired and sweating from heaving the saw back and forth and by noon he was not only tired but also very hungry. By six o'clock, Friedrich and many of the other workers were near collapse. At last, at seven o'clock in the evening the guards again had them all line up in rows four abreast for the march back to the compound. For the evening meal, Friedrich was hoping the rations would be more adequate than the pitiful rations they were allowed at Jasnaja Poljana. Here everyone needed more nourishment to sustain them for the hard work that they had been doing. After standing in line for what seemed like an eternity, he found the only food served was a large bowl of soup that had a strange odour. However, as time went on he would discover from the other slave-labourers that food was a rather minor consideration for the inmates of any of Stalin's camps, be they the kolkhoz camps or any of the evolving variety of Gulags. At the kolkhoz at Jasnaja Poljana, the rations were equally revolting but at least they had one slice of black bread a day. Of course, Friedrich, Henrietta and some of the other inmates at the kolkhoz had been able to supplement their limited rations from vegetable gardens. The food aspect for the slave-labourers was consistent from camp to camp and stayed the same from year to year throughout the history of the Gulag period. Friedrich later told the family after he got back to Jasnaja Polyana what the food was like at the Chelyabinsk Gulag. In his own words he described it as:

"The soup the prisoners were served once, or rarely twice a day consisted mainly of water and its contents were suspect. Often it contained a smattering of rotten cabbage and rarely a few diced potatoes. The main constituents were pieces of pig ears and parts of the heads and intestines of any forest animal that was slaughtered by the kitchen staff. And occasionally, since the Chelyabinsk camp was near a river, the soup contained fish heads and scales. My partner for the day who was a recent recruit from the Crimea kept gagging as he tried to swallow the foul-smelling soup. It seemed he was unable to cross the psychological barrier we all had to face even though he was near starvation."

After several months in the Gulag at Chelyabinsk Friedrich learned through the grapevine that the food provided for the guards and the local administrators was of a far different calibre—pork tenderloin, pork chops, and fillets of trout followed by wine and caviar. These joyful events were common, especially when there were visiting dignitaries from Moscow or some other Gulag. For the inmates, however, the work routine and the food did not change from one day to the next and there was no respite. As winter approached, Friedrich dreaded the thought of again working in deep snow and cold weather with the sparse clothing that he had. As he expected, it was even worse than he had anticipated. He soon saw that when the other worker's shoes wore out and their socks became threadbare, they regularly had frostbite and commonly lost their toes and some even lost their feet. Many of the workers would tie pieces of potato sack around their feet to try to ward off the cold. Fortunately, Friedrich had a relatively warm coat that he had worn by chance on the day of his arrest at Jasnaja Poljana. He also had a heavy pair of socks that Henrietta had knit for him while they were still at Nataliendorf. Clothing was a treasured item to all the inmates. Therefore, it was common for someone to have their coat or shoes stolen by one of the other inmates while they slept. The deep sleep of the totally exhausted made them unaware of being stripped of their most valued possessions. One morning Friedrich woke to find that both his jacket and shoes had been taken from him during the night. However, early the next morning as he awoke shivering from the cold he found the inmate next to him had died during the night so he quietly stripped the body of both coat and shoes. The will to survive became overpowering in the Gulag environment and was uppermost in the minds of the inmates--Friedrich was no exception.

The spring of 1940 was a trying time for Stalin with Hitler's blitzkrieg advancing relentlessly into Russia. Although these were turbulent times for the Communist regime, nothing seemed to change for Friedrich and his fellow inmates at the Chelyabinsk Gulag. It was still work twelve hours a day and seven days a week, although now that spring had arrived wielding the cross-cut saw and chopping limbs from trees was not as soul destroying as doing it in the numbing cold of mid-winter. In early May, the inmates were informed that a new stand of timber was to be harvested and was located about ten miles further into the forest. This meant a much longer daily march for the workers. When they went there for their first day of work and after walking relentlessly for about five miles, they were surprised when they passed another encampment surrounded by a high barbed wire fence. One of the guards told them that it was a Gulag for women who also were logging in the forest where they were to work. The obvious question was "would they be working together?" Since many of the inmates in Friedrich's group had not seen a woman in several years, they were anxious even to be able to look at a member of the opposite sex. However, the lead guard knew what they were thinking and announced that there was to be no contact whatsoever with anyone in the women's group and if anyone was seen making any sort of move in their direction there would be no questions asked and they would be shot on the spot.

Their working days passed on into summer with no change in the daily routine, as well as the long, tiring march back and forth to work. As they would pass the women's Gulag nothing was said about it among the workers, but with the guards, it was always a topic of conversation. The guards were all looking forward to their next payday when they would have the opportunity to visit the women's Gulag, pay the proper bribe to the Gulag administrators, and select whatever woman appealed to them. Apparently, some of the guards chose the same woman each payday, however, these relationships in most cases were short-lived since the women would be rotated to other camps or in many cases would die of overwork or starvation.

With the guards, however, what commonly occurred after the war with Germany began in 1939, was that many of them were drafted into the army and sent to the western front to fight the advancing German army.

For the inmates of the Chelyabinsk Gulag, however, their main concern was looking forward to the agony of the coming winter. Certain inmates, in some way or another had curried favour with the guards or someone in the ruling hierarchy and held positions such as butchers, fishermen, kitchen helpers or servants to senior members of the administration. The relatively easy work for the drivers of the teams of oxen also fell into this category. Late in the fall of 1941, one of the sleds that was used to pull the biggest logs to the river by the oxen, had its steel runners torn off when one of the drivers had carelessly pulled a heavily loaded sled over a rock outcrop at the edge of the river. The driver was immediately demoted and sent back to work wielding an axe with the rest of the ordinary workers. As well, he had his soup ration cut in half for a month. The problem now was that there was no one in the Gulag knowledgeable about working with iron and even if there was, there were no proper tools to repair the runners of the broken sled. Friedrich, seeing an opportunity perhaps to gain favour with the administration, offered his services as a blacksmith to straighten the runners of the sled to get the big logs moved to the river. When he told one of the guards that he had been a blacksmith he was taken in to speak to the Commandant. After a considerable interrogation, Friedrich was allowed to canvass the compound for tools. He found a post-maul that was quite heavy, but would serve as a hammer as well as a length of rail for an anvil. He gathered a pile of wood for a fire to heat the iron but without a blower felt that it would not be hot enough to mould the iron runners. Friedrich knew there was coal on the premises, since coal was used to heat the barracks of the Gulag administrators and the guards. The workers, of course had to heat their barracks with wood. Through several lengthy negotiations with the head administrator Friedrich finally was allowed to use some coal. After several hours of working so close to the heat of the big fire, he finally got the runners straightened and welded back on the sled. The next day Friedrich was put back to work at his usual twelve-hour routine in the forest, but the repair of the sled had been a welcome diversion. It was now near the end of November and the cold weather was setting in for the long hard winter. One day, as they arrived back from their long walk from the logging site, one of the guards ordered Friedrich to follow him to the Commandant's office. This was disturbing to Friedrich for he feared that he might be moved to another Gulag; hopefully it would not be to one in the far north. Some of the other inmates had been at Gulags near Archangelsk and Komi in the Russian Arctic and were relieved now to be at Chelyabinsk. The Commandant looked at Friedrich for a long time and then said, "You have not been here very long, but since you quickly repaired one of the sleds we were able to meet our quota of logs taken to the river, therefore, against my better judgement the NKVD has advised me to discharge you. I must now provide you with travel documents, they will be ready for you within the month and you will be sent back to Jasnaja Poljana. Meanwhile you will carry on with your regular duties."

That evening, while having his standard bowl of soup he was so overcome about thinking of his release from the Gulag that the soup seemed to contain more potatoes and cabbage than usual. Friedrich wondered if it was really true that he would be going back to his family again. The next few days went by quickly for Friedrich and he began counting the days to the end of the month, but when the last day of the month arrived there still was no word from the Commandant about his release. He waited patiently, but another month went by and his documents still had not arrived. It was now well into January of 1942, and each day working in the cold was interminable for Friedrich as he waited and waited. Finally, in early January he was called to the Commandant's office to pick up his travel documents. He then had to wait for a guard to be free to escort him to the railroad station at Chelyabinsk. Of course, during this time he had to continue his logging duties in the forest. After another week of waiting at last, a guard was free to take him to the railroad station. Once he arrived, he was lodged in a barrack with other travellers to wait until there would be enough "passengers" to fill a cattle car—this took another week. The trip to Jasnaja Poljana was no different than the other cattle-car travels he had in the past; wedged together with hungry, desperate and destitute men and women, all shivering in the cold and immersed in their own thoughts of what their lives were like before the rise of the Bolshevik, Leninist, and now the Stalinist reign of terror. Finally, in the early spring of 1942, Friedrich arrived "home" at Jasnaja Poljana and to what was left of his family. When he entered the little sod house that he and his five young grandsons had carved from the earth in the summer of 1938, he was shocked to see a thin and wasted Henrietta lying on the old straw mattress and wondered what the future would hold for them.

When she saw Friedrich her eyes lit up, she smiled and said, "Oh, thank God, you are home again so much has happened while you were away." She then proceeded to tell him the tribulations they had gone through while he was at the Chelyabinsk Gulag. She told him that in June of 1941, the kolkhoz guards discovered their garden and tore out everything they had planted so from that time on they had no vegetables to supplement their rations.

Ottilia had been working on the kolkhoz fields hoeing weeds and cutting hay with a scythe for twelve hours a day, and Wanda had been conscripted to work in the fields. Along with Henrietta, who still was working in the kolkhoz kitchen, the three of them shared their rations with the five young boys, who of course were allowed only half rations. Over a period of time Ottilia, who had the physically most strenuous work and with so little food, she slowly became very weak and thin. Finally, because of her low productivity the Russian foreman cut her food rations in half. This led to even less food for them all to share. In desperation Henrietta, who had always been careful not to take food from the community larder, started secretly to stow food in her clothing to bring a bit more nourishment home. However, it was not long before one of her co-workers saw her taking some potatoes and corn and reported her to the guards. The next day when she arrived at work the Commandant was waiting for her and told her that from now on, she would work at cleaning all of the toilets on the compound and it would be her duty to take the human excrement by wheelbarrow and spread it on the fields as fertilizer. In addition, the Commandant informed her that her food ration was to be cut in half. This left Wanda the only person in the household who had full rations; it was not long before hunger became their constant companion. The struggle to survive was soon to become even more desperate. One day in the autumn of 1942, as Wanda arrived at work at seven o'clock in the morning, the guard informed her that he was taking her to the Commandant's office. When they arrived, Wanda was placed in a chair in front of the Commandant and the NKVD representative at the kolkhoz. The Commandant told Wanda that she was well past the age of the younger people on the compound who were sent to work in the Trudarmee. Since Henrietta had been caught stealing from the kolkhoz kitchen and Friedrich was a criminal serving a sentence at a Gulag, Wanda was to serve a five-year sentence at hard labour working on the railroad from Petrozavodsk to Archangelsk. The NKVD man then informed her that she would be taken to the nearest railroad station the next day along with several others from the kolkhoz.

Fortunately, Wanda did not know what lay ahead for her. Firstly, she did not know that her Aunt Lydia, the wife of Friedrich's brother Emil, would soon be sentenced to five years at hard labour, also on a railroad being built from Archangelsk to the Belomor Canal. Secondly, she did not know that back in 1932, some ten years earlier, when her father Robert Missal was taken away in the middle of the night that he was sent into the Belomor holocaust where he obviously perished. Aftr she left Janaja Polyana Wanda was never heard from again. Undoubtedly, she suffered the same fate as her father and aunt among the nearly 170,000 slave labourers or "enemies of the state" that Stalin had forcibly recruited during the early 1930's for the Belomor Canal project. Their only crime being that they or their ancestors had owned property. When Wanda went back home that evening after her last day of work she dreaded to break the news to the family and wondered if she would ever see them again— possibly a premonition of what the future held for her. When the guards arrived the next morning Henrietta said to her: "Don't worry, one day we will see you back at Nataliendorf because everyone in the family knows where home is and will know where to go when at last we will all be free again." Over the next few years, the only consolation the remaining members of the family would have is the hope that someday they would know where Wanda was sent and they would find her—her fate was never known. Friedrich was again put to work cleaning the livestock barns and what helped somewhat was that he had a full ration of food. Both Ottilia and Henrietta were very weak, so to add a bit more food to their diet he wanted to share part of his ration of watery soup and half a loaf of dry bread. Neither Henrietta nor Ottilia would take any of it and said that the children needed food more than they did. As early summer came, Friedrich took the boys out to the surrounding steppe and they spent hours harvesting the tender grass roots and took them back to the sod house to add to their watery soup. By this time however, Ottilia became very withdrawn. She would not eat at all, and claimed that she could survive on water alone. By July of 1942, she could hardly speak and one morning when young Willi went to wake her, she did not stir. Ottilia was only thirty-seven-years-old and her death was difficult for her three sons to comprehend. They had already seen their father shot to death by the NKVD and now witnessed their mother slowly die of starvation. After work the next day, Friedrich and the boys dug a grave far out on the Kazakhstani steppe and laid Ottilia to rest.

As the summer wore on Henrietta seemed to rally; the boys continued with their summer harvesting of grass shoots, which added somewhat to their daily food. Friedrich found some wire at the barns and devised a snare so that they might be able to catch one of the few rabbits that he had seen while they were picking grass. That night he and the boys set the snare out in their grass field, and after about a week of carefully watching the snare, the boys finally came home with their catch. For their meal that night, they had rabbit stew along with their dry bread and soup. As the days wore on Friedrich continued cleaning the livestock barns until one day the Russian foreman in charge of the barn workers, accused him of not removing all of the manure from the stalls and pointed out places that had not been cleaned. Friedrich thought that he had cleaned each stall thoroughly but in the dim light in the barn, Friedrich had not seen some of the piles of dung. During the last while, he also noticed that in the evenings when he and the boys were searching for grass roots that he could not see well enough to find the little stems of grass.

As the fall and winter of 1942, approached their grass and rabbit food supply began to dwindle and to make matters worse Friedrich was in constant fear of being taken to task for not cleaning the barns properly, since his eyesight was failing more and more every day. He was desperately afraid that he would have his food rations cut in half. This would mean that all seven in the family would be on half rations, which would be a disaster for the coming winter. Every day Henrietta would give part of her half ration to Willi the youngest of five boys, and she soon became even more emaciated. She felt terribly sorry for him since he had so recently lost his mother Ottilia whose burial he had witnessed far out on the desolate Kazakhstani steppe. Late one night in early December, Friedrich heard Henrietta call to him and when he reached her she quietly asked him to stay with her through the night for she knew she would not live until morning. As he lay with her, he thought about their lives together – the death of Eduard, her husband and his older brother, their deportation in 1915 and their struggle to survive the Bolshevik harassment during the Revolution. Then the violence of Lenin and the terror tactics of Stalin led to the agony of this—their lives in the kolkhoz. By midnight, he could no longer hear her breathing and felt her body grow cold. That morning he told the five boys to start digging a grave for their mother and aunt beside that of Ottilia. This would be no easy task on the frozen ground of the Kazakhstani steppe. That night when he arrived home after his day at work, they took Henrietta's body to her final resting place beside Ottilia the mother of the three boys who had helped dig both graves.

The early winter of 1943, was difficult for all of those that remained; the boys were now constantly hungry, especially the teenagers. Sixteen-year-old Arvid who was becoming very thin was becoming despewrate for food and one day told Friedrich that he would prefer to work at anything on the kolkhoz if he could just get a full food ration. Early the next morning, Friedrich took Arvid along with him to his work at the barns and asked the Russian foreman if Arvid could get full-time work with him cleaning the animal stalls. The supervisor said he would check with the Commandant and for Arvid to come with him. They were gone for quite some time and when they returned, the Commandant accompanied by an NKVD representative were with Arvid. The NKVD man told Friedrich that since Arvid was nearly seventeen and his brother Friedbert was almost sixteen that they were ready to be taken into the Trudarmee. He said that since the boys were non-productive at this kolkhoz and consuming half rations of food that they could do more for the Communist cause at a Gulag in the forests of the northern Ural Mountains. In the meantime, Arvid could put in a days work with Friedrich in the barns, but he was to be ready to leave first thing in the morning; a guard would come to where they lived and escort them to the train. With that the guard, the Commandant and the NKVD representative turned and left. The day passed for them both in a state of anxiety. Friedrich was relieved that Arvid was able to point out the piles of manure so that he would not miss any of them, but there was the gripping reality that both Arvid and Friedbert had to leave in the morning. When they got home that night Friedbert happily greeted them with the news that he had trapped a rat that morning and had skinned and gutted it so that they would have some meat to add to their meal that night. Since Friedbert was so pleased to able to add something to everyone's meal that night Arvid dreaded to tell him the news that tomorrow they both were to be sent to work in the Trudarmee at some faraway Gulag.

On the cold and bleak morning of February 15th, 1943, two guards appeared at their door and Friedrich and the three remaining boys bade Arvid and Friedbert farewell. Friedrich told them that when this nightmare was over they would be waiting for them back at Nataliendorf. In a matter of minutes, they were gone; Arvid was never heard from again. Nothing was heard of Friedbert for the next fifty years. However, in 1993 a relative who had recently been allowed to leave Russia heard that Friedbert had survived and had been able to leave. Again, this undoubtedly would have been through the Gorbachev/Kohl agreement allowing the repatriation to Germany of some of the descendents of the German colonists. It is ironic that these people had been Russian citizens who were now many generations removed from the original German colonists that had been invited to Russia by Catherine the Great some two hundred years earlier. In effect, these people were leaving their homeland. After all this time, those of the current generation had never spoken or even heard a word of their native language, since from the time of the October Revolution speaking German had been outlawed. Even back in Tsarist times speaking German had been discouraged by the colonist parents since they wanted their children to be well versed in the Russian way of life.

Friedrich was now left with the last three of his grandchildren: Waldemar, Gerhart, and Willi, who now had to act as his guides since Friedrich's eyesight continued to deteriorate. Each day young Gerhard was assigned to go to the kitchen to get their allotment of half rations for all of the four left in the family. Waldemar and young Willi would mind their trap lines for rats and rabbits. As well in the spring and early summer, the boys would pick the tender young grass blades and roots.

# Chapter 20

## Woroschilograd Tribulations: Taintscha Despair

By 1941, Emil's wife Lydia, with their five remaining children were struggling to survive at the Woroschilograd kolkhoz. With the long hours that she had to spend working in the kolkhoz fields, it not only was exhausting but also left her little time to spend with the children. However, left to roam the fields and bushes the children were able to gather berries and grass, which in turn helped them to survive. The oldest daughter, Antonina, was already twenty-one-years-old and Lydia was thankful that she had not yet been taken away to the Trudarmee. Then, in July of 1941, her next oldest son Richard who had just turned eighteen was approached by men in a Black Maria one morning as he was herding the neighbour's cattle. He was taken away without even being able to take the cattle home or to say goodbye to his family. Richard was never seen or heard from again.

Lydia had little time to wonder where her son was taken, for a short time later she was suddenly pulled from her work in the fields and was told that she was to prepare to leave Woroschilograd. She soon found that she and the children were being sent to a kolkhoz in northern Kazakhstan, and that they would be picked up early the next morning. When a truck arrived the next morning, the NKVD leader would not allow her to take along any belongings or food. Despite being threatened by the NKVD her neighbours rallied and shouted insults at Stalin's police until they let them put some loaves of bread, two small pails of lard and a bit of meat in the wagon for Lydia and her four remaining children. When they got to the

Dniepropetrovsk railway station a train made up of cattle cars, most of which were already filled with human cargo, was waiting for them—again Stalin's established mode of transportation.    An agonizing twenty-six days later, they arrived at the newly established southern kolkhoz at Jasnaja Poljana.    Here they were ushered into a barn-like barrack much like the shelter Friedrich and Henrietta had been provided with when they arrived at Janaja Polyana in 1936. Lydia, Antonina and fifteen-year-old Ergard were immediately put to work at the kolkhoz with each of them working a twenty-four hour shift.    They then would have twenty-four hours off.    This way the new Commandant reasoned that the inmates could use their twenty-four hour free time to provide food for themselves.

However, no thought was given to how these people were to accomplish this feat.    Consequently, the winter of 1941–1942 was difficult for Lydia and the four children.    Nevertheless, they somehow survived.    In early March of 1942, the resident NKVD representative found that Antonina was twenty-two-years-old and was still with her family.    He was incensed that she had gotten away without being sent to the Trudarmee.    Both she and Ergard, who was now sixteen-years-old, were called to report to the Commandant. Both were immediately sent to a slave labour camp somewhere in the Ural Mountains.    Lydia now was left with the two youngest children, fourteen-year-old Gerhard and twelve-year-old Margarita.    And during this time she continued her twenty-four hour shifts working in the fields.    Lydia heard of a Lydia Krampitz (which was her own maiden name) who lived in a sod house not too far away.    Always anxious to hear of and stay in touch with relatives she went to where this Lydia Krampitz lived, but when she found the new Lydia, they discussed their ancestry and could not resolve what the relationship was.    Lydia Krampitz then said that she wanted to be close to the kitchen facility where she worked so that she could check at the Commandant's office because her husband had been sent away to a Gulag for some minor infraction and should have been released some time ago.    She then asked Lydia Fischbuch if she could come and bring her children to stay at her place to look after her baby daughter for a few days.    Lydia agreed, since Margarita or Gerhard could alternate being with the baby, since they were at school and herded cattle for their neighbour inmates at different times. However, a week went by and Lydia Krampitz did not return. During her absence, a man from the NKVD stopped by several times and enquired about Lydia Krampitz. The third time he came he asked Lydia Fischbuch what her name was, and she said that her maiden name was Lydia Krampitz. He immediately said that she was obviously the Lydia they were looking for and arrested her. Lydia Fischbuch was not aware of the other Lydia having earlier been found guilty of "atrocities against the state" and now that the NKVD thought that this was Lydia Krampitz they took Lydia (Krampitz) Fiscbhbuch to serve the five-year sentence at a criminal detention camp.

Margarita and Gerhard were away at school and when they got home, the baby was alone and their mother was gone. They waited patiently for two days. On the third day, Lydia Krampitz returned and it became obvious even to the children that she had gone away leaving their mother there as a decoy—it worked perfectly for her. Thirteen-year-old Margarita and fifteen-year-old Gerhard waited and waitcd until thcy wcrc at last bluntly told by Lydia Krampitz to forget about their mother for she was sent to a far northern Gulag. They never saw their mother again. Lydia Krampitz, probably feeling guilty about her treatment of the children's mother, "graciously" allowed them to stay with her. They continued to go to school and to herd their neighbour's cattle. The little money and the few potatoes that they were given for their work, they carefully stored in a sack in a corner of the Krampitz sod house. About a month after Margarita and Gerhard's mother was taken away, Lydia Krampitz's husband arrived back from his incarceration in the Gulag. Upon his arrival, he was not pleased that there were two additional mouths to feed in his household. After all, they ate more than their allotted amount of food from the community kitchen, so he rudely told them that they must leave. He let Margarita and Gerhard take one small pail of their own potatoes and in return for the money and potatoes that he kept, he told them they could stay in a small dugout at the back of their sod house. Margarita and Gerhard continued to herd cattle for the neighbouring inmates on into the winter of 1942–1943. On a cold day in mid-December, one of the women noticed that Margarita had no shoes and had her feet wrapped in rags. She quickly searched around and gave her an old pair of shoes that had been worn by her son who had been taken away to the Trudarmee. The woman asked where they were staying and where their parents were. She felt sorry for them when she found that they had no parents and that they were living in an unheated dugout. She told Margarita that she and Gerhard could come and stay with her and her husband. She said that they could not pay them any money for herding their cattle and sheep but would give them a warm place to sleep and a bit of food. For this kindness, Margarita and Gerhard were very thankful and for the next three years, they got along well and helped the older couple as much as they could.

In May of 1946, as Margarita was helping the man that they were staying with, plant their potato crop he said that he had heard of someone by the name of Fischbuch that worked at the first established Jasnaja Poljana kolkhoz and if she wished he would go with her to see if they might be some of her relatives. Margarita's spirits rose for she hoped that there might be someone nearby from Nataliendorf, so they decided that on the man's next twenty-four hour break that they would go to see if they could find out if this truly could be a relative. It took nearly the whole day of asking everyone they met if they knew of a Fischbuch somewhere on the kolkhoz. When they finally found the sod house where they were told a Friedrich Fischbuch lived, they were greeted at the door by a woman about forty-years-old. She avoided speaking about Nataliendorf and told them that their name was the same but they would not be related. When Margarita looked into the house, she saw a man with white hair walking toward the door as he felt his way along the wall. The woman said that the man was blind and for them to leave for she had nothing more to say to them. At the time, Margarita thought that the blind man seemed familiar but she did not remember much about her uncle Friedrich, since she was only four-years-old and had only rarely seen him before her mother and her six siblings were taken away in 1934. As Margarita left, she thought that he looked familiar but when she got back to her duties with the old couple, she thought no more about her contact with the blind man. Much later, she would find that it truly was her uncle Friedrich.

In early 1946, Olga and August Krause were sent back to Taintscha to work at the kolkhoz where they were sent in 1934. Olga was concerned about August's heavy drinking, since he was arrested and taken from his work at the kolkhoz because of his drunkenness. He now was on half rations and would commonly trade it for whatever alcohol anyone would offer him. Olga often dreaded to get back to the barrack after work, for August would have beaten and abused their daughter Mehta and Mehta's baby girl. In November of 1946, Olga had heard about her father being held at Jasnaja Poljana, so after recruiting one of her co-workers to work an extra shift for her she went to see if she could locate him. When she got to Jasnaja Polyana, she found Friedrich alone since his three grandsons were away working in the kolkhoz fields. Friedrich told her that after Henrietta died his three grandsons were his salvation and did whatever they could for him. They looked after him well and regularly brought him his share of food from the communal kitchen. When she discovered his official ration was the allotted two hundred grams of food each day, she quickly realized he would be an additional source of food for her and August at their Taintscha kolkhoz. Olga immediately decided to take him back with her. She then went to the office of the Jasnaja Poljana Commandant and got a letter allowing her to take Friedrich to Taintscha. When the three boys: Waldemar, Gerhard and Willi arrived home, their aunt scolded them and said they were not taking care of their grandfather. She told them that she did not want to see her father suffering so she was taking him with her to Taintscha, where she could look after him properly. The boys were angry that she would even suggest such a thing and they said that they were taking good care of Friedrich. Friedrich himself pleaded with Olga to let him stay, but she said that she had already spoken with the Commandant and he had given her a letter allowing her take Friedrich to Taintscha with her. Many years later when Margarita recalled that in her her quest to find a relative, she realized that the woman that came to the door and told them that they were not related was Friedrich's stepdaughter Olga. She could have easily asked Margarita about her parents and probably had even recognized her. Nevertheless, Olga had her own plan in mind and did not want it interrupted by anyone claiming to be a relative.

The next day when Olga was to leave with Friedrich, he wondered if he would ever again have the company of the three grandsons who he cared so much for, and would have to leave them behind at Jasnaja Poljana. It would be a gruelling trip for Friedrich to walk the thirty-five miles to the Taintscha kolkhoz, so to make it easier for him to carry his few belongings the boys made a backpack out of a sack so he would have his hands free to help him keep his balance. The boys made sure that they packed his treasured naval documents and his few clothes in the packsack.

They were careful to include the Cross of St. George that reminded Friedrich so much of his brave naval companions. He had told the boys much about his training on the ships in the Baltic; his help in building the battleship Tsesarevich at Toulon in France; the voyage along the equator to Port Arthur; the Battle of the Yellow Sea; their long stay during the internment of the Tsesarevich at Tsintao and the voyage back to St. Petersburg. Young Willi broke into tears as he said goodbye to his grandfather and said that he would miss him so much, especially the bedtime stories about the navy. Friedrich was shaking with both fear and anger at leaving his trusted grandsons. He called Waldemar, the eldest of the three grandsons, to him and gave him the medallion that was presented to him by the Tsar in 1906 for his service in the Russian Navy. Waldemar kept it with him for the rest of his life. After he immigrated to Germany in 1989, and when he died there in 2007, he left the medallion with his widow Erica, who still has it to this day.

Both Olga and Friedrich were exhausted after their long trek across the cold and barren northern Kazakhstani steppe, and when they arrived at the barracks at the Taintscha kolkhoz they were greeted by a drunken group of workers with August Krause in their midst. Vodka had become as common as tea and was now the opiate of the Russian workers. In the new Communist workplace, people had no sense of accomplishment for their efforts, and went through their days expending as little effort as possible. They knew that all they would benefit from their labours was their meagre ration of food, which would sustain them for only another day. Therefore, any small amount of money they would glean or steal would be spent on an alcoholic tranquilizer that would temporarily ease their frustrations. August Krause, of course had a head start on most of the others since he had already discovered alcohol to drown his frustrations in the early 1930's.

In no time Olga had Friedrich installed in a barrack on a straw-covered cot among a half dozen other incapacitated workers. This became Friedrich's permanent living quarters where once each day Olga would bring him a small part of his food allotment. Any additional food that she had would be sold or traded to supplement August's alcohol consumption. While he was interned at the Gulag August Krause only had access to water, however, vodka flowed freely among the guards and the administration. Therefore, upon his release he pursued his addiction with renewed vigour. It was not long before their daughter Mehta became enthralled with one of August's young drinking cohorts; a man who had come back from Gulag incarceration with August. He had been sent to the Gulag from the Jasnaja Poljana kolkhoz and had been released at the same time as August. He soon found young eighteen-year-old Mehta a willing companion and it was not long before a daughter was born. However, this brought about an impediment to Mehta's social life with her new partner, and consequently, added to the problems that new grandmother Olga had to deal with.

Friedrich continued to languish among the other incapacitated men, but with only a fraction of his allotted food to sustain him he became weaker and weaker and found it difficult to move about in the over-crowded barrack. By early 1946, he asked Olga to try to get him a bit more food because he was constantly hungry, but she said that he was getting his full half-portion and there was nothing more that she could do for him. He asked her for his naval documents and the Cross of St. George, for he wanted to keep them to pass on to his three grandsons. She said that they were useless items and that she had let Mehta's little daughter play with them. She said that she had no idea where they were but in any case, they were useless things to have around anyway.

About a month later when Olga arrived with Friedrich's small ration of food the man in the cot next to Friedrich said that he was not able to rouse Friedrich and that he had stayed in bed all day. When Olga tried to wake him, he did not move and when she felt his face, it was stone cold. The realization flooded over her that her stepfather was dead. This was the man who had helped them through all of the trials since their father had died from his war injuries. She then recalled how Friedrich and Henrietta had tried so hard to keep them from going hungry and comforted her, her sister and her brother during the trying times they had gone through during the 1915 deportation. She now realized that she had neglected someone who had cared deeply for her and she had forsaken his well-being for the sake of her errant husband. Here again arose another case of the basic human instinct to survive. Olga's obsession to accommodate her husband's alcoholism and to provide for his affliction overrode the closeness of family ties that had been instilled in them all by Michel and Justina back in Nataliendorf.

The next day Friedrich's body was loaded onto a wagon with several other bodies of inmates who had recently died. All were carted off to a common unmarked grave in the Kazakhstani wilderness. Sadly, this ended the life of a man who grew up in a family filled with aspirations for a great future for their children. Friedrich's parents felt assured that their diligence and hard work was recognized by their adopted country and they took great pride in the fact that their son was called to serve their country, a country that had given them the opportunity to flourish in a village that took them many years to wrestle from the forest and swampland. And, they were proud that it had become a model settlement for all of Russia to behold.

There was no reward, however, for the six brothers and their families who were sealed behind the Iron Curtain in 1929. After they had served their sentences in the Trudarmee, the Kolkhoz, and the Gulag, they were not even allowed to go back to their native area. They were only allowed to remain near the places where they had been interned. They were forced to reside near whatever insidious correctional facility where they had been held. These were the camps of human fodder that fuelled Stalin's Communist dream and were spread throughout Russia -- in the Siberian wilderness, in the barren Kazakhstani plains, in the frozen Russian Artic, and in the Muslim and Oriental Soviet enclaves to the south and Far East. After their incarceration all the family deportees could do was dream of what it would be like to reunite with brothers, sisters, parents and grandparents. Unfortunately, that dream never came true. The family life together that was such an obsession with Michel and Justina was something that they had all experienced in their youth at their little village of Nataliendorf. It was now just a fading memory. All the surviving descendants of Friedrich and his five brothers were forced to remain in Russia after 1929. However, in 1989 sixty years later Gorbachev's Perestroika allowed some of their descendants to leave Russia.

# Part 2

# The Fate of the Tsesarevich and Friedrich's Naval Associates After 1906

Port Arthur in late 1904, sometime after the defeat of the First Pacific Squadron when Admiral Ukhtomski abandoned the squadron and went back to Port Arthur with five warships during the battle. The five ships are, from left to right: Peresviet, Poltava, Retvisan, Pobieda, and Pallada. All of which were later sunk or captured by the Japanese

TSESAREVICH – The Tsesarevich was designed by Forges et Chantiers Mediterranee de la Seyne; her keel was laid in May of 1899 in Toulon, France.    This armour-clad battleship became the prototype for five Borodino class battleships built at Toulon.    She was built for the Russian Navy under the supervision of Captain Ivan K. Grigorovich.    Friedrich Fischbuch later joined him from the Russian Naval base at Kronstadt to oversee the battleship's propulsion system.    Upon her launching in August of 1903, the Tsesarevich was immediately dispatched to Port Arthur where the Japanese damaged her in a sneak attack in February of 1904.    In

August of 1904, as the flagship of Russia's First Pacific Squadron in the Battle of the Yellow Sea, she was severely damaged and limped to the neutral Chinese port of Tsintao where she was interned until the end of the war. Upon her return to Russia's Baltic naval base at Kronstadt, she became the mainstay of the Baltic Fleet. From 1914 to 1916, she served against attacking German warships in the Baltic Sea. After the Bolshevik Revolution and during the tenuous period of Kerensky's Provisional Government the Tsesarevich was renamed the Grajdanin and was damaged in a battle against the Germans in the Gulf of Riga in 1917. After Stalin became leader of the Communist party in 1924, the Grajdanin was demobilized and sold for scrap in 1925.

GRIGOROVICH – Ivan Konstantinovich Grigorovich was born in 1853, into a family whose naval history went back for two generations. His father had been a Rear Admiral and even though he was not well off financially, he found a way to send Ivan to the Naval Academy. Ivan graduated in 1878, which was some time after his two Baltic naval compatriots had both graduated at the top of their classes: Zinoviev Rozhdestvensky graduated in 1870, and

Stepan Makarov graduated in 1865. Like them, Grigorovich spent much of his early training at sea and unlike many of his other colleagues, he did not seek a plum posting onshore, but rather he took much pride in staying at sea and keeping his ship and sailors in fighting trim. To accomplish this he was a rigid, but thoughtful disciplinarian and consequently was held in high regard by the ordinary seamen under his command. The one positive event in the Russo-Japanese war for Tsar Nicholas was when the Tsesarevich returned to Kronstadt. Through the efforts of its captain and crew, it was the only battleship to survive the disastrous Japanese conflict. The Tsar immediately promoted Grigorovich to Rear Admiral and assigned him as Commander of the Baltic Fleet.

By 1911, Grigorovich had done much to resurrect the Russian Navy and through these efforts, he had been assigned as Commander of both the Baltic and the Black Sea Fleets. He vigorously pursued having new ships brought into Kronstadt and Odessa to bolster the losses resulting from the war with Japan. The Admiralty recognized his naval acumen and in March of 1911, the Tsar appointed Grigorovich as Minister of the Navy, a position he held throughout World War 1. When Lenin overthrew Kerensky's Provisional Government in October of 1917, the Bolshevik Revolution that followed was devastating for the Empire's navy, since most Tsarist government agencies became enemies of the state. Consequently, any government official of the Tsarist regime was sought out by the Bolshevik secret police. Grigorovich, in an effort to protect what he had accomplished for the Russian Navy during his tenure as Minister of the Navy, continued to be very vocal about the need to maintain a strong marine force whatever the political stripe of the Empire. To silence the outspoken Minister the NKVD quickly sought him out, accused him of taking huge bribes from naval suppliers and struck his name from Russian naval records. It was not long before Grigorovich was removed from his naval duties and he was under constant surveillance by the police. Ordinary sailors who had served under him would smuggle food and clothing to him and helped him to escape from his guards. He continued to live hidden by friends and fellow sailors in the St. Petersburg suburbs, always being aware that the NKVD could arrest him, send him to a Siberian slave labour camp or have him executed.  By 1923, he needed treatment for a brain tumour and he could not have this difficult surgery done in Russia for fear of being arrested by the NKVD.  Somehow, Lenin's police became aware of his dilemma and, since they did not know where he was, they posted guards at the Russian borders to prevent his escape.  Members of the Naval Staff, who had not yet been removed by the Bolshevik movement, joined forces to smuggle Grigorovich to France.  Here he had the delicate brain operation.  However, after he recovered he was a destitute outcast in a foreign land.  He subsisted by painting seascapes and selling them to passers-by and when he died in 1930, he was buried in a pauper's grave.

In 2003, his service to Russia as the last Navy Minister of the Russian Empire was again recognized and he was reinstated in the Naval Archives in St. Petersburg.  In July of 2004, two Russian ships, the cruiser Moskva and the frigate Pylky were sent to the French Cote d'Azur to seek out his burial place and bring home the mortal remains of Admiral Ivan Konstantinovich Grigorovich.  Upon the return of the ships to St. Petersburg, his remains were laid to rest in the family vault at the St. Nicholas Cemetery in St. Petersburg.  Some of his descendants were present at the ceremony.  When he left St. Petersburg in 1923, he told those people close to him that his last wish was that he wanted to be buried next to his wife.  However, it took over seventy-five years for his wish to be fulfilled.

WITGEFT – Wilgelm Karlovich Witgeft was born in Odessa in 1847 to German parents whose ancestors had answered the call of Tsarina Catherine II in the early 1800's. They would have travelled the famous Danube route to the Black Sea along with hundreds of other German settlers to the promised land of southern Russia.  Witgeft's name was transliterated to Russian; his first name undoubtedly would have been Wilhelm and his father's name would have been Karl.. After serving on Russian ships in the Black Sea, he became well acquainted in sea-going manoeuvres. By 1868, the Odessa colonists would have been relatively well off and his parents undoubtedly were able to afford to send Wilgelm to the Naval Academy. He was promoted to lieutenant in 1873, and in 1885, was captain of the ship Grosna. In 1892, he was captain of the warship Wajewoda and in 1899, was promoted to Rear Admiral. Upon the death of Admiral Makarov in 1903, he was sent to Port Arthur to command the First Pacific Squadron and remained there until he was killed in August of 1904, in the Battle of the Yellow Sea while on his flagship the Tsesarevich. He was decapitated by shrapnel when a twelve-pound shell from a Japanese battleship struck the bridge of the Russian flagship.

WIREN – Robert Nikolayevich Wiren was the captain of the armour-clad cruiser Bayan that accompanied the Tsesarevich to Port Arthur in August of 1903. In March of 1904, shortly after war was declared and Admiral Makarov arrived as Commander of the Second Pacific Squadron. Makarov sent out the destroyer Strashnyi on reconnaissance and shortly after it was out of the harbour it ran headlong into several Japanese warships. The shore batteries saw what was happening and informed Admiral Makarov who immediately sent two of his fastest cruisers, the Bayan and the Diana, to aid the Strashnyi. When Wiren saw the Japanese closing in on the stricken destroyer, he pushed the Bayan beyond its maximum speed of 21 knots until the vibration shook the entire ship. He braved the encroaching Japanese warships and came alongside the Strashnyi as it began to sink and was able to rescue the entire crew.

In July of 1904, when Admiral Witgeft was sent to Port Arthur to take command of the First Pacific Squadron and as the Japanese forces were encroaching on Port Arthur Witgeft was ordered by the

Tsar to take the First Pacific Squadron to Vladivostok. He left Captain Wiren in command of the port with a skeleton force of a few warships to hold Port Arthur as long as he could. When he left Port Arthur, Witgeft sent word to the Tsar to recognize Wiren's responsibility and a short time later Wiren was promoted to Rear Admiral. The Japanese army was rapidly approaching by land and Admiral Togo's navy was bombarding Port Arthur from the sea, so the defeat of Port Arthur was inevitable. Admiral Wiren, in his new role felt that any open sea battle with Admiral Togo would only hasten Port Arthur's defeat. Therefore, he immediately used his new position to substantially bolster the defences of Port Arthur by using the armament of the five warships that had fled back to Port Arthur during the Battle of the Yellow Sea. He had the sailors and deckhands carry the ships guns and ammunition part way up the mountain slopes to fire at the approaching Japanese land army. In addition, he had several of the smaller Russian warships go out under cover of darkness to lay mines beyond the roadstead. This resulted in the Russian mines sinking four Japanese ships.

By the 19th of September, the Japanese ground forces having siezed the mountain immediately to the east of the port, had a clear view of all of the Russian warships in the harbour, but it took them a month to sink their first Russian vessel. The powder magazine of the battleship Poltava was hit and the ship quickly sank. In the next four days three more battleships and two cruisers were sunk, including the cruiser Bayan that Wiren had brought from Toulon. The Sevastopol was the only battleship to survive and Wiren sent it out into the roadstead to fire at any Japanese warship within range. Amazingly, the Sevastopol along with several destroyers held off the Japanese navy and when they ran out of ammunition, the captain opened the seacocks and scuttled the ship. Finally, on December 20th, 1904, Port Arthur was surrendered to the Japanese and Rear Admiral Wiren was taken prisoner along with the remaining Russian military men.

When Witgeft had been ordered to go to Vladivostok he assumed that Port Arthur would fall within a week. However, through amazing effort Wiren held Port Arthur from August 10th to December 20th, a period of nearly three and a half months.

Eventually Wiren was released by the Japanese and made his way back to St. Petersburg. When interviewed by the Tsar he made it quite clear to his royal highness that the complete Japanese venture was grossly mishandled from the outset.

With the rise of the Bolsheviks, the October Revolution, and eventually the formation of Kerensky's Provisional government, Wiren was consistently outspoken about the rise of Marxism in Russia. On March 1st, 1917, a mob of sailors, steeped in the emerging Leninist ideology, took Wiren from his home in Kronstadt and marched him through the streets where they mocked, ridiculed and beat him. They accused him of the brutal treatment of the seamen that were under his command at Port Arthur. They then shot him as the gathered Bolshevik mob cheered. The ensuing Communist regime had his name crossed from Russian history, his defense of Port Arthur and all records of his naval career were destroyed. Later, however, Wiren's granddaughter Vera Wiren-Garczynski persisted for years to get her grandfather reinstated in Russian naval history. She was finally rewarded in her quest after the Soviet Union fell in 1990. From her efforts today a memorial stands on the Russian Navy's island of Kronstadt honouring the role of Admiral Robert Nikolayevich Wiren in the annals of Russian naval history.

MAKAROV – Stepan Osipovich Makarov was born in 1848 to a father who also had naval credentials. Osip Makarov was a naval petty officer who desperately sought to provide his son with the best naval credentials in Russia. Stepan graduated at the top of his class from the Nikolaevsk Naval Academy in 1865—far ahead of any of his other classmates. He spent every moment he could, studying naval history and battle tactics. During his relatively short naval career, he taught his Russian naval officers on ways of using the new steam-powered ironclad battleships to their full advantage and as well, he tutored them in mine warfare, battle formations and ramming enemy ships. He also designed a collision mat as well as a more effective way to launch torpedoes. During the Russian-Turkish war of 1875–1878, he was decorated for using his torpedo technology to temporarily neutralize the Turkish navy. Ironically, the Japanese navy in their attacks on Port Arthur used many of the battle concepts that they took from his book, "Discussion of Questions in Naval Tactics" that he wrote in 1897, and had been translated into seven languages.

Upon his appointment as Commander of the First Pacific Squadron, he insisted that forty torpedo boats should be disassembled and shipped to Port Arthur via the Trans-Siberian Railway. As well, he requested that the ground defences at Port Arthur should be substantially increased to repel any Japanese land attacks or bombardments from the sea. Nevertheless, his requests were conveniently ignored by the Tsar and his unqualified bureaucrats. Had Makarov not been killed in the sinking of his flagship the Petropavlovsk in March of 1904, he undoubtedly would have had considerable influence in the outcome of the sea battles with Admiral Togo Heihachiro. The loss of Admiral Makarov was recognized by the Japanese navy and they issued a formal statement to the international naval community acknowledging his scientific achievements. Today a statue of Admiral Makarov stands at the Naval Base at Kronstadt in honour of his service to the Russian navy.

ROZHDESTVENSKY — Zinoviev Petrovich Rozhdestvensky was born in 1848, the same year as his compatriot and fellow admiral Stepan Makarov. A fierce competition between Rozhdestvensky and Makarov in their naval careers persisted, until the premature death of Makarov at Port Arthur. However, Rozhdestvensky's major accomplishment came when he took on the monumental task of guiding Russia's hodgepodge

Second Pacific Squadron halfway around the world to confront a rested and well-equipped Japanese navy. Even after his defeat at the hands of Admiral Togo Heihachiro in the Battle of Tsushima, he had won the admiration of naval tacticians around the world for efficiently herding an armada of ill-equipped ships to almost certain defeat. However, had Rozhdestvensky not been struck by a shell fragment that left him disabled and unconscious, leaving the fleet in disarray with no commander, he may have been able to turn the tide of the battle. When the wounded admiral was transferred to an accompanying destroyer it in turn was captured by the Japanese. Rozhdestvensky was then taken to a Japanese hospital where he was well treated and recovered in a relatively short time. In November of 1905, some six months after the battle, the Japanese allowed the Russian transport ship Yakut to take Rozhdestvensky and several other Russian officers to Vladivostok. When they arrived in Vladivostok three days later, the admiral was shocked by what he saw. There was much evidence of rioting and the waterfront appeared to be in a shambles. Several of the waterfront buildings had been gutted by fire and there were only a few small warships anchored in the harbour -- very different from what Rozhdestvensky had seen when he was at Vladivostok in 1890. The rumblings of discontent among Russian citizenry with the Romanov dynasty were already becoming obvious.

As Rozhdestvensky travelled via the Trans-Siberia Railway across eastern Russia on his way back to St. Petersburg crowds of well-wishers greeted him at every stop. Groups of frustrated veteran soldiers, back from the Japanese ground war who were fed up with the Tsar's incompetent handling of the war, crowded around him and shouted that as the martyr of Tsushima he should become the new ruler of Russia. After nearly three weeks of travel, he arrived at St. Petersburg in early December of 1905, and assumed that he would be heralded as a hero and would at the very least be entrusted with rejuvenating and reforming Russia's naval forces. Surprisingly, when he arrived at the railroad station there was no one there to greet him. He soon found that the Tsar and his royally appointed ministers were desperately trying to find a scapegoat for the naval defeats at the hands of the Japanese. Hearing of his popularity among the disgruntled soldiers as his train passed through the Siberian wilderness from Vladivostok, the Tsar and his Admiralty became uneasy, since it was now becoming more and more obvious that they were the ones responsible for the defeat. After all, it was the Tsar and his Admiralty advisors who had insisted that the Second Pacific Squadron leave in such a hurry without proper training, minimal artillery practice and only a limited amount of ammunition. They were stalled for over two months at Madagascar, as well as an agonizing month delay in Indochina. And, to add to the admiral's frustration, he had to take plodding old ships and fragile pleasure craft that were of little value in a sea battle. To absolve themselves of any responsibility Nicholas and his incompetent advisors were now heaping total responsibility for the defeat on Rozhdestvensky.

In January of 1906, the Tsar's attention was momentarily diverted from his responsibility in the Far East debacle by the return of the good battleship Tsesarevich. This gave him an opportunity publicly to reward Captain Grigorovich and Chief Engineer Friedrich Fischbuch for bringing back at least one of Russia's battleships to St. Petersburg. However, he still had to save face in Russia and abroad and vowed to show that the admiral and the officers in charge of the Second Pacific Squadron were completely responsible for the naval defeat with Japan -- they must be punished. In June of 1906, Rozhdestvensky was court-martialled along with all of the staff officers of his flagship the Suvorov. As well, the captains and officers of four other warships of the Second and Third Pacific Squadrons that had surrendered to Admiral Togo to avoid even more bloodshed were also arrested and tried. The Tsar and the Admiralty were of the opinion that no Russian warship should have done the cowardly act of surrendering to the enemy. Rozhdestvensky refused to have legal representation and stated that he was fully conscious throughout the entire battle. As he stood in court, he stated that as commander of the fleet he was solely responsible for the defeat and that the other officers were acting under orders directly from him and should be released immediately. However, evidence from other officers and the ship's doctor made it obvious to the court that the admiral was incapacitated and unconscious from being struck by shrapnel as the flagship was hit by the first salvo of heavy shells from the Japanese battleships. Rozhdestvensky grudgingly was acquitted. However, four of his officers were sentenced to death, as was Admiral Nebogatov, the late arriving commander of the Third Pacific Squadron who had surrendered four unscathed Russian warships to the Japanese. As Tsar Nicholas became more and more engrossed with the disintegration of the Romanov dynasty he relented and commuted the sentences to prison terms. After the trial, Rozhdestvensky surprisingly had little to do with Russia's navy or politics and lived quietly surrounded by friends and family. He died suddenly, probably of a stroke on January 1, 1909, in St. Petersburg.

# Afterword

There are not many events during the rise of the autocratic Romanov dynasty in Russia in which the citizens of the Tsar's vast domain could take pride. Under the Tsar's all-powerful rule, no one was able to rise to fame or fortune from the vast population of serfs and peasants that made up nearly ninety per cent of the population. Even after Tsar Alexander II freed the serfs in 1861, they remained uneducated and unskilled and roamed the countryside as itinerant Mouzhiken. As a result, the only people that could rise in Russian society were those that were members of the Romanov dynasty, the church, the nobility or the aristocracy to be eligible for the Tsar to anoint them to any position, be it an ordinary or privileged post. Certainly, among those at the top of the Tsarist hierarchy there were some spectacular accomplishments.

Tsarina Catherine II in her shrewd rise to power made commendable strides to develop the agricultural potential of southern Russia by inviting German workers. And, even when engrossed in her titillating love affairs made aggressive territorial expansion of the Empire.

As well, one cannot overlook the foresight of Tsar Peter the Great who brought experienced artisans to Russia, not only to train his unskilled subjects in worldly trades, but also to build an architecturally unique city. He located and built his capital city that he christened St. Petersburg on the delta of the Neva River where it flows into the Baltic Sea. It was not long before it became Russia's gateway to the outside world. Nevertheless, these were individual accomplishments of Romanov rulers who had the foresight to improve the lives of the ordinary Russian people. However, with the advent of Bolshevism and Communism whatever reminded them of the hated Tsarist dynasty was demolished.

In the midst of the stifling Tsarist autocracy, there was one segment of Russian society that was able to rise above the Romanov shackles. Since trade schools and institutions of higher learning were non-existent, some ordinary Russian citizens realized that to attend the Naval Academy was an institution where ordinary citizens could study. Most important of all, it was not as expensive as it was to become an army officer. Consequently, many people strove to send their sons to train as naval officers. It followed that many of these sailors were the ones who after graduation stayed at sea. Whereas, those of royal or aristocratic background who had been brought up in St. Petersburg's high society found sea-going duties rather harsh and immediately sought less demanding shore duties. However, even though these ordinary citizen officers had honed their seagoing skills they still had to manoeuvre their way carefully through the Tsar's bureaucratic naval maze.

Once they reached their goal of captaining a ship these seaoned and well-trained sailors far outshone captains and admirals who were appointed at the whim of the Tsar. Then, finally, when their ships reached the open seas away from the Tsar's fawning bureaucrats and relatives they became masters of their own destinies and many of these captains and admirals of the Russian Navy gained international recognition. It is not that there were any spectacular Russian naval victories for there were very few. Nevertheless, heroics of some individual sailors and their warships were admired and respected by other navies around the world. Many of Russia's naval craft that were sailed by these well-trained captains and admirals had crews with backgrounds all the way from royalty, to aristocrats, to colonists to itinerant ex-serfs. It followed that whenever a ship was piloted by a competent commander who had fought his way through the academy, had spent years at sea and had struggled through the Tsarist bureaucratic maze, it was not long before a spirit of respect for the commander grew and a special camaraderie arose. As they served together, the crews formed a lasting partnership on "their" sea-going vessel. Despite their different backgrounds, this comradeship instilled a sense of accomplishment among the sailors all the way from the captain, to the gunner, to the stoker and to the deckhand. In this way, each crew in working as a cohesive unit made their warship a battle-ready machine. What was happening back in Russian politics drifted from their minds as they steamed further and further out to sea and away from St. Petersburg.

On the other hand, ships that were commanded by Tsarist appointed captains or admirals, many of whom had little or no naval training, were often so poorly operated that they commonly ran aground, collided with other ships or in some cases faced mutiny. Nevertheless, some royal appointees did become worthy naval commanders despite their swollen egos and their lack of naval training.

## The Fate of Friedrich's Descendents, His Thirteen Brothers and Sisters and Their Descendents After 1928

It was decreed by the Communist Party that no ethnic German would ever be allowed to go back to their native Russian community, so once they were deported from their properties from the early 1930's to 1990, none of the six brothers who remained in Russia or their descendants were allowed to return to their home villages. They also were required to report to the authorities every month solely because they were of alien German heritage. Even if they wished to go from one neighbouring village to another, wherever they remained after their Siberian exile, they had to apply for a travel visa and wait to have it processed, which commonly took as long as two years. However, they were given somewhat increased freedom to travel and shorter waiting times after Stalin's death in 1953. Even then, they were never allowed to go back to their home villages.

EDUARD – Eduard Fischbuch was the oldest son of Michel and Justina and was born in 1874, in Nataliendorf. He married Henrietta (Yeta) Wolltmann about 1901, and they had three children: one son and two daughters. Eduard died in 1916, from wounds sustained in WW1 in the Crimea. Friedrich, his younger brother married his widow, Henrietta, and adopted the three children after their gruelling deportation in 1915 to 1917.

JOHANN – Johann Fischbuch was born in 1876, at Nataliendorf, he married Wilhelmina Reinas in 1898. Their two youngest children died of starvation in the deportation of 1915 to 1917. Their oldest daughter died in a slave labour camp in the early 1930's. Johann and Wilhelmina, with their remaining two sons, Reinhold and Arnold and one daughter came to Canada in 1928. The daughter Elfrieda was born in 1906, and lived in Nataliendorf until 1928. In 1982, she provided me with pictures and historical events of the family from her younger days, their 1915 deportation and her family's survival under the Bolshevik-Stalinist regime from 1915 until they left Russia in 1928.

AUGUST – August Fischbuch was born in 1878, at Nataliendorf. He married Ottilia Kahler in 1901. Two sons, Friedrich and Reinhold died at birth in Nataliendorf in 1902 and 1903. A daughter, Antonia was born in Nataliendorf in 1905. August was sent to Canada in 1906, by his father because of his indiscretion with his fourteen-year-old sister-in-law. The baby son died in childbirth. His wife Ottilia and daughter Antonia followed him to Canada in 1907. Antonia burned to death in a tragic accident in Winnipeg in 1909. August and Ottilia had eleven more children after Ottilia arrived in Canada: Otto born 1908, Erna born 1910, Elsie and Emil (twins) born 1912, Frieda born 1913, Herman born 1915, Edwin and Martha (twins) born 1917, Violet born 1923, Meta born 1925 and Norman born 1931. August died of internal bleeding in 1934 when he was kicked by a horse. The widowed Ottilia nurtured her family of eleven children through the poverty and hunger of the Great Depression that lasted from 1929 to 1939. She died in 1943.

Shortly after August was killed in 1934, when Ottilia was faced with providing for her remaining eleven children, she was hand-delivered a letter from Russia from the husband of her sister Emma. In the letter, he said that Emma had died of starvation, but their three little girls were still alive and could Ottilia send money for their fare to come to Canada because he had found a way to leave, but needed money for travel—even if it was just enough to send the children. However, Ottilia was in a crisis herself with the death of August and eleven children to feed in the depth of the Great Depression. She wept for her three nieces, but could do nothing.

During this time, many pleas for help came to North America. Some of these cries of help to relatives in North America were searched out by Dr. Samuel Sinner who published them in his work entitled "Letters from Hell." One of the many letters he unearthed reads as follows:

"Our large village is half empty. As the horses have died people would fight and argue over small pieces of horsemeat that had gone bad. But now there are no horses left. The parents now go to the Soviet Office and ask permission to eat their children who have starved to death. Everything can't be written, that would be an evil."

"We have now ended a seventy-year experiment with socialism with little more to our credit than tens of millions of corpses."
...Eugene Genovese, Professor of History
Rutgers University.
(Former American Communist)

Friedrich & Henrietta (Yeta) Fischbuch
Nataliendorf, Volhynia 1918

FRIEDRICH – Friedrich Fischbuch was born in 1879, at Nataliendorf. After his brother Eduard's death Friedrich married Eduard's widow, Henrietta (Wolltmann) Fischbuch in 1917, and adopted the three children, Robert, Olga and Ida. During Stalin's time of the Great Terror through the 1930's these three children and their families were engulfed in the Communist reign of death. The first family member to be taken away in 1931 was Olga along with her husband and their three children. Initially they were sent to a kolkhoz at Taintscha in northern Kazakhstan and a short time later, they were sent to a detention slave labour camp north and east of the Ural Mountains. However, they were later returned to the Taintscha kolkhoz.

In 1932, the other daughter Ida starved to death at their Missal home in Annette. She had made a vain attempt to provide enough food for their growing children by only taking little or no food for herself. Not long after his wife's death late one night in the latter part of 1932, Robert Missal was woken by the NKVD at his door and they immediately arrested him. He quickly sent his three young children to stay with their grandparents, Friedrich and Henrietta. Robert Missal was sent to work at Stalin's Belomor Canal project where he either froze to death or starved to death along with hundreds of other slave labourers. Nothing was ever heard of him again.

In 1937, Friedrich and Henrietta's son Robert was shot to death when the NKVD were arresting him. Later his wife, Ottilia and their three children also were arrested and sent to the same kolkhoz at Jasnaja Poljana that Friedrich and Henrietta were sent in 1935. Some time after she arrived at Jasnaja Poljana she slowly died of starvation because of her attempt to provide extra food for her children from her own limited ration. Friedrich and Henrietta now had these three young grandsons as well as Ida's three children with them and looked after them at the Jasnaja Poljan kolkhoz. After Henrietta died in 1942, and when Ida's three grandchildren reached the age of seventeen they were taken away to the Trudarmee to work at other kolkhozes, Gulags or some other detention camp. Robert and Ottilia's three sons who still were under seventeen years of age: Waldemar, Gerhard, and Willi were with Friedrich when he went blind while they were at the Jasnaja Poljana kolkhoz in Kazakhstan. Every day when they brought his half ration of food to him and as they ate together, he told them many stories about his life in the navy. Friedrich died in 1948, at the Taintscha kolkhoz where his stepdaughter Olga had taken him in 1946. He now lies buried in an unmarked common grave somewhere on the bleak steppe in northern Kazakhstan. His body, along with the bodies of some of his fellow inmates had been unceremoniously and uncaringly dumped into an open pit, which was immediately ordered to be covered with earth by other kolkhoz slave labourers so that there would be no evidence of their demise once it was overgrown by grass. This had now become the routine disposal method of the mounting number of deaths from exhaustion, over work and starvation in Stalin's penal colonies. The only purpose for their existence was to further Stalin's quest to build his Communist Empire and would enhance his image abroad.

4a) WALDEMAR – Friedrich's oldest grandson Waldemar Fischbuch was born December 25, 1929, in Nataliendorf, Russia. From 1946 to 1948, Waldemar continued to work in the kolkhoz Trudarmee at Jasnaja Poljana. From 1948 to 1950, he apprenticed as a sheet metal worker and from that time on worked in the sheet metal industry. In 1952, Waldemar married Erica Zimmer whose grandfather was August Fischbuch a brother to Michel Fischbuch Waldemar's great-grandfather. The NKVD also had sent Erica's parents to Jasnaja Poljana. In 1978, Waldemar and his family were allowed to move to Tokmak, Kirgistan where they lived until 1989 when they were allowed to immigrate to Germany with their family, two sons and two daughters. I met Waldemar, Erica and their family in 2002 at which time they told me much about their lives in Kazakhstan, and Waldemar spoke about what Friedrich had related to the boys about his life in Russia's Navy. I wanted to visit him again and hear more about his life with Friedrich and Henrietta. Unfortunately, Waldemar died in 2007. However, during a visit with Erica and the rest of the family in 2008 I learned more about their lives with Friedrich in Jasnaja Poljana.

4b) GERHARD – Friedrich's next grandson Gerhard Fischbuch was born on February 20th, 1931, in Nataliendorf, Russia. After Friedrich was taken to Taintscha, Gerhard and his brother Willi remained at Jasnaja Poljana where they continued to go to school while their older brother Waldemar worked at the kolkhoz. Since Gerhard had done very well at his studies his teachers recommended him to be sent to a university at Alma Ata, a city far to the south near Kirgistan. Here he studied physics and mathematics and lectured there for a time. He was later sent to teach at Taljati, but during this time he went blind and was retired. In 2007 Gerhard with his wife and son were allowed to leave Russia and now live in Bremen, Germany. I spoke to him briefly in 2008.

4c) WILLI – Willi Fischbuch, Friedrich's youngest grandson was born February 12th, 1933, in Nataliendorf, Russia. In 1946, after his aunt Olga took Friedrich to Taintscha, Willi and his next oldest brother Gerhard continued to go to school at the Jasnaja Poljana kolkhoz. Like his brother, he excelled at mathematics and when he finished his required schooling at the kolkhoz, he was sent to study at the university at Petropavlovsk, a city north of Jasnaja Poljana near the northern Kazakhstan border with Siberia. Here he studied mathematics and physics like his brother Gerhard had at Alma Ata. He taught mathematics and physics for two years and then was sent to Usunkol, northern Kazakhstan where after two years he became the director of scientific studies at an institute of higher learning at Usunkol. He was there for the next twenty-two years. Willi married Ida Beimler in 1957, and they had three children; they later were divorced and Willi married a Russian woman and they had two children. Willi died in Kazakhstan in 2000 and his second wife and children still live in Kazakhstan. His first wife and their three children now live in Berlin, Germany.

GUSTAV – Gustav Fischbuch was born in 1882, at Makowetz, Russia. He married Maria Bekker in 1903; she was from the village of Dermanka a German settlement southwest of Novograd Volinskiy. They had two sons and one daughter. Their mother, Maria (Bekker) Fischbuch died of starvation in 1923. They had two sons, Bernhard and Reinhold, who both served sentences of five to ten years in Siberian Gulags. They survived and upon their release, they remained in Kazakhstan, and died there in 1972 and 1977. The daughter, Lilli, died of starvation in 1921 during the Lenin era of confiscation.

In 1926, Gustav had married again to Auguste Arndt; they had two sons who both survived Gulag imprisonment. Both of these sons, Wilhelm and Oskar, remained at Siberian communal farms until the mid 1950's when, even though there was the threat of imprisonment, they returned to their native village of Dermanka where they lived until their deaths in 1990 and 2007. Gustav died about 1950, somewhere near where he had served in a forestry Gulag in the Ural Mountains.

JUSTINA-GUSTEL – Justina-Gustel Fischbuch was born in Nataliendorf, Russia in 1884. She married Dmitri Bolislav in 1906 at the time when Friedrich got back from St. Petersburg after he was discharged from the navy. After her marriage to her Russian husband she disappeared into the Russian community. Nothing was heard from her during the Bolshevik Revolution and the rise of Lenin and Stalin. She died in 1920, but the family only heard of her death some ten years later.

MICHEL Jr. – Michel Fischbuch Jr. was born in 1887, at Nataliendorf, Russia. He married Emilia (unknown) in 1911. They had three sons and one daughter who were born between 1915 and 1925. There is no record of the fate of Michel Jr.'s family after they were sent to slave labour in 1934 somewhere in the eastern part of the Ural Mountains.

Emil & Lydia (Krampitz) Fischbuch 1915

EMIL – Emil Fischbuch was born in 1889 at Nataliendorf, Russia. He married Lydia Krampitz in 1915, just before leaving to serve in the Russian army; they had five sons and two daughters. In 1934, Emil was declared a kulak and in 1936 was sentenced to 10 years at hard labour at Tomsk, deep in the Siberian wilderness. Lydia and their seven children were taken from Nataliendorf to work at a kolkhoz at Woroschilograd in the Dnieper-Donetz area. Here the youngest son Erwin died of pneumonia or starvation. In May of 1937, the oldest son Reinhold was sentenced to 10 years at hard labour in the Russian arctic to work on a railroad to the Belomor Canal. In September of 1937, Lydia received a letter from

Emil that was brought to her by another Tomsk inmate who had just been released and arrived at Woroschilograd. In the letter, Emil said that he was forced to feed pigs, eat, and sleep with them. The letter was not finished but someone wrote on it that Emil had died in his confined quarters among the pigs. Reinhold survived his ten-year sentence and eventually became a chef and was sent to work as head chef at a hospital in Kirgistan. In 1992, he and his three children were allowed to come to Germany; he died there a year later. In 1941, Lydia's next oldest son Richard, who was then eighteen-years-old was taken away to an unknown slave labour camp and was never heard from again.

Later in 1941, Lydia and the four remaining children were put on a cattle train without even being allowed to take along their few belongings. After a twenty-six day travel ordeal from Woroschilograd, they were delivered to a recently enlarged kolkhoz at Jasnaja Poljana in northeastern Kazakhstan. Shortly after their arrival the oldest daughter, Antonina who by this time was twenty-two-years-old and had been overlooked earlier by the NKVD overseers, was taken away along with her eighteen-year-old brother Ergard. They were both sentenced to serve five-years at a slave labour camp in the Ural Mountains. After their release in 1946, Antonina and Ergard both married, but by Stalin's decree regarding German subversives had to remain in the area where they were released.

After Antonina and Ergard were taken away, Lydia remained at the expanded Jasnaja Poljana kolkhoz with the two youngest children, fourteen-year-old Gerhard and twelve-year-old Margarita. In early 1943, Lydia heard about another Lydia Krampitz (Krampitz was her own maiden name) in the same compound and went to see if she was a relative. When she arrived they could not establish a relationship, but the other Lydia asked Lydia Fischbuch to bring her children to her place and look after her daughter for a few days. She was going to see about her husband who had been sent to serve a sentence at a far-away Gulag for some minor infraction at the kolkhoz. During Lydia Krampitz's absence the NKVD appeared and assuming that this was Lydia Krampitz, arrested Lydia Fischbuch and sent her to a Gulag to work on a railway at Archangelsk. This is where she either froze to death or starved to death in October of 1944. The Lydia Krampitz that Lydia Fischbuch went to see undoubtedly used her namesake as a decoy. Margarita and Gerhard now alone had to fend for themselves and survived through the help of other benevolent inmates who let them herd their cattle and sheep for food and shelter. In the winter of 1946 both Gerhard, who now was eighteen-years-old, and Margarita who was sixteen-years-old were assigned work at the kolkhoz. Each of them were on the usual twenty-four hour on, twenty-four hour off, shifts seven days a week. Gerhard had to look after a team of oxen and drive them during the day; horses had all been taken away to be used in the war effort. Margarita had to work in the fields carrying sacks of grain for men to plant and she had to help dig the rows for the grain to be sown. As the plants grew, she was required to hoe and weed between rows of grain and vegetables.

Hunger was a constant companion with all of the workers and when harvest time arrived Margarita, in the darkness of the late evening, would quietly rub grain out of the wheat sheaves and slip it into her pockets; she would share this with Gerhard and since there was no time to cook it they would eat it raw. However, it was not long before Gerhard was given notice that he soon would be sent to the Trudarmee to work in the coalmines at Karaganda. The day that he was notified to leave, he quickly gave Margarita an address where he thought he would be at the mines so that by chance she might be able to contact him.

The shoes that she had been given by the old people with whom they had lived earlier were worn out. Since she now was working barefoot, there was no problem during the summer and fall. However, by early November her feet were frostbitten nearly every day. By January, even though she bound her feet in rags, she could hardly walk; finally, she pleaded to the foreman for help. He grudgingly arranged for her to go to the hospital. When she arrived there, they did nothing for her feet but gave her massive doses of some experimental drug. What it was and why they gave it to her was never divulged. In a few days, she became very ill and began to put on weight as they continued to administer the drug. Finally, whenever they put the needles into her arms she would pull them out. When at last she was discharged and sent her back to work in the fields she could hardly walk. Her feet, knee and weight problems plague her to this day.

In early 1950, when Margarita was still working at the kolkhoz a young man by the name of Otto Krieger, who was interned at the coalmines at Karaganda, had obtained a visa to come to Jasnaja Poljana to visit his parents who had just recently been sent to the kolkhoz barracks where Margarita was working. When he met Margarita, he came to see her nearly every day during his short leave. Before he left he asked her to marry him, but he had no idea when he would be back again. They decided that they would get married the day of his departure. Of course, she was not able to go with him and she knew that it would be a long time before he would be able to get back. It took over a year for him to get another visa to be able to come to Jasnaja Poljana. When he arrived, he immediately walked to the NKVD registry, which was some forty miles away, to get a visa for Margarita and by the time he returned it was he had to leave and get back to the coalmines at Karaganda. Margarita then had to wait a month to report her marriage and get permission from the Commandant to go to Karaganda. On her twenty-four hours off, she had to walk twenty miles to get to the NKVD office where she had to wait two days to see the Commandant; during this time, she was kept in a jail cell. When she got back to her barrack, she was told that she had to keep on working in the fields until the authorities would allow her to join her husband. She and other brides then had to wait until there were enough of them to fill a cattle car to tramsport them to Karaganda. Margarita then worked and waited another month. When enough brides had accumulated, they were taken to the railroad station in an open wagon and after a long train trip, the women finally arrived at Karaganda.

Upon their arrival, they were each interviewed for several hours while the others were left to wait. The process took several days until at last they were released. They were then faced with the problem of where to look for their husbands. None of them had ever been informed as to where their husbands lived or even where they worked, so they began wandering the streets and asking passers-by if they knew of anyone who knew the men. Margarita had carefully kept the address where her brother Gerhard lived. Finally, a man on the street pointed them in the direction of Gerhard's barrack. They found the large barn-like structure and were fortunate that Gerhard was there. He then helped them all to search for their respective mates and a matter of trial and error united them all with their husbands. When Margarita and Otto finally were together, they both again had to report to the Commandant – many papers had to be signed until the marriage process at last was over. Margarita and Otto's marriage ordeal was not unique, any Russian-German marriage was a long and complicated matter. Couples always had to be careful not to get together before all documentation was in place; if they tried to meet secretly and it was discovered, or if they were reported, they were both sentenced to an automatic jail term or banished to a Gulag. In 1956, three years after Stalin's death in 1953, Kruschev gave the Russian-German's an amnesty of sorts, but they still needed documents to travel from one village to another and were never allowed to return to their native villages.

Gerhard worked deep in the underground coalmines until 1952 when he was reassigned to a somewhat easier job at driving a truck hauling coal. One day his truck stalled on a railway crossing and a train demolished it. For this misdemeanour, he was sentenced to three years at hard labour. After he was released in 1955, he married and by 1959, they had three children: Elsa, Gerhard Jr., and Frieda. Gerhard died in 1961 when he was only thirty-three-years-old. His children and their mother were able to go to Germany in 1987, where Gerhard Jr., died at the age of forty-nine.

Margarita's husband Otto worked twelve-hour shifts seven days a week in the coal mines from 1948 until they finally were allowed to leave in 1991, a period of forty-three years. Today he is nearly blind and suffers from black lung disease. During this time, Margarita also worked at different jobs at Karaganda kolkhozes. During their time at the Karaganda coalmines from 1953 to 1970, they had six children: Eduard, Lydia, Alexander, Waldemar, Elvira, and Irma all of whom were forced to live in the Soviet nuclear testing area of northeastern

Kazakhstan from the time that they were born until they finally were allowed to leave Russia in 1991. Their memories of what transpired during their lives in Russia provided many of the facts recorded in this book.

ALBERT – Albert Fischbuch was born in 1891 in Nataliendorf, Russia. He was conscripted into the Russian army at the beginning of World War I and was sent to fight in the Crimea against the Turks As the Tsar's armies were collapsing Albert was either killed in action or starved to death. By chance, his body was discovered by his older brother, Eduard when his army unit happened to be passing through a Turkish held area in the Crimea.

ROBERT – Robert Fischbuch was born in 1893 in Makowetz, Russia. He married Elsa Missal in Makowetz in 1923. Robert had become a tailor and worked in Makowetz. Robert and Elsa had two sons and two daughters. In 1936, Robert was arrested and sent to an eastern Kazakhstani kolkhoz. In 1939, Elsa had a letter delivered to her by a Ukrainian inmate who had been released from the kolkhoz. In the letter, Robert said that he was very ill and that his feet and hands were too swollen to work and now, with his food ration cut in half he was getting very weak. The Ukrainian then told her that Robert had died. Elsa and the children were then sent to a kolkhoz in Kazakhstan. In 1941, Elsa and the two daughters were sent to Mongolia where they were forced to stay for the rest of their lives. In 1941, when her two sons were seventeen and eighteen-years-old they were sent to a Gulag east of the Ural Mountains, the younger son was never heard from again. Gregor, the oldest son was released after five years; he could not get a visa so had to remain in eastern Kazakhstan. In 1948, he married Alma Leicht, they had two children and in 1992, they were allowed to immigrate to Germany. In 2005, I met Gregor and he told me much about his life in Russia during the Stalinist era; he died at Hochstadt, Germany in 2007.

ZAMEL – Zamel Fischbuch was born in 1895 in Nataliendorf, Russia. He married Beate Lauch in 1920. Zamel became a butcher and had a butcher shop in the nearby village of Marianin. In 1935, Zamel, Beate and their four children, two sons Ernst and Artur, and two daughters Zelfia and Maria, were arrested because they were "wealthy kulaks" and deported to Kareliya, a Gulag high in the Russian arctic northeast of St. Petersburg. Here they worked as slave labourers cutting down trees with handsaws and axes. The winters lasted from September to May so potatoes and cabbage were the only vegetables grown, since they could be planted in mid-June and harvested by the end of August. When Zelfia and Maria reached the age of fourteen they were put to work in the forest cutting trees. No food was provided at the work site so they would take part of their daily ration of potatoes in their garments to keep them from freezing; they cooked them at noon in the fires that the workers would build to keep warm.

Many of the people that did not fill their work commitment were put on half rations and would eventually get swollen limbs and stomachs, and soon died of starvation. An old woman who was weak from hunger went to the Commandant and asked for food; he laughed and told her to eat the lice that were crawling on her head. All of the slave labourers were treated in this manner, but ethnic Germans were singled out to work until they died. In 1941, all in the family were sent to Komi, which was even further into the cold north. Here they served time until 1948, when they finally were given freedom to find work on their own. In 1954, Zamel and Beate got visas to live Syktyvkar, a city in the nearby Komi area; this is where Zamel died in 1981 and Beate died in 1990. Ernst became a Lutheran minister and lived there until he died in 2007. Artur worked at an airfield and still lives in Syktyvkar. Zelfia was married in Syktyvkar and she and two of her four children were able to get to Germany in 1992. Her sister Maria with her husband also now live near Hannover in Germany with their three children.

LYDIA – Lydia Fischbuch was born in 1896 in Nataliendorf, Russia. She married Emil Krampitz in 1919. They, with their two children, Alma who was eight-years-old, and Meita four-years-old, left for Canada in late 1928 along with Lydia's brother Johann and their sister Olga and their respective families. Lydia and Emil had son Albin who died of starvation during the famine resulting from Lenin's confiscations in 1923. During their long wait in Latvia, waiting for a ship to take them to Canada, little Meita died probably of Typhus. In early 1929 they arrived at Leader, Saskatchewan at the home of Lydia's brother August. A short time later Emil and Lydia started a tailor shop at Empress, Alberta and it was here where another daughter Melita was born. In 1934, they sold their tailor shop and moved to Vancouver, British Columbia. They retired at Kelowna, British Columbia in 1970 and this where Lydia died in 1971 and Emil died in 1976. Two children of their oldest daughter Alma, a son Albin and a daughter Millie still live in the Vancouver area.

HERMAN – Herman Fischbuch was born about 1899 in Nataliendorf, Russia and died of unknown causes sometime before 1910.

OLGA – Olga Fischbuch, the last of Michel and Justina's fourteen children, was born at Nataliendorf, Russia in 1901. She married Ewald Degen in 1921 and they had two children in Russia, Arvid who was five-years-old, and Lilly who was two-years-old when they left for Canada in 1928. Shortly after they arrived in Saskatchewan, they applied for a homestead in northern Alberta where they had two more sons, Oscar who was born in 1931 and Paul born in 1937. Olga died during childbirth in 1943 and Ewald died in 1970 at Barrhead, Alberta, where they had taken their homestead in 1929. Their oldest daughter Lilly died in 2000 at Barrhead. Her husband Raymond Ruhl, Arvid, Oscar and Paul and their families still live at Barrhead, Alberta.

# Afterword

Stalin's atrocities not only persisted, but also systematically escalated from the time that Friedrich and the other families were taken away from their treasured village of Nataliendorf in the mid 1930's until 1989, a period of nearly ninety years. Finally, Perestroika marked the end of the Communist regime in Russia.    Before Friedrich died in 1948, he may have felt that the Stalinist years were coming to an end, but little did he know that Stalin's devastating legacy would continue for over forty more years, not only for the descendants of all German colonists who had been deported helter-skelter across the country, but also for much of the Russian population.   Friedrich's three grandsons: Waldemar, Gerhard and Willi and later their children, as well as the descendants of his five brothers, by Communist decree were not allowed to leave northern Kazakhstan. From the early 1950's to 1990, the families were obliged to live in the three northern oblasts (provinces) of Kazakhstan: Semipalatinsk, Karaganda, and Pavlodar, which had been designated as Russia's nuclear testing range. The residents were never told about any of the secret nuclear trials that were to be performed among them. They would hear great explosions and see massive clouds of ash which unknown to them was nuclear fallout.

For periods of one to two weeks, the residents of the villages closest to test areas were ordered to remain outside, dress lightly and watch the explosions.  Others were ordered to remain in the cellars of their homes or in their adjacent root cellars.  After their release, the authorities would appear and briefly examine the people that lived in the villages near the explosion.  During the forty years that testing took place the equivalent of twenty thousand Hiroshima bombs were exploded with the people completely uninformed or of the consequences.    Economic hardship was common to the population before the testing began, but became worse as time went on.  During these forty years, the farmers would unknowingly herd their cattle and sheep over ground that was covered with nuclear ash after and even during each explosion. Periodically, when people would gather mushrooms or berries in the fields or would take vegetables from their gardens the military police would come by and confiscate their produce with no explanation. Eighteen thousand square kilometres of land in the three oblasts was covered with nuclear fallout. Yet when Friedrich's oldest grandson Waldemar, his wife Erica and their four children were allowed to leave Russia for Germany in 1989, it was only then they became aware of the fact that they were deliberately used as guinea pigs for Russia's nuclear experiments. The Communist cover-up was so complete that while they were living in Russia they had not even heard of Chernobyl

Kazakhstani authorites have recently revealed that the thousands of people exposed to radiation in the three oblasts had, and still have serious health problems, such as genetic mutations, i.e., human birth defects—eight times the normal average; mental retardation—three times the normal average; cancer—five times the normal average; as well there are many other frightening statistics.

# References

Photos courtesy of www.cityofart.net  www.bigbadbattleships.com

Atakhanova, Kaisha – "The Monster of Semipalatinsk." Atomwaffentestgelande Semipalatinsk, from the NCO Ecocenter, Karaganda, 2004.

Aitimov, Chingiz – "The Day Lasts More Than a Hundred Years." English translation by E. J. French in 1983. Published by Novyi Mir in Kazakhstan in 1980. Published in English by Indiana University Press, 601 North Morton Street, Bloomington, Indiana, 1983, 352 pages

Applebaum, Anne – "Gulag." A History. Published by Doubleday, a division of Random House, Inc. New York in 2003, 677 pages

Arndt, Nikolaus – "Die Deutschen in Wolhynien." Ein kulturhistorischer Uberblick. Die Deutsche Bibliothek – CIP-Einheitsaufnahme, 1994, 96 pages

Bachmann, Berta – "Memories of Kazakhstan." A Report on the Life Experiences of a German Woman in Russia. Translated from the German Edition by Edgar Duin, American Historical Society of Germans from Russia, Lincoln, Nebraska, 1983, 110 pages

Bender, Ida – "The Dark Abyss of Exile: A Story of Survival." Germans from Russia Heritage Collection, North Dakota State University Libraries, Fargo, North Dakota, 2000, 195 pages

Biberdorf, Emil – "Spreading Branches." Private Publication, Printed in Aldergrove, British Columbia

Bullock, Alan – "Hitler and Stalin, Parallel Lives." McClelland & Stewart Inc., 481 University Avenue, Toronto, Ontario, 1993, 1089 pages

Collections/Belomorkanal – "The White Sea Canal: A Hymn of Praise for Forced Labour." International Institute of Social History.

Courtois, Werth, Panne, Paczkowski, Bartosek, Margolin – "The Black Book of Communism, Crimes, Terror, Repression." Harvard University Press, Cambridge Massachusetts. London England, 1999, 858 pages

Das, Nelly – "Gone Without a Trace." Translated by Nancy Bernhardt Holland. Published by the American Historical Society of Germans from Russia, 631 D Street, Lincoln, Nebraska, 232 pages

Dmitriew, Helen – "Surviving the Storms, Memory of Stalin's Tyranny." The Press at California State University, Fresno, California, 1992

Fischbuch, Norman – "Unsere Leute" Private Publication, Calgary, Albera, 2003, 404 pages

Giesinger, Adam – "From Catherine to Kruschev." Marian Press, Battleford, Saskatchewan, 1974, 443 pages

Hohenecker, Jacob – "In the Russian Army During the Russo-Japanese War." Translation by Herman Wildermuth, Heritage Review, vol. 11, no. 4, North Dakota Historical Society of Germans from Russia, Bismarck, North Dakota, 1981

Hough, Richard – "The Fleet That Had to Die." Published by Birlinn Limited 8 Canongate Venture, 5 New Street, Edinburgh, EH8 8BH, 2000, 237 pages

Kizny, Tomasz – "Gulag." Life and Death Inside the Soviet Concentration Camps. Translated from the Polish by Antonia Lloyd-

Jones. Published originally in 2003 by Balland/Editions Acropole, Paris. Published in Canada in 2004 by Firefly Books Ltd., 66 Leek Crescent, Richmond Hill, Ontario, 2004, 494 pages

Kruger, Alfred – "The Deportation of the Volhynian Germans." Translated by Adam Giesinger, Journal of the American Historical Society of Germans from Russia, vol. 2, no. 1, Lincoln, Nebraska

Kurth, Peter – "Tsar." The Lost World of Nicholas and Alexandra. A Madison Press Book, Produced for Back Bay Books, Little, Brown and Company, Boston, New York, Toronto, London, 1995, 229 pages

Mai, Brent Alan – "The Expropriation of Land from the Germans in Volhynia, 1915." American Historical Society of Germans from Russia, 631 D Street, Lincoln, Nebraska

Miller, Donald N. – "Under Arrest." Repression of the Russian Germans in the Zhitomir Region, Ukraine, in the 1930's. Published in Zhitomir, Ukraine, Printed by Volyn, 2004, 238 pages

Parsons, Elsie (Fischbuch) – "Memories of my Mother – Ottilia (Kahler) Fischbuch", Private Publication, 1987, 54 pages

Pleshakov, Constantine – "The Tsar's Last Armada." The Epic Voyage to the Battle of Tsushima. Published by Basic Books, 10 East 53rd Street, New York, NY 10022-5299, 395 pages

Rink, Friedrich – "The German Settlements in Volhynia." Translated by Adam Giesinger, Journal of the American Historical Society of Germans from Russia, Work Paper no. 23, Lincoln, Nebraska, 1977

Roleder, Emil J. – "The Volhynian Germans as I Saw Them During the First Decade of the Communist Era." Journal of the American Historical Society of Germans from Russia, vol. 2, no. 2, Lincoln, Nebraska, 1979

Semenoff, Vladimir – "Coaling at Sea, 1905." Modern History Sourcebook

Semenoff, Vladimir – "The Battle of the Yellow Sea." War Times Journal

Semenoff, Vladimir – "The Battle of Tsushima." War Times Journal

Shevardnadze, Eduard – "The Future Belongs to Freedom." Sinclair-Stevenson Limited, 7-8 Kendrick Mews, London, England, 1991, 204 pages

Sinner, Samuel D. – "Letters from Hell." Letters written by the starving during the famines of 1921 and 1933, The American Historical Society of Germans from Russia, 1998, 14 pages

Sobelow, W.S., Director of Russian Marine Archives, St. Petersburg, Russia — "Naval Record of Engineer 1st Class Friedrich Michael Fischbuch." Nr. of N203548, Navy roll N152, recorded April 26, 1906

Solzhenitsyn, Alexandr – "The Gulag Archipelago Two." Translated from the Russian by Thomas Whitney. Harper and Row, Publishers, New York, 1995, 712 pages

Stumpp, Karl — "The Emigration from Germany to Russia in the Years 1763 to 1862." Published by the American Historical Society of Germans from Russia, Lincoln, Nebraska, 1978

The Russo-Japanese War Research Society, — "The Battle of the Yellow Sea."

Wentland, Theodore C. – "Torn Roots." Private Publication, Urbana, Illinois, 1976, 115 pages

Wikipedia.org, the free encyclopedia – "Battle of the Yellow Sea"

# Postscript

Apparently, time and human manipulation heals all wounds. This is now happening with the sordid legacy of the Soviet Union. This year Russian students will read their history from new and revised textbooks. Russian Prime Minister Vladimir Putin has been instrumental in introducing new state-approved history textbooks depicting Stalin as, "one of the most successful leaders of the USSR". These new textbooks are now required reading for history students in all of Russia. Documented facts of Russian history have been distorted and modified by the Putin administration to fit the new political agenda. Russia's Rossiya TV recently held a contest to select Russia's most popular historical figures; 50 million people voted. Stalin came in third narrowly edged out by Peter Stolypin who was head of one of the most successful Dumas; this was a government selected by the people. Stolypin was assassinated in 1911.

During the six years of the Second World War, Hitler was responsible for the killing of six million Jews and is rightfully condemned worldwide. On the other hand, Stalin in the thirty years of his reign was methodically instrumental in the death of at least thirty million people and is now heralded as a hero. In the new Russian history books, Stalin is no longer regarded as a paranoid mass-murderer, but as an "efficient manager" who defeated the Nazis and saved Europe. Nothing is said of how Stalin used human fodder from his slave labour camps, the Trudarmee, the Gulags and the kolkhozes to further his brutal conquests. Nor is there any mention made of the 170,000 labourers most of whom, in the mid 1930's, perished high in the Russian arctic while building the Belomor Canal with their bare hands. Most of them either froze to death or starved to death. This included at least three of Friedrich's family members: his sister-in-law Lydia Fischbuch, his son-in-law Robert Missal, and his granddaughter Wanda Missal. His nephew Reinhold Fischbuch also was sentenced to ten years at hard labour working on a railroad to the Belomor Canal, but miraculously survived. Reinhold arrived at the Belomor project on a cattle train containing one-hundred slave-labourers. Of the one-hundred slave-labourers only two survived -- Reinhold was one of the two.

The cruel occupation of Eastern Poland, the siezure of the Baltic states and Romania, and the invasion of Finland is now considered as a well-thought-out, logical and necessary move made by Stalin to further his quest to build a great world power.

One new textbook, *History of Russia from 1945 to 2008 for 11th Graders,* states that; "The Soviet Union was not a democracy, but in terms of social policy and programs it was the best model of a fair and just society for millions of people around the world."
Vladimir Ryzhkov, an historian and former Russian politician has gone on record to say that, "The new history textbooks are intended to ideologically prepare an entire generation of young people to loyally and complacently serve the Russian ruling class. The strong admiration for the Soviet regime is the golden thread running through the textbook. Just like during the Soviet period, repression, authoritarianism, militarism and the creation of spheres of influence and satellite states are justifiable prices to pay for building a great nation."

Irena Karatsuba, another historian from Moscow State University has stated that, "Soviet textbooks have now hidden what actually happened. But now Stalin's terror is presented as not only necessary, but useful."

Mr. Putin, the former KGB agent when he became president in 2000, immediately brought back symbols of the Stalinist era. He had the Russian Central Bank strke commemorative silver coins bearing Stalin's portrait. During ceremonies marking the 55th anniversary of the end of the Second World War, he unveiled a plaque honouring Stalin for heroic leadership. Later, Mr. Putin approved the placement of a bust of Stalin in Moscow's Victory Hill War Memorial. He also had parliament restore the old national anthem that was commissioned by Stalin in 1943. In 2007, when Putin orderd Russian educators to produce new and revised history textbooks, he said, "But other countries have also known their bleak and terrible moments. In any event, we have never used nuclear weapons against civilians and we have never dumped chemicals on thousands of kilometres of land or dropped more bombs on a tiny country than were dropped during the entire Second World War as was the case in Vietnam."

The Russian nuclear testing area at Jasnaja Polyana, Karaganda, Pavlodar and Semipalatinsk in northern Kazakhstan where so many of the Fischbuch families were forced to live is conveniently forgotten. Obviously, his own citizens, the human guinea pigs that lived in northern Kazakhstan during the forty years of nuclear testing, can be dispensed with and are not worth mentioning.

Now that Putin's rehabilitation of Stalin is underway, most Russians are feeling that the collapse of the Soviet Union was a humiliation. They experienced the sudden loss of the Empire as a loss of their own identity and many now resent that their country was stripped of its superpower status. During the chaotic flirtation with democracy that followed the collapse of the Soviet Union the Russian people longed for the return of an authoritarian leader – enter Vladmir Putin.

If one day, a statue of Adolph Hitler appeared in Berlin Germans would be ouraged. However, in China Mao Zedong, one of the cruelest tyrants in history, starved or murdered nearly seventy million people. Yet, I have personally seen the prominent protrait of Chariman Mao, as well as the Mausoleum housing his remains; both are placed in a dominant part of Beijing's renowned Tiananmen Square.

Similar adulation is now being fostered in Russia for Josef Stalin, which comes through the words of an authoritative leader who hides the Russian populace from the documented facts of their history. While actual events of the Stalinist era are being vocally clouded and manipulated by the new political elite, the agony of Stalin's victims cannot be heard – most of their sufferings have been silenced by death.